UTOPIAN ROAD TO HELL

UTOPIAN ROAD TO HELL

ENSLAVING AMERICA AND THE WORLD
WITH CENTRAL PLANNING

WILLIAM J. MURRAY

 WND Books

UTOPIAN ROAD TO HELL

Published by WND Books, Washington, D.C. WND Books is a registered trademark of WorldNetDaily.com, Inc. ("WND")

Book designed by Mark Karis

Front cover photographs (top row: Vladimir Lenin, Joseph Stalin, Adolf Hitler; middle row: Benito Mussolini, Mao Zedong, Pol Pot; bottom row: Karl Marx, Margaret Sanger, Saul Alinsky)

WND Books are available at special discounts for bulk purchases. WND Books also publishes books in electronic formats. For more information call (541) 474-1776 or visit www.wndbooks.com.

Scripture quotations are from the Holy Bible, King James Version (public domain).

Softcover ISBN: 978-1-944229-08-5
eBook ISBN: 978-1-944229-09-2

Library of Congress Cataloging-in-Publication Data

Names: Murray, William J. (William Joseph), 1946-
Title: Utopian road to hell : enslaving America and the world with central planning / William J. Murray.
Description: New York, New York : WND Books, [2015] | Includes bibliographical references and index.
Identifiers: LCCN 2015026149| ISBN 9781944229085 (softcover) | ISBN 9781944229092 (e-book)
Subjects: LCSH: Utopian socialism--History. | Totalitarianism--History.
Classification: LCC HX626 .M87 2015 | DDC 335/.0209--dc23
LC record available at http://lccn.loc.gov/2015026149

Printed in the United States of America
16 17 18 19 LBM 9 8 7 6 5 4 3 2

To the tens of millions who lost their lives to the misguided twentieth-century efforts to create Utopia here on earth, whether that be the Nazi "Thousand-Year Reich" or the failed Soviet experiment with communalism, and to the hundreds of millions more who suffered through starvation and enslavement.

CONTENTS

ACKNOWLEDGMENTS

I thank my ever-suffering editor, my wife, Nancy Murray, who has proofed not only this work, but countless millions of words in several other books and hundreds of articles, columns, and newsletters.

INTRODUCTION

Being a "Red diaper baby" gives me a unique perspective on the magic thought involved in the twentieth-century utopian movement known as Marxism. For those who are not familiar with the term, "Red diaper baby" was a common twentieth-century expression describing those born into Marxist families. My early teen years were spent in Marxist–Leninist study groups in the basement of either my family's home or those of other Marxist families. As a teenager I met the chairman of the Communist Party USA, Gus Hall, as well as many of the other American "Socialist heroes."

The view of the world from a true Marxist home is very different from the reality of humanity. In my Marxist upbringing, competition was an evil and all were expected to work for the common good with no selfish desires. All things material were to belong to the state for shared use by all. The view of humankind can truly only be described as *magic think* because it defies all of human history. Had man, from the time of his creation, never hunted game or worked the land for food to feed his family, perhaps there is a 1 in 10,000 chance human society today could be what the Marxist utopians believe it should be. The concept simply defies human nature—and the very nature of all living things struggling for survival.

Along with the Marxism in my family came atheism. This is necessary because Marxists must have a godless, relative value system by which any action, no matter how cruel, is justified if it serves to advance the end result of a new and perfect society. What must be done cannot be justified according to a Judeo-Christian belief system. With utopianism, the means—even mass murder—are always justified by the ends. In 1960 my family actually attempted to defect to the Soviet Union, believing it was close to achieving the utopian state we so desired.

My eyes began to open to the evils of central government when I received my first paycheck and saw the amount of tax removed to support others who could not or would not work. Years later, my eyes were further opened when I realized that the only utopia possible is not of this earth, but of the one God who rules in His heaven. Reality looks far different from the utopian foolishness of changing the very nature of humanity to achieve a society so equal that personalities cease to exist. It is with this background, having served nearly equal periods of my life on opposing sides of reality, that I present this work.

There is currently, and has been for centuries, an ongoing material and spiritual war between the liberty of the individual and the central control of society by elitists who believe they can best determine the optimum course for the life of each individual in the population.

The battle is always between those who believe in individual liberty and government that is the least coercive, and those who hold that government can replace God and create a perfect system, managed by elitists, wherein all human needs can be determined and met.

These arrogant elitists proclaim that they can provide for humanity through a centrally planned system that relies primarily on collectivism. Regardless of what the system may be called, it relies on taking from the productive and redistributing to all. Though dating back to Sparta, the latest collectivist mantra sums up the centrally planned collectivist utopian plans that have plagued the world, particularly in the twentieth century: "From each according to his ability, to each according to his need."

Nowhere in that mantra do the words *want* or *desire* appear.

Collectivists, whether fascist, Communist, or religiously motivated, have no faith in the individual or his ability to provide for his own needs and create value to trade for other desires. Collectivists view people as best suited to be part of a centrally planned system created and managed, of course, by themselves. Most often, those who reject their collectivist systems face the hangman's noose, the guillotine, or the firing squad.

Those who seek centralized power typically do so by proclaiming some utopian scheme that they claim will perfect mankind and eliminate competition, greed, poverty, and war.

The politically driven utopian tyrants invariably achieve their goals by killing off vocal opponents and terrorizing the remaining populace into submission. This was as true in the French Revolution and Reign of Terror instigated by Robespierre, as it was in ancient Greece's Sparta.

Energizing most utopians is a militant atheism, a belief that a better society can be created on earth, perhaps through their own personal brilliance, than any deity could create. When the belief in man as a creation in the image of God is completely rejected, the use of slavery and mass execution can be justified in the name of the creation of a utopian state for the masses.

Utopian tyrants such as Lenin, Stalin, Mao, and Pol Pot all shared a near-supernatural hatred of God and His creation, as if driven by satanic forces. They used the creation of a new, uniform humanity as an excuse to murder tens of millions of people collectively.

Hitler and Mussolini were no less utopian than the Communists of the twentieth century. They also viewed themselves as creating a centrally planned civilization that would be superior to any that had ever existed on earth. For Mussolini, the effort to centralize control of all means of production by the state was described as a spiritual goal.

At the root of all the utopian planners seems to be the satanic logic that a human hand can replace the hand of God in determining the fate of humanity. The utopianists of the twentieth and twenty-first centuries have a particular hatred for Jesus Christ because of His teachings that God frees people rather than enslaves them. A few, rather than being atheistic in their denial of God, have openly shown their belief that Satan is the heir of Earth.

Each of these utopian tyrants has tried to create a counterfeit of God's ultimate rule on the earth during Jesus Christ's thousand-year reign.

As this relates to America, the Founders, several of whom were pastors, held the biblical belief that man was sinful and prone to mischief. Indeed, half of the signers of the Declaration of Independence had some divinity school training, according to Larry Schweikart, professor of history at the University of Dayton and coauthor of *A Patriot's History*. Well educated and aware of the dangers of a Platonic system such as that described in *The Republic*, they authored a Constitution for the nation that maintained checks and balances in government. Their goal was to create a smaller federal government, with guaranteed wide-ranging powers reserved for state governments at a more local level, where politicians were more accountable to the people. That system is now endangered by an encroaching imperial presidency and a growing militarized police force.

In addition to the political utopian tyrants, this work also deals with the cultural utopians who have brought untold suffering into the world because of their ideas about morality, the environment, and the human condition. Among those are militant atheist Margaret Sanger, the amoral founder of Planned Parenthood—a group specifically created to eliminate nonwhite races in the United States.

Even environmentalists are utopian and believe that humankind is a cancer on the earth that must be controlled. In that discussion, Rachel Carson's *Silent Spring* helped bring about the banning of DDT, and thus the deaths of millions of human beings from malaria in poorer tropical nations.

Much of the successful work of the current crop of cultural and environmental utopians has been accomplished inside a relatively democratic process. Keep in mind that Adolf Hitler was actually elected to office. In Friederich von Hayek's works, which we will explore, he discusses *democratic totalitarianism*, the process of taking away the sphere of individual liberty in the name of such morally high-sounding concepts as "social justice" and "economic justice."

We begin this journey through the history of utopian tyrannies by examining the satanically driven, godless utopians of the Soviet Union and then examine the root philosophies and history that drove this twentieth-century utopian nightmare. In Western civilization those roots can be traced as far back as Sparta and the writings of Plato.

Sadly, this is no mere history of utopian totalitarianism; the battle for freedom rages on today, even in the United States, where "social planners" believe government can better determine the human outcome than either the individual or God.

1

SATANIC INFLUENCE IN UTOPIAN TYRANNIES

Utopians running for office promise a perfect and equal life for all. Rather than simply promising equal opportunity, however, they guarantee the unobtainable goal of an equal outcome for everyone. Once utopians are in power, their inability to deliver an equal outcome leads very quickly to totalitarianism because their utopian vision requires central control of all resources. To guarantee everyone equal amounts and quality of food and shelter, the free marketplace can never be trusted because some people must inevitably acquire less than others. Another aspect of the desired equality is that work must be provided for everyone who wants a job, even if it is work that does not need to be done. Nowhere is there more documented proof of the failure of utopian central planning than in Eastern Europe under imposed Communist rule.

The late Lutheran pastor Richard Wurmbrand, having endured torture at the hands of those who believed they could replace God with government, described the utopian Communist era under which he suffered as being satanic. Wurmbrand lived to tell of his torture, but more than 100 million died at the hands of the central planners who referred to themselves as Marxists in the late nineteenth and twentieth centuries.

Wurmbrand first suffered under Nazi central planners in World War II, and then spent fourteen years in Communist prisons in Romania.

Pastor Wurmbrand was repeatedly tortured while in prison and came to believe that the real force behind Karl Marx's hatred of Christianity was Satan himself. In fact, his persecutors often as much as admitted that they were motivated by a satanic hatred of Christianity.

Upon his release from prison and subsequent emigration to America, Wurmbrand founded the faith-based organization Voice of the Martyrs and worked on behalf of the underground church in nations that were enslaved by the then-Communist entities of the Soviet Union and Red China. He also wrote nearly twenty books, including his classic *Tortured for Christ*; *In God's Underground*; and *Marx and Satan*.

In *Marx and Satan*, Wurmbrand carefully documents the fact that Karl Marx, Vladimir Lenin, and Joseph Stalin had all once pursued a faith in Jesus Christ, but at some point had rejected Christ and embraced Satan instead. From that point on, their lives were given over to the most unspeakable evils and destructive agendas—agendas that have since resulted in the torture and deaths of millions of men, women, and children. Wurmbrand also details the satanic path that Adolf Hitler took, and the antireligious hatred that led Mao Tse-tung into a decades-long bloodbath in China.

As Wurmbrand stated in *Tortured for Christ*, "We wrestle not against flesh and blood, but against the principalities and powers of evil. We saw that communism is not from men but from the devil. It is a spiritual force—a force of evil—and can only be countered by a greater spiritual force, the Spirit of God."[1]

Wurmbrand went on to say:

> The cruelty of atheism is hard to believe. When a man has no faith in the reward of good or the punishment of evil, there is no reason to be human. There is no restraint from the depths of evil that is in man. The Communist torturers often said, "There is no God, no hereafter, no punishment for evil. We can do what we wish." I heard one torturer say, "I thank God, in whom I don't believe, that I have lived to this hour when I can express all the evil in my heart." He expressed it in unbelievable brutality and torture inflicted on prisoners.[2]

This maniacally evil guard and others like him gladly followed the lead of the man by whom they were inspired, Karl Marx. Yet, according to Wurmbrand, Marx was never really an atheist. He believed in God, but hated him and chose to cast his lot with Satan. It became Marx's lifelong goal to destroy organized religion, and in his efforts he brought untold suffering on the world. Of course Marx himself believed that he was building "utopia," a perfect society for all people, which he alone possessed the knowledge and ability to create.

One wonders if Karl Marx actually made a deal with the devil. He certainly wrote about it.[3] According to Wurmbrand, though Marx professed to be a Christian as a teenager, not long after his high school graduation he began writing a series of anti-Christian and anti-God poems. One of them included the line "I wish to avenge myself against the One who rules above."

In Marx's poem, "Invocation of One in Despair," he spoke as though he were Satan himself:

So a god has snatched from me my all,

In the curse and rack of destiny.

All his worlds are gone beyond recall.

Nothing but revenge is left to me. . . .

I shall build my throne high overhead,

Cold, tremendous shall its summit be.

For its bulwark—superstitious dread.

For its marshal—blackest agony.

Who looks on it with a healthy eye,

Shall turn back, deathly pale and dumb,

Clutched by blind and chill mortality,

May his happiness prepare its tomb.[4]

In another poem, Marx wrote:

Then I will be able to walk triumphantly,

Like a god, through the ruins of their kingdom.

Every word of mine is fire and action.

My breast is equal to that of the Creator.[5]

In a poem titled *The Player*, Marx wrote:

The hellish vapors rise and fill the brain,

Till I go mad and my heart is utterly changed.

See this sword?

The prince of darkness

Sold it to me.

For me he beats the time and gives the signs.

Ever more boldly I play the dance of death.[6]

Writing in his play *Oulanem*, Marx described his ultimate objective in life:

If there is a Something which devours,

I'll leap within it, though I bring the world to ruins—

The world which bulks between me and the abyss

I will smash to pieces with my enduring curses.

I'll throw my arms around its harsh reality,

Embracing me, the world will dumbly pass away,

And then sink down to utter nothingness,

Perished, with no existence—that would be really living.[7]

Wurmbrand believed Karl Marx was himself inspired by a satanic madman, the Marquis de Sade, who penned vile pornography and died insane in prison. It was de Sade who said, "I abhor nature. I would like to split its planet, hinder its process, stop the circles of stars, overthrow the globes that float in space, destroy what serves nature, protect what harms it—in a word, I wish to insult it in my works. . . . Perhaps we will be able to attack the sun, deprive the universe of it, or use it to set the world on fire. These would be real crimes."[8]

Marx's writings were filled with similar rantings, but in Wurmbrand's mind they were not the words of an atheist, but of a man who had given his life over to Satan to be his servant on earth.

Eugene Methvin, in *The Rise of Radicalism: The Social Psychology of Messianic Extremism*, wrote about Marx's incredible capacity for hatred:

> Even as a child, Karl Marx's first recorded response to human society revealed an underlying hostility. His outstanding trait was a fierce hate. As with so many young radicals in our day, Marx's language of hate appeals to them more than his logic. Marx's sister Sophie recalled that Karl was "a terrible little tyrant" who turned his remarkable gift of words into a fearsome weapon, fashioning cruelly cutting lampoons and satirical verses with which he would bully playmates. Repeatedly his imperious and volcanic hostility struck others who knew him. The Russian liberal, Paul Annenkov, found Marx at 27 "haughty, almost contemptuous. His sharp voice rang like metal, remarkably suited to the radical judgments he habitually delivered on men and things. His tone expressed his own firm conviction that his destiny was to reign over men's minds, dominate their wills and dictate their laws. Before my eyes stood the personification of a democratic dictator." A few months later during Germany's 1848 revolution Marx similarly impressed the Cologne democratic congress. "Never have I seen a man of such offensive, insupportable arrogance," recorded 19-year-old fellow delegate Carl Schurz, who later emigrated to America and became a noted journalist and political leader.[9]

A Prussian officer who knew Marx at age thirty said of him, "He laughs at the fools who join in his proletarian litany. If he had as much heart as intelligence, if he could love as intensely as he can hate, I would go through fire for him. But personal ambition in its most dangerous form has eaten away anything that was good in him. Everything he does is aimed at the acquisition of personal power."[10]

Marx was energized by a satanic hatred not only of God and Christianity but of organized Western civilization. It was his goal to destroy everything he could. In fact, one of his favorite quotes, from Mephistopheles in *Faust*, was "Everything in existence is worth being destroyed." Interestingly, Satan of the Judeo-Christian Bible, would seem to agree. His very purpose is to steal, kill, and destroy. (See John 10:10.)

Two of those who followed Marx in believing that central planning can create utopia on earth also had a hatred for God. Vladimir Lenin and Joseph Stalin were both energized by a demonic hatred of Christianity and the one true God.

There was much propaganda from the Communist Party in the Soviet Union to convince the young to reject God. It is rumored that at age sixteen Lenin tore a cross from his neck, spat on it, and stomped on it in a violent statement of his hatred of God. Although that story cannot be confirmed, its existence shows the degree of hatred for Christianity that was fostered in the Lenin/Stalin era of the Soviet Union.

Lenin became a committed Marxist during his teen years and modeled his life after his older brother, Alexander, who had plotted to kill Czar Alexander III with a bomb hidden in a medical dictionary. Police discovered the plot just before the bomb was ignited, and Alexander was arrested and hanged. After his brother's death, Lenin immersed himself in Marxist writings and dedicated himself to the overthrow of the czarist regime.

As Lenin became more radicalized by Marxism, his hatred of Christianity became more intense. Karl Marx became his god, in a sense, and Marx's writings became his bible. Lenin often referred to religion as the enemy of materialism, and vice versa. He professed the Marxist axiom that religion is an "opiate" for the peoples repressed under capitalism. As a staunch Marxist, he did "not believe in eternal morality."[11]

"Religion is a kind of spiritual gin in which the slaves of capital drown their human shape and their claims to any decent human life," Lenin stated, mirroring Karl Marx.[12] "We must combat religion—this is the ABC of all materialism and consequently, Marxism."[13]

Lenin had the blood of many innocents on his hands during the creation of his version of utopia, which could not even manage to keep the lights on in Moscow once the Marxists came to power. Seeing that Lenin's utopian dream could never be realized with anything less than brutal force, Stalin determined to carry forward the dream no matter the cost in human life.

Lazar Kaganovitch, Stalin's brother-in-law and the ruthless butcher who engineered the murder of millions of farmers in the Ukraine, wrote of him in his diary:

> I started to understand how Stalin managed to make himself a god. He did not have a single human characteristic. . . . Even when he exhibited some emotions, they all did not seem to belong to him. They were as false as the scale on top of armor. And behind this scale was Stalin himself—a piece of steel. For some reason I was convinced that he would live forever. . . . He was not human at all. . . .
>
> Rosa [his wife] says he makes her climb a tree wearing nothing but stockings. I have a feeling he is not human at all. He is too unusual to be a regular human being. Although he looks like an ordinary man. Such a puzzle. What is it I'm writing? Am I raving mad, too?[14]

Kaganovitch continued:

> Many times Stalin spoke of religion as our most vicious enemy. He hates religion for many reasons, and I share his feelings. Religion is a cunning and dangerous enemy . . . Stalin also thinks that separation from children should be the main punishment for all parents belonging to sects, irrespective of whether they were convicted or not.
>
> I think he secretly engaged in astrology. One peculiar feature of his always astonished me. He always talked with some veiled respect about God and religion.
>
> At first, I thought I was imagining it, but gradually I realized it was true. But he was always careful when the subject came up. And I was never able to find out exactly what his point of view was. One thing became very clear to me—his treatment of God and religion was

very special. For example, he never said directly there was no God. . . .

People ceased somehow to be their own selves in his presence. They all admired him and worshiped him. I don't think he enjoyed any great love of the nation: he was above it. It may sound strange, but he occupied a position previously reserved only for God.[15]

In fact, during Stalin's reign of terror in the Soviet Union, he created a cult of personality for himself. He became "god" in place of the one true God, even demanding to be worshipped as a god.

Pastor Richard Wurmbrand, who suffered so dearly under Marxist tyranny, wrote:

> Hitler killed millions of Jews, including babies, with the excuse that Jews had done harm to the German people. For the Communists it was a matter of course to imprison and torture the family members of a person they considered guilty. When I was jailed, it was taken for granted that my wife must be jailed too, and that my son must be excluded from all schooling.
>
> Marxism is not an ordinary sinful human ideology. It is Satanic in its manner of sinning, as it is Satanic in the teachings it purveys. Only in certain circumstances has it openly avowed its Satanic character. [16]

Collective punishment is a hallmark of leftist ideology and indeed satanic. In this case Wurmbrand expected the punishment of his family for his actions. In broader settings central planners, utopians, and those leaning in their direction require collective punishment to achieve social goals.

UNSPEAKABLE PRISON TORTURES AGAINST CHRISTIANS

In his writings Pastor Wurmbrand described not only experiencing firsthand the tortures meted out by God-hating Communists of Eastern Europe, but also witnessing the torture of many other believers. Christians were specifically targeted for the most obscene brutalities, which also involved the desecration of Bibles and other religious artifacts.

Wurmbrand was repeatedly put into a frozen locker and left to chill to the point of death. He would then be removed, warmed up, and then repeatedly shoved back in the locker to freeze again. At other times, he was placed in a coffin-like box with nails driven through the outside. If he moved inside the box, the nails would pierce him.

One Romanian Orthodox priest named Roman Braga had his teeth knocked out one by one with an iron bar in order to force him to blaspheme God. Here are some other instances of torture Wurmbrand recounted:

> A theology student was forced to dress in white sheets (in imitation of Christ's robe), and a phallus made out of soap was hung around his neck with a string. Christians were beaten to insanity to force them to kneel before such a mocking image of Christ. After they had kissed the soap, they had to recite part of the liturgy.
>
> Some prisoners were compelled to take off their trousers and sit with their naked bottoms on open Bibles.
>
> Such blasphemous practices were perpetrated for at least two years with the full knowledge of the Party's top leadership. What have such indignities to do with socialism and the well-being of the proletariat? Were their anti-capitalist slogans not merely pretexts for organizing Satanic blasphemies and orgies?
>
> Marxists are supposed to be atheists who believe in neither heaven nor hell. In these extreme circumstances, Marxism has lifted its atheistic mask to reveal its true face, the face of Satanism. Communist persecution of religion might have a human explanation, but the fury of such perverse persecution can only be Satanic.
>
> In Romanian prisons and in the Soviet Union as well, nuns who would not deny their faith were raped anally, and Baptist girls had oral sex forced on them.[17]

HITLER AND THE OCCULT

Many collectivists in the West who still dream of a utopia under central planning disown one of the greatest central planners of all, Adolf Hitler, proclaiming him to be part of the "far right." Atheists and critics of the church in America claim that Adolf Hitler was a Christian. Nothing could be further from the truth. He was indeed a National Socialist, but his evil was associated with the occult.

Hitler claimed to have regularly heard voices inside his head, giving him directions about what he was to do. His reliance on these "voices" began back when he served as a *gefreiter* (lance corporal) in the Bavarian Army in World War I, and continued throughout his life.

Hitler wrote about these voices:

> I was eating my dinner in a trench with several comrades. Suddenly a voice seemed to be saying to me, "Get up and go over there." It was so clear and insistent that I obeyed automatically, as if it had been a military order. I rose at once to my feet and walked twenty yards along the trench carrying my dinner in its tin can with me.
>
> Then I sat down to go on eating, my mind being once more at rest. Hardly had I done so when a flash and deafening report came from the part of the trench I had just left. A stray shell had burst over the group in which I had been sitting, and every member of it was killed.[18]

While in a hospital at Pasewalk, suffering from blindness from the effect of a gas attack, Hitler wrote, "When I was confined to bed, the idea came to me that I would liberate Germany, that I would make it great. I knew immediately that it would be realized."[19]

Hitler bragged about himself in later years:

> I carry out the commands that Providence has laid upon me.
>
> No power on earth can shake the German Reich now, Divine Providence has willed it that I carry through the fulfillment of the Germanic task.
>
> But if the voice speaks, then I know the time has come to act.[20]

Slowly, but surely, Hitler began to compare himself to Jesus Christ, although he personally detested Christianity and the Savior of the world.

Hermann Rauschning, a Prussian aristocrat who knew Hitler during the 1930s, wrote *Hitler Speaks* in 1939, describing Hitler's obsession with destroying Christianity and how he viewed himself as a Germanic messiah. In 1940 the book was published in America as *The Voice of Destruction*. It was a prophetic warning to the West about Hitler's demonic plans for the world.

Describing one encounter with Hitler, Rauschning quoted him as saying:

> The religions are all alike, no matter what they call themselves. They have no future—certainly none for the Germans. Fascism, if it likes, may come to terms with the Church. So shall I. Why not? That will not prevent me from tearing up Christianity root and branch, and annihilating it in Germany. The Italians are naive; they're quite capable of being heathens and Christians at the same time. The Italians and the French are essentially heathens. Their Christianity is only skin-deep. But the German is different. He is serious in everything he undertakes. He wants to be either a Christian or a heathen. He cannot be both. Besides, Mussolini will never make heroes of his Fascists. It doesn't matter there whether they're Christians or heathens. But for our people it is decisive whether they acknowledge the Jewish Christ-creed with its effeminate pity-ethics, or a strong, heroic belief in God in Nature, God in our own people, in our destiny, in our blood . . .

He continued:

> Leave the hair-splitting to others. Whether it's the Old Testament or the New, or simply the sayings of Jesus, according to Houston Stewart Chamberlain—it's all the same old Jewish swindle. It will not make us free. A German Church, a German Christianity, is distortion. One is either a German or a Christian. You cannot be both. You can throw the epileptic Paul out of Christianity—others have done so before us. You can make Christ into a noble human being, and deny his divinity and his role as a savior. People have been doing it for centuries. I believe there are such Christians today in England and America—Unitarians they call themselves, or something like that. It's no use, you cannot get rid of the mentality behind it. We don't

want people who keep one eye on the life in the hereafter. We need free men who feel and know that God is in themselves. . . .

Hitler went on to say:

You can't make an Aryan of Jesus, that's nonsense . . . What Chamberlain wrote in his Principles is, to say the least, stupid. What's to be done, you say? I will tell you: we must prevent the churches from doing anything but what they are doing now, that is, losing ground day by day. Do you really believe the masses will ever be Christian again? Nonsense! Never again. That tale is finished. No one will listen to it again. But we can hasten matters. The parsons will be made to dig their own graves. They will betray their God to us. They will betray anything for the sake of their miserable little jobs and incomes.[21]

Rauschning described Hitler's apparent encounter with demonic spirits while attempting to sleep:

His sleeplessness is more than the mere result of excessive nervous strain. He often wakes up in the middle of the night and wanders restlessly to and fro. Then he must have light everywhere. Lately he has sent at these times for young men who have to keep him company during his hours of manifest anguish. At times these conditions must have become dreadful. A man in the closest daily association with him gave me this account: Hitler wakes at night with convulsive shrieks. He shouts for help. He sits on the edge of his bed, as if unable to stir. He shakes with fear, making the whole bed vibrate. He shouts confused, totally unintelligible phrases. He gasps, as if imagining himself to be suffocating.

My informant described to me in full detail a remarkable scene—I should not have credited the story if it had not come from such a source. Hitler stood swaying in his room, looking wildly about him. "He! He! He's been here!" he gasped. His lips were blue. Sweat streamed down his face. Suddenly he began to reel off figures, and odd words and broken phrases, entirely devoid of sense. It sounded horrible. He used strangely composed and entirely un-German word-formations. Then he stood quite still, only his lips moving. He was massaged and offered something to drink. Then he suddenly broke out—

"There, there! In the corner! Who's that?"

He stamped and shrieked in the familiar way. He was shown that there was nothing out of the ordinary in the room, and then he gradually grew calm. After that he lay asleep for many hours, and then for some time things were endurable.[22]

What Rauschning was describing is demonic possession or oppression. In fact, he compared Hitler to a medium who channels evil spirits!

There is an instructive parallel—mediums. Most of these are ordinary, undistinguished persons; yet suddenly they acquire gifts that carry them far above the common crowd. These qualities have nothing to do with the medium's own personality. They are conveyed to him from without. The medium is possessed by them. He, himself, however, is uninfluenced by them. In the same way undeniable powers enter into Hitler, genuinely daemonic powers, which make men his instruments. The common united with the uncommon—that is what makes Hitler's personality so desperate a puzzle to those who come into contact with him. Dostoevsky might well have invented him, with the morbid derangement and the pseudo-creativeness of his hysteria.

I have frequently heard men confess that they are afraid of him, that they, grown men though they are, cannot visit him without a beating heart. They have the feeling that the man will suddenly spring at them and strangle them, or throw the inkpot at them, or do something senseless. There is a great deal of insincere enthusiasm, with eyes hypocritically cast up, and a great deal of self-deception, behind this talk of an unforgettable experience.[23]

Hitler, as it turns out, was greatly influenced in his thinking about his messianic role in Germany by a British occultist named Houston Stewart Chamberlain. He loved Germany so much that he became a naturalized German citizen. According to William L. Shirer, author of the classic *The Rise and Fall of the Third Reich*, Chamberlain

> was given to seeing demons who, by his own account, drove him
> relentlessly to seek new fields of study. . . . Once in 1896, when he
> was returning from Italy, the presence of a dream became so forceful
> that he got off the train at Gardone, shut himself up in a hotel room
> for eight days and . . . wrote feverishly on a biological thesis until he
> had the germ of the theme that would dominate all his later works:
> race and history . . . Since he felt himself goaded on by demons, his
> books . . . were written in the grip of a terrible fever, a veritable trance,
> a state of self-induced intoxication, so that . . . he was often unable
> to recognize them as his own work.[24]

Chamberlain wrote extensively against the Jewish people and in 1899 published *Foundations of the Nineteenth Century*, which he claimed was dictated to him by demons. It became the bible of the Nazi movement.

Occultist Lewis Spence described Hitler as one possessed by evil spirits:

> As Adolf Hitler has advanced in life there has steadily grown up within
> him another man, rather an evil spirit, of the most violent and deadly
> kind, to whose daily expansion he has offered little or no resistance.
>
> In a word, the malign power has seen in this base and pitiless crea-
> ture, utterly lost to all human sensibility, and moved only by crude
> and elementary emotions of revenge and mock sentiment, precisely
> the kind of vehicle which it sought, and which it ever seeks to carry
> out its infernal purpose . . . That he is impelled by forces the true
> nature of which he does not comprehend is plainly obvious . . . [It
> is] evident that he is under the domination of influences of which he
> is only the mouthpiece.[25]

Hitler wasn't the only demon-driven Nazi. Heinrich Himmler, the head of the SS (*Schutzstaffel*, Hitler's special bodyguard unit), was notorious for his interest in the occult, and he used demonic means to promote the ruthless murder of hundreds of thousands of Jews and other perceived enemies of the Third Reich.

The devastating results of the Nazi abandonment of Christ and their value system based on occultism are still physically evident today at the notorious Auschwitz death camp in Poland. This collectivist Nazi "utopia" of the twentieth century gave us the most notorious slave and death camp in modern history. In November 2014 I personally witnessed the aftermath of this horror with Governor Mike Huckabee when he led a group of evangelicals through the gates of the Nazi horror of Auschwitz.

The experience of visiting Auschwitz and then Auschwitz II, also known as Birkenau, is so emotional that it is very difficult to write about. A total of 1.5 million human beings walked through those same gates and into a hell on earth. Many did not die in the gas chambers but were kept alive on starvation diets to work with toxic chemicals and do other manual labor until they were too weak to continue.

Once useless as laborers, they were killed or simply allowed to starve to death.

The vast majority of the victims arriving in cattle cars and kept in sheds designed for horses were Jewish. In sheds designed to hold perhaps a few dozen horses, up to 700 human beings slept on bare wooden racks. Following Governor Huckabee through the horror-filled rooms, I kept my composure until I arrived in an area where thousands of children's shoes found by the Russians when they liberated Auschwitz in 1944 are displayed in hundred-foot-long cases.

Birkenau, not Auschwitz, was the true slaughterhouse with the first gas chambers and crematoriums specifically designed to eradicate an entire race of people. Those separated out by the infamous Dr. Mengele for the Birkenau Camp were dead within an hour after their arrival in closed rail boxcars. Funneled into what they thought were showers after their heads were shaved, they were gassed up to seven hundred at a time.

It could take fifteen minutes or more for these innocent victims of Hitler's imagined Jewless utopia to die—their bodies then were cremated. Their hair was sent back to Germany to mix with cotton and wool to make clothing, and the human ashes were used as fertilizer. This is the ultimate example of the inhumanity of a society that abandons God.

While at Birkenau, Governor Huckabee noted that the Germany of the 1930s and '40s was the most scientifically advanced and educated society in the world; yet they had abandoned God for a value system that allowed them to seek an end by any means. He reminded us that, unlike those who died there, we would be able to exit through the gates we had just entered. He asked, "If you were to take a message from those who could not leave, what would that message be?"

At a dinner in Krakow on the group's final night in that city, Governor Huckabee declared that "Auschwitz came into existence because God had been removed from Germany's culture." While reminding those present that the Nazis had brutally murdered millions, Huckabee noted that, in the United States, 55 million of the "most innocent who should be in the safest place in the world, their mother's wombs," have died at the hands of abortionists.

Huckabee said that the removal of God from Western society can have devastating consequences, as proven in Nazi- and Communist-run nations. Huckabee's comments on the horror visited on humanity by Hitler's attempt to establish his utopian "Thousand-Year Reich" is a chilling reminder of the descriptions given of the godless Communist society by Pastor Wurmbrand.

HIMMLER'S OCCULTIST STORM TROOPERS

Heinrich Himmler was one of Hitler's most ruthless killers—a man who ran the feared SS and was driven by a fascination with the occult and ancient Germanic warrior cults.

Bill Yenne, author of *Hitler's Master of the Dark Arts: Himmler's Black Knights and the Occult Origins of the SS*, describes Himmler this way:

> Hitler was the charismatic madman who brought Nazism to power. Himmler was the ruthless figure in the shadows, the man who took the philosophies that were at the roots of Nazism and methodically shaped and codified them. Himmler is the man whom General

Heinrich Hossbach described as "Hitler's evil spirit, cold, calculating and ambitious . . . undoubtedly the most purposeful and most unscrupulous figure in the Third Reich."[26]

Himmler was a disciple of occultist Karl Eckhart, who believed that each person is part of a soul group and is reincarnated repeatedly within the group. Himmler ordered twenty thousand copies of Eckhart's book *Temporal Immortality,* but the order was canceled after members of Hitler's inner circle convinced him that such occultism was damaging his efforts to co-opt the Christian church in Germany.

Nevertheless, Himmler promoted occult practices in the SS, and it became the most brutal element of the Nazi regime. It was he who established the hideous concentration camp Dachau and approved of grisly experiments on Jewish prisoners.

Himmler was undoubtedly one of the most evil men ever to walk the earth—and he and Hitler were both seen to be dedicated to serving voices or demonic spirits. Their hatred resulted in the torture and killing of millions throughout the world. Jesus Christ said that "the thief," referring to Satan, came into the world for one purpose: to steal, kill, and destroy (John 10:10). Regrettably, Himmler and Hitler's purpose was the same.

In the following chapters, I will chronicle the human suffering brought about by demonically controlled men like Hitler, Stalin, Mao, Robespierre, and others who have sought to create utopian societies on earth. What they have always inevitably created were demon-inspired, hellish societies resulting in hundreds of millions of deaths. Satan has effectively brought hell to earth through these men.

The ongoing war against utopian tyrants is more than physical; it is spiritual as well. The most brutal killers in history were firmly committed to defying God in the same way Satan himself did. In pages to come, I will describe the human carnage they caused.

2

SIR THOMAS MORE'S *UTOPIA*

In the twentieth century the term *collectivism* was often associated with Communism because of the notorious works of Karl Marx and Friedrich Engels. But collectivism, which is merely a form of utopianism, encompasses more systems than Marxism and has existed in one form or the other under various names for many centuries. This is clearly evident in the works of Friedrich Hayek, who, in *The Road to Serfdom*, stated, "The various kinds of collectivism, communism, fascism etc., differ among themselves in the nature of the goal toward which they want to direct the efforts of society. But they all differ from liberalism and individualism in wanting to organize the whole of society and its resources for a unitary end and refusing to recognize autonomous spheres in which the ends of the individuals are supreme."[1]

Whether it be an ancient Chinese emperor or an elected despot such as Venezuela's now-deceased Hugo Chávez, centralized control to achieve equal outcome is always the goal of the utopian autocrat. Although attempts at a utopian society under tight central control date back to ancient Greece, the modern term was coined by Thomas More, an official in the Court of Henry VIII, the king of England who created a schism in the Catholic Church over issues of the flesh.

Adolf Hitler was no less a utopian than Karl Marx or Pol Pot. All of these murderous and fanatical central planners had ideological roots tracing back to a rather obscure work of fiction authored by Thomas More and first published in Greek. Though many refer to it, far too few have read it, much less understand it.

Modern utopian tyrannies have knowingly or unknowingly modeled themselves on the ideas expressed in Sir Thomas More's *Utopia*, which was first published in 1516. Of course, many other books have been written on ideal collectivist or centrally planned societies, but More's, because of the name it coined, is often the most recognized. Although rarely read today, it had great influence on the collectivist leaders of the twentieth century. Vladimir Lenin championed More's *Utopia* as worthy of honor in his newly created worker's paradise of the Soviet Union. Being honored by a ruthless dictator such as Lenin confirms the totalitarian concepts of centralized collectivism portrayed in *Utopia*.

Critics have argued over More's true purpose in writing on a centrally planned utopian system. Some scholars claim his *Utopia* was a critique of collectivist movement within the church. Given translations of character names and places from Greek into English may confirm in the minds of many that it was indeed a parody of collectivism birthed in Europe. So its original title was far more descriptive of its purpose than scholars may want to admit. (It wasn't until 1551 that the first English translation of the book was published. It was titled: *On the best State of a Commonwealth and on the new Island of Utopia a Truly Golden Handbook, No Less Beneficial than Entertaining by the Most Distinguished and Eloquent Author Thomas More Citizen and Undersheriff of the Famous City of London.*[2])

Sir Thomas More's life and ignominious death were portrayed in the 1966 movie *A Man for All Seasons*. He was a brilliant lawyer, jurist, and Catholic scholar. He also served as a member of Parliament in 1504, and as an undersheriff in London.[3] He eventually became Lord Chancellor of Britain.

From an early age, it was clear that Thomas More was a natural leader. At nineteen, he attended Canterbury College in Oxford, where he mastered Greek as a student of William Grocyn and Thomas Linacre, the first to bring Greek studies from Italy to England. (Linacre, a physician, was founder of the College of Physicians.) After attending Canterbury College, More went on to study law. He was a devoted Catholic who at one point even studied for the priesthood, wore a hair shirt, and whipped himself as a way of subduing his flesh.

One biographical sketch of More detailed his philosophical leanings:

> With respect to his philosophy, Thomas More belonged very much to the early or Erasmian period of the English Renaissance in his emotional and intellectual attitudes—toleration of eclecticism, search for simplicity, stress on ethics, return to Greek sources, and desire for reform: social, political, educational, religious, and philosophical. These traits appear not only in his highly imaginative and durably significant creation, *Utopia*, but also in his most pertinent pronouncements in real life.[4]

More was a serious student of the Greek philosophies of Platonism, Aristotelianism, Stoicism, and Epicureanism (which involved pleasure seeking.) Several of these philosophies influenced More's observations of collectivism and central planning in the writing of *Utopia* and other theological works. The utopian society he wrote about somewhat resembles that of Plato's *Republic*.

In 1518, two years after *Utopia* was published, More became a member of King Henry VIII's Council and a valued adviser to the king. But More vehemently opposed the Protestant Reformation, and it was this association, coupled with his strong stance against rebellion of the Church of Rome, which had condemned Henry's desire to divorce his wife and marry his mistress, that ultimately led to More's beheading.

More's troubles began in 1534, during one of Parliament's darkest hours, when England passed the Succession Act. The act required More to take an oath that repudiated the pope and declared that King Henry's marriage to Catherine of Aragon was invalid. It also acknowledged that the children of Henry and mistress Anne Boleyn would be the legal heirs to the throne. More refused to take the oath and as a result was charged with treason, placed in the Tower of London, and beheaded in 1535. His head was then parboiled and hung on London Bridge. It is believed that somehow, perhaps through bribes, his daughter, Margaret Roper, retrieved his head. She also published a series of prison letters that he had written while languishing in the Tower, awaiting execution. These letters were addressed, not just to More's daughter, but to the British citizenry, as he clearly wanted to explain his position before losing his head to King Henry's wanton desires of the flesh.[5]

Margaret's husband, William, later wrote one of the first biographies of Thomas More, *The Life of Sir Thomas More*, in 1557. Roper portrayed More as a man of "singular virtue" and a "clear, unspotted conscience."[6]

MORE'S COLLECTIVIST UTOPIA

In *Utopia*, More describes a fictional conversation with Raphael Hythloday, a man who traveled around the world with Amerigo Vespucci. (Incidentally, Raphael is the name of a guardian angel and "Hythloday" is a compound of Greek words meaning "peddler of nonsense.") Hythloday tells the story of his five years as a guest on the island of Utopia, which means "nowhere" in Greek. He claims to have studied every aspect of Utopian culture and describes it in detail to More.

Thomas More's own political and cultural views are expressed both directly and indirectly through the characters, who carry on a lengthy philosophical conversation about Utopia and what makes an ideal form of government.

The book is divided into two sections. The first section is a rambling discussion of politics, religion, and philosophy between More, Hythloday, and More's friend Peter Giles. The second is a detailed description by Hythloday of his experiences in Utopia. The second section, which also details Utopian culture and government, was actually written first. More's book has become a classic description of a so-called perfect society, where all live in harmony with one another and willingly share their wealth with every member of the society.

More describes his version of Utopia essentially as a collectivist society, where private property is shunned, profit is frowned upon, and the acquiring of money is regarded as needless and the cause of wars and greed. In his planned economy there is the pretense of a democratic system, but in actuality it is a dictatorship of the proletariat run by self-appointed elitists.

More's writings indicate a clear understanding of Plato's *Republic* and the regimented culture of ancient Sparta under the tyrannical system devised by Lycurgus, which resembles Utopian society in many ways, as we will see later. Utopia also resembles the regimented tyrannies of the twentieth century, including the former Soviet Union, North Korea, and China under Mao. Human beings in More's Utopia are regarded as worker bees in a hive, not individuals with God-given rights.

Literary critics have tried to explain More's purpose in *Utopia* with much conflict. Some have suggested that it is a satire of British society in the 1500s; others have looked at it as serious social commentary on the inequalities More saw in England at the time. Some even wondered if More's purpose was to present Utopia as a model of government for future kings in England. What really matters today is the concepts described and the attempted implementation of them since.

Karl Kautsky, one of the most prominent Communist theoreticians of the late nineteenth and early twentieth centuries, wrote a critique in 1888 of Thomas More's *Utopia* and had high praise for what he saw as More's socialist system. In his book, *Thomas More and His Utopia*, Kautsky wrote: "As a Humanist and a politician, More was in the front rank of his contemporaries, as a Socialist he was far ahead of them all. His political, religious, and Humanist writings are to-day only read by a small number of historians. Had he not written Utopia his name would scarcely be better known to-day than that of the friend who shared his fate, Bishop Fisher of Rochester. His socialism made him immortal."[7]

Thomas More was considered a hero by Lenin, the ruthless dictator who died in 1922 shortly after the Russian Revolution. Lenin even ordered that More's name (shown as "T. More") be inscribed on a monument in Moscow's Alexandrosky Garden. It is one of eighteen names, along with "Karl Marx," on the monument.[8]

COLLECTIVIST PERFECTION

A further examination of More's work delivers an understanding of Lenin's admiration. The mythical Raphael Hythloday describes the Utopian culture as one free of poverty and the lust for money, a perfect collectivist society. The island paradise of Utopia was formerly part of a continent, but after the ruler Utopus conquered the land, he forced the inhabitants to dig a fifteen-mile-wide channel to separate the area from the continent.

Utopus's goal was to build a perfect society without being infected by other cultures. It was this very logic, of building purity from scratch, that led Pol Pot to murder one out of every three citizens in Cambodia in an attempt to return to a pure state of the proletariat from which to build his version of Utopia.

Utopus, Hythloday says, was determined to create a culture where everyone lived in harmony and peace with their neighbors and where the normal temptations associated with money were eradicated. Utopus designed a culture that valued equality above all else: equality in clothing (think, the gray uniforms of Mao's China), housing, and social status. There was no real possibility of personal advancement, as equal outcome was also assured.

According to Hythloday: "Utopus, that conquered it (whose name it still carries, for Abraxa was its first name), brought the rude and uncivilised inhabitants into such a good government, and to that measure of politeness, that they now far excel all the rest of mankind. After Utopus separated his island from the rest of the continent, he then required the inhabitants to build large cities—all within twenty-four miles of each other—so citizens could travel from one to another in a day. Every city was designed exactly the same so there would be no reason for an individual to move from one to another. All of the homes were built exactly alike as well, each having front and back doors (folding) that were always unlocked. Anyone could enter whatever home he or she wished, as no one was allowed to claim to have such a thing as 'private property.'"[9]

Uniformity was demanded and expected of all citizens and, oddly enough, they willingly accepted the demands without complaint. This, of course, defies human nature as bestowed by God in the form of free will. More offered no explanation for the people's lack of desire to practice that free will.

The citizens of Utopia are controlled from the cradle to the grave by magistrates who are chosen from among the people, who are in turn ruled by a prince who serves for life. Utopians have little freedom in choosing their own careers, as they are forced by the government to work part of the time as farmers and other times as laborers in the cities. In the Pol Pot version in Cambodia and in Mao's China, city dwellers were sent to the rural areas to farm as well.

The concepts of individual freedom or human rights are unknown in the culture described by Hythloday. Every person is considered to be a tool of the all-powerful, benevolent central government, which controls the person's life from the moment he rises in the morning until he goes to bed at night. In essence, the citizens of Utopia are happily enslaved, working their entire lives in service to a government that controls every aspect of their existence.

The description of Utopia in More's work is much like the dictatorship described in George Orwell's *1984*, but without the electronic surveillance systems. Utopians live in what amounts to a police state, but it is more benign and invisible than the brutal dictatorship Orwell described. In both systems, however, people are forced to conform to the will of the rulers or face the consequences. In the Orwellian nightmare, individuals who sought to break free of the dictatorship were systematically tortured and brainwashed into submission. If they refused to submit, they would be killed. In Utopia, these individuals would be enslaved or banished from the island.

The system of government in *Utopia* is totalitarian in nature and rejects such basic concepts as freedom of speech, freedom of conscience, freedom of choice, and freedom of movement. No one owns his own property and everyone must share all of their produce with their fellow citizens. In the cities, citizens must eat together in huge mess halls, just as Spartan soldiers did. (In Sparta, soldiers were permanently separated from their wives. In Utopia, wives eat in the same mess halls, but at different tables.) They are summoned to these mess halls by the blowing of a trumpet; thus they are also required to eat at the same times each day. During these communal dinners, the citizens are required to listen to sermons on morality.

Population control is strictly enforced in More's Utopia, and children are removed from homes and sent to live with other families if there is a perceived imbalance in the populations of various cities. The Utopians would have recognized Hillary Clinton's belief that "it takes a village" to raise a child and that each child was actually the property of the state rather than the parents, whose own role was more like paid babysitters than legal guardians and decision makers. Perhaps the basis of Hillary Clinton's book *It Takes a Village* was conceived from More's *Utopia*.

In addition, whole groups of individuals can be forcibly moved into other sections of Utopia or to a neighboring continent to set up colonies. According to Hythloday, "They draw out a number of their citizens out of the several towns and send them over to the neighbouring continent, where, if they find that the inhabitants have more soil than they can well cultivate, they fix a colony, taking the inhabitants into their society if they are willing to live with them."[10]

Furthermore, all Utopians "wear the same sort of clothes, without any other distinction except what is necessary to distinguish the two sexes and the married and unmarried."[11] This text may very well have been the source that led China's Mao Tse-tung to dictate the drab gray semi-uniforms for every man, woman and child in his version of utopia.

The ultimate goal of the culture is to enforce equality of income, appearance, and moral values. No one is to have more than anyone else, and no one is to try to be better than anyone else in the culture. This is again clearly "equal outcome" rather than "equal opportunity."

What More describes is a totalitarian system that suppresses the natural desires of humanity and kills any desire to create, build, or invent new products or services. His version of Utopia stagnates industry much as was done in the Soviet Union, with the classic example being the "people's car," the Lada.

Whether fictional or real, this type of environment destroys innovation and discourages the natural instincts in men and women to generate value for reward. There is no incentive to create or be productive because the products are equality distributed regardless of quality.

MORE MARXIST PRAISES FOR *UTOPIA*

As stated earlier, the Utopians' daily lives are rigidly controlled by rulers known as "Syphogrants" (magistrates) who divide the day into six hours of work—three in the morning and three after dinner, eight hours for sleep, and the rest of the time unstructured. However, the people are not permitted to use this time for "idleness," and of course, the rulers determine what is considered idleness. In More's world, useless, idle individuals include religious professionals, rich gentlemen, noblemen, the bodyguards of noblemen, and beggars!

Communist philosopher Karl Kautsky was pleased that More's views on working hours were similar to those of Karl Marx. Wrote Kautsky, "It is interesting to compare More's views with those of Marx regarding the curtailment of working hours in a communistic society. A similar train of thought will be found in both. In *Capital* we read: 'Only by suppressing the capitalist form of production could the length of the working-day be reduced to the necessary labour-time.'"[12]

J. H. Hexter, in his 1952 book, *More's Utopia: The Biography of an Idea* (published by Princeton University Press), also expressed pleasure with More's communistic ideas. He called More a "Christian humanist" and said that the most important part of *Utopia* is More's economic view, a view that abolishes private property and an economy based on money.

Another writer, Russell Ames, in *Citizen Thomas More and His*

Utopia (1949) considered him a Communist who was concerned about the social conditions facing the poor in the sixteenth century. He expressed regret that more has not been made of More's economic views that were influenced by early Christian Communism and the thinking of the humanists of his time—including his friend Erasmus, the humanist philosopher.[13]

UTOPIANS REJECT MONEY

In More's *Utopia* money is worthless and never used except to pay for mercenaries to fight wars. Precious metals, such as silver and gold, are also viewed with disdain. In fact, they are so valueless that they are used to make chamber pots (toilet bowls) and other crude items. Gold is held in such contempt it is used to make the chains that bind Utopia's slaves.

In this socialist utopia, the concept of free enterprise is unknown, as there is no way to buy and sell anything. All is held in common and each person is free to take what he wants out of local storehouses where farmers deliver their crops and where city dwellers bring their products.

Of course, this is a totally unrealistic and unworkable situation in the real world. Human greed and sin always play a role in human conduct. Some will always take far more than needed and leave others with little or nothing. This explains the constant shortages and long lines in the old Soviet Union and the Venezuela of today, as fixed, low prices, which are supposed to benefit all, leave shelves empty. More presented a cultural climate of benign and loving cooperation that has never existed and, by the very nature of the free will of man, can never exist.

He also presented a world that condemns rewards. Yet, the Bible describes rewards and punishments both in this world and in the next. And there is no sin in using one's labor to create value in a product or service that can in turn be sold or traded to meet one's needs and desires. Jesus's parable of the talents was clearly designed to teach His disciples that it's good to take something of value and add more value to it (see Matthew 25:14–30).

The current entitlement systems in Europe and the United States have quite a lot in common with the Utopian practices of communal "sharing." The system robs people of the desire to produce value for reward and causes generations of welfare dependency.

UTOPIAN MEDICAL CARE

In More's Utopia the government offers free medical care to every citizen at four hospitals built at various locations throughout the island. But, there's a dark side to this medical care. When a person becomes too ill, he is urged by the government leaders to commit suicide, either by starvation or by a lethal dose of drugs. In Utopia, it is a citizen's duty to not die too old or too sick. It may seem odd that those in Utopia would accept this as a norm, but assisted suicide in Europe is now encouraged and common for the chronically ill. It is supported by a majority of Europeans.

TRAVEL RESTRICTED

No one is free to travel without permission in More's Utopia. Travel inside and outside of Utopia is permitted only if the person first obtains a passport from the rulers. The passport limits how long the citizen may be gone from his home and from his state-imposed duties. Once a citizen's travel has been preapproved, the rulers supply the traveler with a free wagon and a slave. The traveler carries no provisions along with him because he's given free food and lodging all along the way. He must, however, work for it.

Anyone who travels without getting a passport is punished severely. If he commits a second offense, he's put into slavery.[14] Utopians prefer to put the offender into slavery instead of prison so he can be useful.

WARFARE

More's Utopians avoid fighting their own battles if they can. They prefer to hire mercenaries to fight and die for them. They also engage in political propaganda inside the enemy's territory to spread disinformation and offer rewards to anyone in the enemy camp who will kill the prince of that nation or those close to the prince in power. High salaries are paid to a race of warriors known as "Zapoletes," who will fight for any country for a price. More uses this to show why Utopians had a hatred for the profit motive. Paying the warriors indicated they had no set moral standards and would kill for the country that pays the most. The love of money trumps any true allegiance to a nation or its cause, according to the Hythloday account.

The Utopians place no value whatsoever on the lives of the Zapoletes. They consider it a benefit to all of the countries nearby that Zapoletes die in battle. The fewer of them, the better, is the Utopian belief.

As Hythloday puts it, "As soon as they [the Utopians] declare war, they take care to have a great many schedules, that are sealed with their common seal, affixed in the most conspicuous places of their enemies' country. This is carried secretly, and done in many places all at once. In these they promise great rewards to such as shall kill the prince, and lesser in proportion to such as shall kill any other persons who are those on whom, next to the prince himself, they cast the chief balance of the war."[15]

The Utopians also offer money to those who are willing to commit treason against the other country's leaders—another slap at the profit motive, but this sounds vaguely as if More had read *The Art of War* by Sun Tzu.

Utopians don't pursue a defeated enemy or destroy cities or burn fields. They also don't go to war against a nation that has cheated them in commerce, since they don't value products anyway. Only in nations that value private property do people get hurt when their trading partner cheats them, according to Utopian thinking. "Economic" crimes are irrelevant to the Utopians.

In yet another slap against private property, the Utopians don't permit any soldiers to claim booty from a battle. All items confiscated in battle become "common" property controlled by the Utopian rulers! In the twentieth century Hitler's drive to create a utopia required funding far past the ability to tax the German people. Initially he robbed Jews of their property to finance his dream. His lust to create his utopian empire of a Thousand-Year Reich later led to raiding art museums in occupied areas. However, looting has been a part of war throughout the history of mankind.

RELIGIOUS PRACTICE IN UTOPIA

Though the Utopians have a variety of individual religious beliefs, the best and brightest among them believe in one overarching "God." According to Hythloday:

> There are several sorts of religions, not only in different parts of the island, but even in every town; some worshipping the sun, others the moon or one of the planets. Some worship such men as have been eminent in former times for virtue or glory, not only as ordinary deities, but as the supreme god. Yet the greater and wiser sort of them worship none of these, but adore one eternal, invisible, infinite, and incomprehensible Deity; as a Being that is far above all our apprehensions, that is spread over the whole universe, not by His bulk, but by His power and virtue; Him they call the Father of All, and acknowledge that the beginnings, the increase, the progress, the vicissitudes, and the end of all things come only from Him; nor do they offer divine honours to any but to Him alone. . . .
>
> These are their religious principles:—That the soul of man is immortal, and that God of His goodness has designed that it should be happy; and that He has, therefore, appointed rewards for good and virtuous actions, and punishments for vice, to be distributed after this life.[16]

The Utopians practice religious tolerance, and many of them warmly embrace Christianity. The only problem with Christians, however, emerges when one of the newly baptized believers begins condemning other Utopians to hell for not becoming Christians. He is banished from the community for his evangelical efforts. According to Hythloday, "This is one of the ancientest laws among them—that no man shall be blamed for reasoning in the maintenance of his own religion."[17]

Hythloday said of one zealous Christian:

He being newly baptised did, notwithstanding all that we could say
to the contrary, dispute publicly concerning the Christian religion,
with more zeal than discretion, and with so much heat, that he not
only preferred our worship to theirs, but condemned all their rites as
profane, and cried out against all that adhered to them as impious and
sacrilegious persons, that were to be damned to everlasting burnings.
Upon his having frequently preached in this manner he was seized,
and after trial he was condemned to banishment, not for having dis-
paraged their religion, but for his inflaming the people to sedition.[18]

When King Utopus originally created Utopia, he expressed two
basic convictions about religion: (1) that it would be destructive for any
person to use violence or coercion to bring another man into acceptance
of a religious belief; and (2) that the truth about any religious faith
would eventually be revealed. Utopus also was convinced that a person
was subhuman if he believed that the soul dies when the body dies and
that life in this world is merely the result of a random accident. He
required all the citizens of Utopia to believe that there is a reward for
goodness and punishment for evil in the afterlife.

***

Sir Thomas More was aggressive in his attacks on the leaders of
the Protestant Reformation. For example, he was responsible for
denouncing William Tyndale as a heretic for being a Protestant and
publishing an English-language version of the Bible.[19] Some would cite
the fact that *Utopia* was written two years before the official beginning
of the Protestant Reformation as proof More was not at the time referring to that group. However, there had been an ongoing Protestant
movement in Europe for decades prior to Luther. In More's *Utopia*
priests were married and women could become priests. This indicates
a knowledge of the many demands in and outside of the church that
Thomas More as an educated man was aware of and perhaps, as a
devout Catholic, feared. This may have been more of a warning to

the Church of "This could be you" than a modeling of his beliefs.

THE DYSTOPIAN REALITY

Thomas More's *Utopia* inspired many future thinkers and science fiction writers to create their own versions of utopian societies or dystopian societies (societies characterized by poverty, oppression, and totalitarianism). Contriving idealized and perfect societies in fiction is harmless, but the evil results become clearly evident when a utopian zealot attempts the creation of such a society in real time in a real world. What inevitably ensues is a hideous Dystopia, not a Utopia. People die, productivity is killed, and human freedom is extinguished, often for decades or longer.

George Orwell, writing in *1984* and *Animal Farm*, Aldous Huxley in *Brave New World*, and Yevgeny Zamyatin in *We*, created dystopian futures that were based on real-life totalitarian systems or on emerging technologies that could be used to enslave entire populations.

Orwell and Huxley both seem to have drawn on the 1923 novel by Zamyatin that describes a totalitarian world in the twenty-sixth century. George Lucas's 1971 movie, *THX 1138*, appears to be based on this dystopian novel as well.

In *We*, Zamyatin has created a world that sounds eerily similar to More's Utopia, the warrior state of ancient Sparta, and the vicious totalitarian state created by Lenin in Russia (without the technological advances of the twenty-sixth century). In the dystopian world created by Zamyatin, all on Earth are ruled by totalitarian Guardians, and citizens live in glass houses so they can be constantly watched. Individuality has been wiped out to the point that people don't have names but rather numbers to identify themselves.

In this dystopian society all wear identical uniforms and consume synthetic food. Each day, the Earth residents are forced to engage in recreation, consisting of marching together while the anthem of the "Single State" is blared over loudspeakers. Marriage is nonexistent, but citizens are permitted to lower curtains around their glass houses for what's known as the "sex hour." Children are not raised in families, but rather, in the "it takes a village" model spoken so highly of in leftist circles today. Every moment of a person's life is ordered by "the Tables of Hourly Commandments."

Capital punishment in the One State is accomplished through use of the Guillotine—not the crude one used in the French Revolution to maintain the "virtue" of Robespierre's dictatorship, but a modernized version that kills the person by evaporating him into a pool of water.

George Orwell reviewed *We* in 1946 for the *British Tribune* and noted: "The guiding principle of the State is that happiness and freedom are incompatible. In the Garden of Eden man was happy, but in his folly he demanded freedom and was driven out into the wilderness. Now the Single State has restored his happiness by removing his freedom."[20]

We ends badly for the main character, who falls in love with a freedom fighter, much as the main character Winston Smith did in *1984*. Neither character comes out victorious against the all-powerful surveillance state. They both eventually become reabsorbed into the system after their failed attempts to break free. The quest for human freedom is crushed.

Orwell's tragic character is tortured into submission, while Zamyatin's character becomes the victim of brain surgery which removes the section of his brain that controls imagination. Both are reenslaved and their freedom of thought is suppressed by their masters.

The tyrannical system Zamyatin envisioned is a world of advanced technology that is used to keep its subjects in slavery. The nightmarish future in *1984* is one of technological and cultural decay, where elevators don't work but Big Brother still has enough technology working to put telescreens in party members' apartments to keep constant watch on them.

In Huxley's *Brave New World*, citizens are kept in subjection through the use of drugs, and a rigid caste system is in place. Morons are deliberately created to do menial labor in this technological dictatorship.

The Orwell/Huxley/Zamyatin views of the future are far more likely than the perfect society envisioned by Thomas More or others like him. Human beings are granted by their Creator free will, which can't be bred out or changed by imposing social systems upon them by a totalitarian leader—benevolent or otherwise.

The Hunger Games trilogy by Suzanne Collins also describes a dystopian future government that controls everyone's life in a North American dictatorship called Panem. In this book trilogy and movie series, the North American continent is ruled by a city known as the Capitol, which controls twelve separate districts. The Capitol itself was a utopian state, financed by the brutal treatment of the districts.

No one could leave a district without permission, and the residents were kept in abject poverty. Each district produced a particular product for the Capitol, but the residents were not allowed the fruits of their labors. At one point, there were thirteen districts, and they rebelled against their tyrannical leaders. The rebellion was defeated, and allegedly District 13 was completely destroyed. The totalitarians have since ruled Panem with an iron fist for more than seventy years.

To punish the remaining twelve districts each year for their rebellion, the Capitol holds "the Hunger Games," a televised event that brings a boy and girl from each district to fight to the death in a controlled outdoor environment. Only one victor can emerge. Twenty-three teenagers must die for the entertainment of the hedonistic citizens who live in the utopian Capitol.

In this dystopian world, human freedom has been extinguished, and the heartless citizens of the Capitol enjoy watching teenagers brutally killing each other in various heinous manners. Unlike More's *Utopia*, the ending of Collins's trilogy is more realistic to the norm: after causing untold suffering and death to maintain a utopian existence inside the Capitol, the brutal system is brought to its knees in defeat.

The various dystopias portrayed in these and other fictional accounts more aptly describe the results of attempted utopian rule than does Thomas More's *Utopia*. History has revealed that utopian leaders, regardless of their intent, inevitably become tyrants who infringe upon human rights and the very dignity of mankind granted in the image of God to fulfill their utopian visions. Coercion, most often deadly, is always required to cause men and women to give up their freedom and become mere cogs in a state-run machine.

In the late nineteenth and early twentieth centuries, Utopian writers like Edward Bellamy, who penned *Looking Backward*, and Woodrow Wilson's alter ego, Colonel Edward Mandell House, who wrote *Philip Dru: Administrator*, described utopian societies seemingly based on Thomas More's concept of Utopia. Bellamy and House, whom we will discuss in a later chapter, both inspired others to turn their Marxian ideas into public policy.

Utopian visionaries, while claiming a high moral ground, are typically amoral and even more ruthless than those described in *1984*, *Brave New World*, or *Hunger Games*. Far from the model of More's Utopia is the reality of Nazi Germany and the Soviet Union.

As we continue, we will look at other origins of utopian thinking, how it has devastated various cultures, and what we must do to fight its reappearance. The menacing chance of it reemerging again as a government, perhaps even in the United States, is a terrifying thought that should inspire all those who love freedom to stay on guard and to stop its advance at first sight.

3

SPARTA AND PLATO'S *REPUBLIC* INSPIRE UTOPIAN

TYRANTS

The Grecian city-state of Sparta and Plato's descriptions of the supposedly perfect society in his *Republic* and in the *Laws* (a twelve-book series) have been the inspiration for utopian tyrants throughout history. Sparta was a collectivist, centrally planned city-state. Individuality was discouraged, and all were expected to live their lives in obedience to the dictates of the totalitarian leadership. Boys were raised from birth to be soldiers and not much more.

Sparta moved to utopian tyranny under the rule of Lycurgus, who imposed a series of laws on the Spartans around 800 BC. Lycurgus turned Sparta into a disciplined war machine, a country where freedom was nonexistent and where cultural creativity died. Regrettably, his influence over this nation-state lasted some five hundred years. Sparta eventually decayed from within, and outside invasions decimated its population.

Before Lycurgus imposed his draconian laws upon Spartan's citizens, there had been art and creativity in the city-state's culture; however, Lycurgus ordered all Spartans to disregard art (with the exception of some martial-style songs, music, and poetry). He taught them to distrust philosophy and to avoid excess in all things. Even their speech patterns were restricted to avoid pointless chatter, gossip, or too much speaking of any kind.

Lycurgus banned most of the arts, in exchange for a militaristic society that regimented the lives of all citizens. Every boy was raised to be a ruthless, disciplined soldier who would blindly follow orders and die, if needed, for the state. The Spartans became a feared military force in Greece, but a society lacking freedom of thought, action, or inventiveness.

The historian Plutarch described how Lycurgus traveled to other parts of the known world to study various forms of government and cultures before returning to Sparta to implement his totalitarian plans. He searched for a society based on virtue and a warrior ethos. Lycurgus then traveled to the Greek Oracle of Delphi (a priestess of the god Apollo) to obtain instructions from the "gods" on how to rule Sparta, or at least claimed that as his purpose.

According to Plutarch, the oracle taught Lycurgus that he himself was a "god" and confirmed his ruthless plans for governing Sparta as purposed by the gods.

With apparent "divine" approval through this mystical oracle, Lycurgus began to remake Sparta in the utopian image he imagined. Plutarch related how he first established a council of elders who would have an equal vote with the two kings who ruled Sparta at the time. According to Plutarch, "eight-and-twenty elders would lend the kings their support in the suppression of democracy, but would use the people to suppress any tendency to despotism."[1]

Long before Karl Marx, Lycurgus was the ideal collectivist and central planner. He believed that Sparta's citizens were the property of the state and that they had no higher purpose than to obey the dictates of the rulers throughout their lives. The concept of individual liberty and of freedom of conscience and action soon became nonexistent in Sparta. The state rather than the family was the center of each person's life.

Unlike Marx or Lenin, Lycurgus never produced an overall doctrine in writing for Sparta. Using this tactic, he could add to the rules or change them as he pleased, just as other despotic rulers over Sparta did who followed after his death.

As a good collectivist, Lycurgus hated wealth and private property, so he decided that wealthy landowners should be stripped of all their property so it could be given to the poor. He engaged in what current collectives describe as "redistributing" the wealth. In the twentieth century, Communists called this land-theft process "agrarian reform." According to Plutarch, Lycurgus accomplished this without murder:

> Lykurgus abolished all the mass of pride, envy, crime, and luxury which flowed from those old and more terrible evils of riches and poverty, by inducing all land-owners to offer their estates for redistribution, and prevailing upon them to live on equal terms one with another, and with equal incomes, striving only to surpass each other in courage and virtue, there being henceforth no social inequalities among them except such as praise or blame can create.[2]

Lycurgus also hated the concept of money because it supposedly resulted in greed and avarice. His solution was to abolish the use of gold and silver money and to make iron money the only legal tender in his city-state. The iron money was so large that it had to be carried by a yoke of oxen. The destruction of the gold and silver standard also made it impossible for Sparta to effectively trade with other countries. No other country recognized Sparta's iron money, and few people even wanted it. The abolition of gold and silver money effectively isolated Sparta from the supposed corrupting influences of strangers from other nations.

According to Plutarch:

> After this, he ordered a general expulsion of the workers in useless trades. Indeed, without this, most of them must have left the country when the ordinary currency came to an end, as they would not be able to sell their wares: for the iron money was not current among other Greeks, and had no value, being regarded as ridiculous; so that it could not be used for the purchase of foreign trumpery, and no cargo was shipped for a Laconian port, and there came into the country

no sophists, no vagabond soothsayers, no panders, no goldsmiths or workers in silver plate, because there was no money to pay them with. Luxury, thus cut off from all encouragement, gradually became extinct; and the rich were on the same footing with other people, as they could find no means of display, but were forced to keep their money idle at home.[3]

Foreigners who had made a living selling their goods and services in Sparta departed from the city-state since Sparta's iron money was useless to them. Spartan businessmen couldn't freely market their goods in neighboring cities, and Sparta became an isolated military base.

Because the state was more important than the family in the lives of the people, Lycurgus moved to stop them from eating together in their homes. He instituted common mess halls, where citizens were required to eat together. His objective was to make Spartans think of themselves as members of a larger family known as the state. The traditional family structure was basically abolished under this type of tyrannical rule.

Groups of fifteen Spartans would eat together at tables in the common mess hall and would be required to bring food to share with others. After the evening meal, the Spartans were forced to return to their homes without torches to guide them so they could be taught to walk fearlessly in the dark.

Lycurgus controlled every aspect of Spartan life. There were even precise regulations as to how a Spartan home could be roofed. The beams of each house had to be constructed with an axe, while the doors had to be built with a saw and no other tools.

His regulations for marriage were equally bizarre. Husbands (all of whom were trained for war) were forced to live apart from their wives and children most of their lives. Plutarch wrote:

> Their marriage custom was for the husband to carry off his bride by force. They did not carry off little immature girls, but grown up women, who were ripe for marriage. After the bride had been carried off the bridesmaid received her, cut her hair close to her head,

dressed her in a man's cloak and shoes, and placed her upon a couch in a dark chamber alone. The bridegroom, without any feasting and revelry, but as sober as usual, after dining at his mess, comes into the room, looses her virgin zone, and, after passing a short time with her, retires to pass the night where he was wont, with the other young men. And thus he continued, passing his days with his companions, and visiting his wife by stealth, feeling ashamed and afraid that any one in the house should hear him, she on her part plotting and contriving occasions for meeting unobserved. This went on for a long time, so that some even had children born to them before they ever saw their wives by daylight. These connections not only exercised their powers of self-restraint, but also brought them together with their bodies in full vigour and their passions unblunted by unchecked intercourse with each other, so that their passion and love for each other's society remained unextinguished.[4]

Lycurgus was an advocate of infanticide, which became an institution in Sparta. Whenever a child was born, it was considered state property and, if a boy, he was destined to spend most of his life training or engaging in warfare against Sparta's enemies. Thus, he had to be strong and indifferent to pain and privation. Babies that appeared to have defects or weakness at birth were eliminated, as they could not serve the Spartan state and thus had no value.

The manner of death of the unwanted babies was not as sterile as it is today at a Planned Parenthood clinic. Newborns were taken to a group of elders for examination. If those elders chose a child for disposal, it was taken to the top of a mountain cliff and thrown off, to be eaten by wild animals.

Boys in Spartan culture were taken from their families at age seven to live in military-style barracks and there ruthlessly trained for combat. According to Plutarch, these boys had only one garment to wear after their twelfth year and were forbidden to take warm baths. They didn't sleep on mattresses, but on beds of rushes they had picked from the banks of a local river. Every day of their lives in training was filled with floggings and hardships to prepare them for a life on the battlefield. They were forced to be on active duty in the Spartan army until age sixty, which was well past life expectancy at the time.

Often the younger boys were deliberately starved and were encouraged to steal in order to survive; however, if caught, they were flogged for having failed to steal successfully. According to Plutarch, "The boys steal with such earnestness that there is a story of one who had taken a fox's cub and hidden it under his cloak, and, though his entrails were being torn out by the claws and teeth of the beast, persevered in concealing it until he died. This may be believed from what the young men in Lacedaemon do now, for at the present day I have seen many of them perish under the scourge at the altar of Diana Orthias."[5]

Sparta developed sophisticated military systems, and its soldiers are forever memorialized in history at the Battle of Thermopylae, where three hundred Spartans stood their ground, delayed the advance of thousands of Persian troops for three days, and inflicted twenty thousand casualties upon the Persians.

Lycurgus forbade free travel, and outsiders were discouraged from coming to Sparta. He feared that if free travel in and out of the country were permitted, the Spartans might become infected with the thoughts and practices of other cultures. Such restrictions are typically imposed by totalitarian governments based on central planning even today. North Korea is a modern-day equivalent of Sparta.

The Spartans were also strictly divided into classes, with slaves known as the Helots at the bottom of the system who outnumbered the Spartans at least ten to one. Their only reason for existence was to supply crops and services to the Spartan elites. To keep the Helots enslaved and in constant fear, Sparta's leaders created a secret police much like the Soviet KGB or the Nazi Gestapo to terrorize them on a regular basis. This force was called the Krypteia. Plutarch described their activities:

> The Krypteia was this: the leaders of the young men used at intervals to send the most discreet of them into different parts of the country, equipped with daggers and necessary food; in the daytime these men

used to conceal themselves in unfrequented spots, and take their rest, but at night they would come down into the roads and murder any Helots they found. And often they would range about the fields, and make away with the strongest and bravest Helots they could find. Also, as Thucydides mentions in his History of the Peloponnesian War, those Helots who were especially honoured by the Spartans for their valour were crowned as free men, and taken to the temples with rejoicings; but in a short time they all disappeared, to the number of more than two thousand, and in such a way that no man, either then or afterwards, could tell how they perished.[6]

The Helots had once been free in their own area, known as Messenia, but Sparta coveted their land and productivity, so they invaded it and conquered it. Spartan soldiers then spent twenty years working to keep the Helots in submission. These farmers became property of the city-state, and Spartans were constantly on guard against Helot uprisings or conspiracies to break free of their bondage.

Sparta had to deal with both internal strife and outside enemies. As it expanded its territories, it also had to subdue its new slaves—and keep them subdued. It was constantly at war, and its armies were constantly training, fighting, and dying.

During the twenty-seven-year Peloponnesian War against Athens, Spartans "butchered as enemies all whom they took on the sea, whether allies of Athens or neutrals," according to historian Thucydides.[7] It was a relentless war but ultimately resulted in Spartan victory.

EVERYONE—EXCEPT SLAVES—IS EQUAL

In Lycurgus's utopian system, everyone was to be equal, and the person who stood out as better than others often forfeited his life by refusing to be average in his accomplishments.

Sparta, under the utopian ideology of Lycurgus, could not and would not adapt to changing times. It declined because of its inability to reform its institutions or provide any sort of flexibility for its citizens. There was no innovation because Spartans were forbidden to think for themselves. There was, of course, no reason to invent or work harder at a project to create value for trade. Without this incentive economic activity declined.

Friedrich Schiller, a German dramatist and student of totalitarian systems such as those in Sparta, gave a speech on Lycurgus and Spartan culture at the University of Jena in August 1789. In his speech, "The Legislation of Lycurgus and Solon," he compared the difference between oligarchical government and republican governments, saying one favors freedom of the individual, and the other glorifies an all-powerful state.

Schiller condemned the Spartan totalitarian system for its denial of human freedom and its destruction of human progress. Lycurgus, noted Schiller,

> founded his state on the ruin of morality; in an entirely different way, too, he worked against the highest purpose of humanity, in that, through his well thought-out system of state, he held the minds of the Spartans fast at the level where he had found them, and hemmed in all progress for eternity.
>
> All industry was banned, all science neglected, all trade with foreign peoples forbidden, everything foreign was excluded. All channels were thereby closed, through which his nation might have obtained more enlightened ideas, for the Spartan state was intended to revolve solely around itself, in perpetual uniformity, in a sad egoism.
>
> The business of all its citizens together was to maintain what they possessed, and to remain as they were, not to obtain anything new, not to rise to a higher level. Unrelenting laws were to stand watch, that no innovation take grip upon the clockwork of the state, that the very progress of time change nothing in the form of the laws. To make this condition perpetual, it was necessary to hold the mind of the people at the level where they stood when the state was founded.
>
> But we have seen that progress of mind should be the purpose of the state.
>
> Lycurgus's state could persist under but one condition, that the mind of the people stagnate, and he was thus only able to sustain

his state by trespassing against the highest and only purpose of the state. Thus, what is cited in praise of Lycurgus, that Sparta would only flourish as long as it followed the letter of its laws, is the worst one might say about it.[8]

Schiller stated further, "This most remarkable [Spartan] constitution is contemptible to the highest degree, and nothing more sad could befall humanity, than that all states be founded on this model."[9]

One virtue above all was established in Sparta, said Schiller: love of fatherland. It was to this artificial impulse that the most natural and the most beautiful emotions of mankind were sacrificed.

> Political merit was sought at the expense of all moral emotions, and the capacity to attain this political merit was the only capability inculcated.
>
> In Sparta there was no marital love, no mother's love, no child's love, no friendship—there were nothing but citizens, and nothing but the virtue of citizens.

Schiller continued his analysis of the despicable nature of Spartan culture by noting:

> Universal human emotions were smothered in Sparta in a way yet more outrageous, and the soul of all duties, respect for the species, was irrevocably lost.
>
> A law made it a duty of the Spartans to treat their slaves inhumanely, and in these unfortunate victims of butchery, humanity was cursed and abused.
>
> The Spartan Book of Laws itself preached the dangerous principle, that people be considered as means, not as ends—the foundations of natural law and morality were thereby torn asunder, by law.
>
> Morality was utterly sacrificed to obtain something, which can only be valuable as a means to this morality.[10]

This Spartan utopian tyranny, of course, inspired Adolf Hitler and other totalitarian systems. *Sparta in Modern Thought*, edited by historians Stephen Hodkinson and Ian MacGregor Morris, describes how Spartan culture was used by such tyrants as models for their dictatorships. In 1940, for example, Hitler had a textbook printed for German youth, titled *Sparta: The Life-Struggle of an Aryan Master-Race*, by archaeologist Otto-Wilhelm von Vacano. Sparta's history was to be an inspiration to German youth in order to create Hitler's thousand-year reign on earth. Nazi youth were to be educated in the same way that Spartan youth were. Both were to pledge their total obedience to the state and were to spend their lives spreading the totalitarianism envisioned by Hitler and his Spartan role models.[11]

Stephen Hodkinson, in *Sparta: The Body Politic*, wrote:

> Even before they came to power in 1933, National Socialist thinkers began to build on these longstanding analogies between Sparta and Germany. The battle of Thermopylae and the connection between the Spartan warrior state and the Nordic master race played important roles in Nazi propaganda and self-representation, alongside other aspects of the Spartan system such as its brutal treatment of the helots, its supposed eugenic policies and racial purity, its educational system, and its state control over landownership.[12]

Hitler's Gestapo was very similar to the Krypteia, the secret police established by the Spartans to terrorize its Helot population into submission. Lenin also established a Krypteia-like terror system, known as the Cheka, when he first seized power. The Cheka engaged in a systematic reign of terror on all Russian citizens in order to bring them into total submission to his tyrannical rule. The Cheka eventually became the KGB in the former Soviet Union police state. And, of course, when Mao Tse-tung was leading a Communist revolution in China during the 1920s, he told his followers that it was "necessary to bring about a . . . reign of terror in every county." He said that "anyone who has land is a tyrant, and all gentry are bad." They were the targets of his hatred of private property and wealth. In the cities, Mao set up an elaborate secret police system to control the Chinese—a system that still exists today.[13]

The German preoccupation with Sparta's collectivist, central-planning nature actually predated Hitler by two centuries. The Prussian Empire headed by Frederick II in the mid-eighteenth century was known at the time as the "Sparta of the North" for its fascination with Sparta's military discipline. In fact, Frederick II (Frederick the Great) molded his Prussian Army on the Spartan model and introduced state-run schools to fashion young men and women into servants of the state. Prussia was characterized under Frederick the Great as an army with a country, rather than a country with an army.

Voltaire, the atheist who became a friend of Frederick's, described Prussia as Sparta in the morning and Athens in the afternoon because at least the Prussian leader didn't shun the arts or creativity, as Lycurgus had.[14] Even so, Prussia remained an imperialistic superpower that demanded military discipline of its citizens and a willingness to die so the empire could expand by subjugating other nations.

Spartan tyranny actually served as an inspiration to the Swiss atheist philosopher Jean-Jacques Rousseau, who lived in the eighteenth century. Rousseau was one of the first self-styled intellectuals, according to historian Paul Johnson. He considers Rousseau the most influential of all "intellectuals" and certainly one of the most destructive of civilized countries and Christian morality.

Rousseau was the promoter of the idea of the "noble savage"—the eighteenth-century version of a radical environmentalist. He and other self-appointed critics of society believed they could reject the existing Christian order and replace it with their idea of the perfect society. Unfortunately, many of them were successful in doing just that. As a result, millions have died over the centuries.

Rousseau was clearly a totalitarian central planner who preached that a free society had to be replaced by an all-powerful State and that this State would reflect the "General Will." This "General Will" had to be obeyed by all subjects in the state. However, as Paul Johnson observed in *Intellectuals*:

Though Rousseau writes about the General Will in terms of liberty, it is essentially an authoritarian instrument, an early adumbration of Lenin's "democratic centralism." Laws made under the General Will must, by definition, have moral authority. "The people making laws for itself cannot be unjust." "The General Will is always righteous." Moreover, provided the State is "well-intentioned" (i.e., its long-term objectives are desirable) interpretation of the General Will can safely be left to the leaders since "they know well that the General Will always favours the decision most conducive to the public interest."[15]

In fact, Rousseau began reading about Lycurgus when he was only six years old and became deeply impressed by the central planning of the totalitarian Spartan culture. His rejection of Christianity and his natural rebellion were fertile ground for his embracing this totalitarianism.

Rousseau associated the arts and culture with decadence, so he was pleased that Sparta's rulers banned most of the arts:

> Could I forget that in the very heart of Greece rose that city as renowned for its happy ignorance as for the wisdom of its laws, that republic of demi-gods rather than men, so superior did their virtues seem to human nature? O Sparta! You eternally put to shame a vain doctrine! While the vices which accompany the fine arts entered Athens together with them, while a tyrant there so carefully collected the works of the prince of poets, you chased the arts and artists, the sciences and scientists away from your walls.[16]

Rousseau died a decade before the 1789 French Revolution, but many of his contemporaries held him responsible for the slaughter that resulted from his writings. Robespierre, the cruel despot who ruled for a time after the French Revolution, said of the philosopher, "Rousseau is the one man who, through the loftiness of his soul and the grandeur of his character, showed himself worthy of the role of teacher of mankind."[17]

Thanks in part to Rousseau's nihilistic philosophy, the leaders of the French Revolution became known for their ruthless use of the guillotine to punish their enemies. Robespierre oversaw a Reign of Terror between

1793 and 1794 that resulted in nearly seventeen thousand deaths. In various other revolts and wars in France between 1793 and 1796, nearly half a million people died. The slogan of the French revolutionaries was "Liberty, Equality, and Fraternity," and the symbol of the revolution was the guillotine and state-sponsored terrorism.

Paul Johnson wrote in *Intellectuals* of Rousseau's hatred for private property, a typical Spartan and collectivist viewpoint:

> The evil of competition, as he saw it, which destroys man's inborn communal sense and encourages all his most evil traits, including his desire to exploit others, led Rousseau to distrust private property, as the source of social crime. His fifth innovation, then, on the very eve of the Industrial Revolution, was to develop the elements of a critique of capitalism, both in the preface to his play *Narcisse* and in his *Discours sur l'inégalité*, by identifying property and the competition to acquire it as the primary cause of alienation. This was a thought-deposit Marx and others were to mine ruthlessly, together with Rousseau's related idea of cultural evolution.[18]

The Jacobins, who led the French Revolution, idolized Spartan tyranny as the model for their overthrow of the French monarchy. As historian Jennifer Tolbert Roberts has noted:

> The extent to which it was either possible or desirable actually to resurrect ancient institutions in modern France was the topic of considerable disagreement among the revolutionaries, and individual thinkers often changed their mind from one week to the next. Jacobins on the whole enjoyed setting up Sparta as a model; Billaud-Varenne contrasted the solidity of Sparta under the Lycurgan system with the disastrous effects of the weak and trusting Solon on Athens.[19]

One of the most brutal Jacobins at the time of the Reign of Terror was Jacque Nicolas Billaud-Varenne, who held Sparta as his role model for the sort of government that he envisioned for France. He said of the terrorism during the French Revolution, "No, we will not step backward, our zeal will only be smothered in the tomb; either the Revolution will triumph or we will all die." Thousands of Frenchman died to protect the revolution from its perceived enemies.[20]

Robespierre made it clear that terror was an instrument of central planning and collectivization: "The principle of the republican government is virtue, and the means required to establish virtue is terror."[21]

Rousseau's writings inspired not only the monstrous killers who engineered the French Revolution; they also inspired the former Cambodian dictator Pol Pot. He had studied and admired Rousseau in Paris when he was a college student in the 1950s. He eventually conquered Cambodia and murdered three million people in his quest for a new utopian order. The population of Cambodia before Pol Pot seized power was just seven million. He and his killers wiped out nearly half of the population in order to fashion the perfect dictatorship of the proletariat. Those who were left alive faced starvation and slavery. Rousseau would have been pleased.

Philipp Blom, a student of the European Enlightenment, describes Rousseau and his impact on Pol Pot in *A Wicked Company: The Forgotten Radicalism of the European Enlightenment*: "Utopians are always religious at heart, and it comes as little surprise that Rousseau was a direct inspiration not only for Robespierre but also for Lenin and Pol Pot. The latter studied Rousseau's works in Paris during the 1950s, before his murderous campaign forced Cambodia back into the Iron Age, under the guise of creating a society of virtuous peasants isolated from the corrupting influences of higher civilization."[22] Of course, by religious he meant devoted to the rigid formation of totalitarian government.

Rousseau's influence also inspired Adam Weishaupt to create the Order of the Illuminati on May 1, 1776. Weishaupt was a professor of canon law at the University of Ingolstadt in Bavaria. According to James Billington, in *Fire in the Minds of Men: Origins of the Revolutionary Faith*, this order was "secret and hierarchical," modeled on the Jesuits (whose long domination of Bavarian education ended with their abolition by the papacy in 1773) and dedicated to Weishaupt's Rousseauian vision of leading all humanity to a new moral perfection, freed from all established religious and political authority. "Weishaupt did not so much invite intellectuals to join his new pedagogic elite as taunt them to do so," wrote Billington. "He radiated contempt for men of the Enlightenment who 'go into ecstacies over antiquity, but are themselves unable to do anything,' and insisted that 'what is missing is the force to put into practice what has long been affirmed by our minds.'"[23]

A year after the founding of the Illuminati, Weishaupt began infiltrating Masonic lodges, hoping to use them to foment his own utopian revolution in Germany. Some historians have suggested that Weishaupt's Illuminati served as the catalyst for the French Revolution.

The utopian tyranny established by Lycurgus lived on in the depraved mind of Rousseau, in the leaders of the French Revolution, and in Pol Pot's genocidal campaign in Cambodia. Like the Spartan terrorist campaign waged against the Helots, the Jacobins under the leadership of Billaud-Varenne and Robespierre conducted their own terror campaign against the French people. The goal, of course, was to create a "virtuous" dictatorship to be ruthlessly controlled by Robespierre.

Clearly, utopian ideas have consequences, and those consequences usually end in brutal deaths, slavery, poverty, and misery for those who are victims of leaders like Robespierre, Lycurgus, Hitler, and Pol Pot. Sparta set the stage for future genocides and dictatorships.

PLATO'S *REPUBLIC* AND THE *LAWS*

If Plato had lived in the early nineteenth century, he would likely have become a dedicated Marxist.

Plato was born in 429 BC. In the early years of his life, Athens was fighting Sparta in the twenty-seven-year Peloponnesian War. He came of age around the time of Athens's defeat by Sparta. Athens was in military, political, and social chaos at the time.

Plato sat under the teachings of Socrates, and began a prolific career as philosopher and writer. In 387 BC, he founded a philosophical school in the grove of the Greek hero Academus. Plato's Academy became the lifelong "think tank" of Aristotle, who came to the academy when he was seventeen and who then taught there for twenty years. Many of Plato's writings apparently originated in his lectures at the Academy.[24]

Two of Plato's books, *Republic* and the *Laws*, discuss his ideas on how to create the perfect utopian city, where justice and peace reign supreme. Everyone would have a job to do and would do it willingly for the good of the all-powerful state. No one would want for anything, because all would be held in common. There would be no greed, no striving for status or power in these mythical cities. The phrase for this in modern Marxism is "From each according to his ability and to each according to his need."

In *Republic*, Plato described two different kinds of utopian societies. The first of his theoretical societies is described as a "true and healthy" model for utopian life. In this ideal society the city-state's government provides for only its citizens' basic needs, including food, shelter, clothing, and shoes. The people have no luxuries, such as meat, entertainment, and furniture.

Plato admitted that this wasn't a workable society. No one would want to live in it. So, he created a second one that he described as feverish and "luxurious." This became his model for a totalitarian central planning system. There, a rigid caste system includes the breeding of perfect citizens, euthanasia, arranged marriages, and relentless brainwashing of the citizens to keep them in line.

This ideal society is run by a group of elitists known as "Guardians," and the city-state is protected by a warrior class called "Auxiliaries." To protect the land from outside influences and subversion from within, Plato invented what politicians often use today: the "noble lie."

One of the "noble" lies that Plato suggested should be used in this totalitarian society is that children are born of the earth, not from women. Citizens are also to be told that they should submit their personal wants and desires to the will of the Guardians.

As political commentator Mark Levin explains in *Ameritopia*:

Indoctrination is also crucial to controlling the citizenry. The City consists of a comprehensive "education" system. In addition to the "noble lie," censorship is widely practiced. For example, myths and music are suppressed to avoid any stories where authority is challenged or the Guardians are presented as anything other than good (379c). The style of music is regulated. Only certain modes and rhythms are approved, for "rhythm and harmony most of all insinuate themselves into the inner most part of the soul and most vigorously lay hold of it" (401d). Freedom of expression is banned for the Ideal City's health is more important than self-expression.[25]

The Guardians are in charge of the sexual reproduction of its citizens in much the same way Communist central planners in China enforce the one-child policy. To maintain a pure race, the Guardians determine who may have sex with whom. In fact, the Guardians themselves are encouraged to engage in wife swapping to make sure only the purest of the race can reproduce.

Plato abolished the traditional family in his ideal society. He forced men, women, and children to live in communes and removed children from the homes so they could be educated in government-run schools.

THE PERFECT COLLECTIVIST DICTATORSHIP

Plato also abolished private ownership among the Guardians because he believed that private property was a corrupting influence on their ability to lead.

Lifelong American socialist Harry W. Laidler devoted a lengthy chapter to Plato's Republic in his 1944 book, *Socio-Economic Movements*. In it, he pointed out that common ownership of property (including wives) in Plato's society made it "possible for the state to develop the science of eugenics, 'to bring together the best of both sexes as often as possible, and the worst as seldom as possible'; to abandon the inferior offspring and to prevent irregular alliances. [Plato] goes into considerable detail regarding the relations which should be permitted and those which should be restrained 'if the flock is to attain the first-class excellence.'"[26] Laidler clearly had no philosophical problem with eugenics to weed out "inferior" humans and to permit only the most perfect specimens to breed.

Plato's selective breeding plan for his Guardians became a horrific reality under Adolf Hitler, who exterminated millions of Jews, Gypsies, Slavs, and others in order to erase these supposedly "inferior races" from his new utopian order. Eliminating inferiors was just one part of Hitler's plan for a thousand-year tyrannical reign. In 1935, Hitler set up the Lebensborn association, which became a Nazi breeding program for the Aryan race. The system was run by the SS. "Racially pure" German girls had babies in secret and turned them over to the SS to be trained to be good Nazis. This bizarre program ended in 1945 when the Nazis were defeated by the Allied Forces.[27]

PLATO: THE SOCIALIST BEFORE SOCIALISM HAD A NAME

Harry Laidler devoted his entire life working to destroy the free enterprise system in America and to institute a Platonic collectivist or socialist system. He was clearly pleased with Plato's concepts of government and control of the individual. According to Laidler, "in his condemnation of gross economic inequalities, Plato set up ideals which have been a source of inspiration to later thinkers. And the world is beginning to give serious heed to the problems of eugenics and of the functional organization of society which Plato raised."[28]

Laidler continued in his kudos to Plato:

Plato['s] *Republic* indicates the truth of the contention that utopias are built up by the social dreamers out of the warp and woof of the social and economic institutions in which they live. Plato's picture of a future ideal state was inevitably limited by his environment. He could not possibly have envisaged a utopia with railroads, telephones, automobiles, aeroplanes [*sic*], skyscrapers, steel mills, and ten-cent stores. The picture he had in mind could never come true in an age like this. Nevertheless, certain great principles of justice and social organization which he enunciated could well be applied, and with revolutionary effect, to our modern social structure.[29]

Laidler could clearly see in Plato's writings the makings of a socialist utopia with elitists such as himself as one of the Guardians running the country. In fact, Laidler did have a considerable impact on our nation during the early part of the twentieth century. He was a cofounder of the Intercollegiate Socialist Society (ISS) with Upton Sinclair, Jack London, and others. He was also a prolific writer on the subject of socialism, and his *History of Socialistic Thought* was used as a college textbook throughout the United States. He was also friends with socialists inside the Woodrow Wilson and later the Roosevelt administrations.

In 1921 the Intercollegiate Socialist Society changed its name to the League for Industrial Democracy, which was a less threatening title, especially during the twenties, when Americans began learning about the dangers of Soviet Communism.

THE WORTHLESSNESS OF THE INDIVIDUAL

In Plato's central planning dictatorship, the individual could expect to die a painful and senseless death if chronically ill. Under Plato's plan none of the chronically ill would receive medical treatment because they had lost value to the city-state. Plato's views on treating the ill emerged with a vengeance in the 1920s among German doctors, who began to advocate that the ill, weak, or handicapped be eliminated because they were a financial drain on the German state. Germany had begun a universal medical care program similar to systems such as Obamacare as far back as the Health Insurance Bill of 1883, passed through by Otto von Bismarck. As a result there was real cost to the state. This horrific devaluing of human life eventually led to the Nazi death camps and the ovens where millions died. Antilife ideas like these have consequences—and those consequences are often repeated in centrally planned utopian-leaning societies.

THE GUARDIANS DETERMINE GOOD AND EVIL

Plato's Guardians were to be philosopher-kings, who alone could judge what is good and what is false or evil. A child who was selected to be a Guardian must spend the first twenty years of his life being trained in arts and literature. At twenty, he would begin a training regimen in astronomy, philosophy, harmonics, geometry, and math to prepare him to make decisions regarding good versus evil.

From among these elites, a smaller group would eventually be picked to spend five years studying philosophy and had to spend another fifteen years studying government. After meticulously building arguments for his ideal State, Plato at last confessed that such a place would be impossible to create or to maintain, given mankind's natural imperfections.

Plato concluded, "Just as the philosopher is the best and happiest of men, so the aristocratic State is the best and happiest of States; and just as the tyrannical despot, the slave of ambition and passion, is the worst and most unhappy of men, so is the State ruled by the tyrant the worst and most unhappy of States."[30]

Clearly, Plato preferred a "benevolent" dictatorship run by philosopher-kings to a democratic system where citizens actually participated in the governmental process. In his city-state system, freedom was nonexistent and citizens existed only to serve the state. Totalitarians throughout history have adopted his flawed ideas for how people should be governed. It inevitably results in suffering, starvation, and death, especially when these dictatorships take control of an economy. We'll deal with the devastation caused by central economic planning in the Soviet Union and China in a later chapter.

THE *LAWS* AND A TOTALITARIAN CITY-STATE

In the *Laws*, Plato has a fictional discussion on government with three individuals: one from Athens who is unnamed but is actually Plato; one from Crete named Kleinias; and one from Sparta named Megillus. Plato created an imaginary constitution for a city-state on an island he called Magnesia. In it, he drew heavily from the totalitarian system already in place in Sparta.

The *Laws* is considered to be Plato's last writing before his death—and accordingly it is unfinished and may have actually have been published after his death.

At the end of book 3, the Cretan announces that the leaders in Crete had decided to build a new city in an abandoned part of Crete—and he asks the unnamed Athenian to help him build it. In books 4–12, the Athenian outlines what he believes will be the best form of government for this new city.

In Magnesia, land was to be distributed equally among the citizens. These plots of land were not owned or farmed in common, but each owner should consider the land to be the common property of the entire city. There was to be neither poverty nor riches because everyone would supposedly have the same amount of land to till.

Plato established four classes of people in this utopian city. The first class could have assets worth three to four times the value of the lots they owned; the second class, between two and three times the value, and on down to the lowest class. He also forbade the use of gold and silver by the inhabitants of the city, and they were only allowed to use tokens as currency. This of course allowed deficit spending, as the Magnesian government could easily mint these tokens at little actual cost, just as the current US Federal Reserve system produces dollars with "quantitative easing."

Plato also borrowed the concept of common mess hall meals from Sparta in his utopian city-state. Women not only ate with the men, but were expected to serve in battle with them as well.

Also like the Spartans, Magnesians were forbidden to engage in trade or commerce with other entities, and they had a separate monetary system similar to that of Sparta. Likewise, Plato's perfect society banned travel outside of the island unless granted permission by the authorities. He feared strangers infecting his island paradise with foreign ideas.

But Plato's island utopia isn't completely like the tyranny of Sparta. It also includes elements from the Athenian government system.

Plato's city features an "Assembly," composed of all citizens who have served or are serving the military. The second government entity is the "council," which includes the Guardians of the laws and the courts. Another element is the Nocturnal Council, which meets daily from dawn until sunrise. This body functions, in part, as a rehabilitation program for those who have broken Magnesia's laws through ignorance. Lawbreakers are imprisoned for five years and must sit through daily teachings by council members to reform their thinking. This sounds a lot like the Communist "self-criticism" meetings where Communists were required to confess their failings to party leaders or be publicly ridiculed for their crimes against the state.

The Nocturnal Council includes the ten oldest Guardians in the city, the general superintendent of education, examiners (who check qualifications for office), and citizens who have traveled abroad for the council on fact-finding missions.

In this city-state, the individual has little or no real freedom of action or choice. He is subject to the whims of the Guardians, the Assembly, and the Nocturnal Council.

Plato's *Republic* and the *Laws* have planted the seeds of utopian totalitarianism in the minds of many writers, philosophers, and political activists throughout the centuries. These utopian ideas have resulted in tremendous suffering for millions of men, women, and children.

The only reality about a utopian society is that one can never *really* be expected to exist.

No system devised by man can eliminate all poverty, all hunger, all fear, all inequalities, and all wars. To believe such a system is possible is a childish fantasy that would require an imaginary population. Individuals who claim they can create such a society in reality have a messiah complex. They must be vigorously exposed and opposed.

On this earth, the closest thing to "utopia" is a society that respects individual freedom, punishes wrongdoers, embraces a free enterprise system, allows private property, and encourages independence and self-government. The Founders of the United States brought forth precisely such a system in the form of a *constitutional republic*.

4

UTOPIAN TOTALITARIAN RULERS

Maximilien de Robespierre was one of the most ruthless (and short-lived) utopian political leaders in the eighteenth century. It was Robespierre, along with his revolutionary allies in the Jacobin Club, who engineered the French Revolution in 1789, which resulted in the overthrow of King Louis XVI and ultimately his execution.

By temperament, Robespierre was a natural rebel who rejected all legitimate authority. He attacked the monarchy and promoted "equality" and "freedom" for the French working class. Robespierre carefully nurtured a public perception that he was deeply concerned about the poor and was eventually elected to high public office. He was also a leader of the Jacobins, a group of radicals who promoted "virtue," equality, and sacrifice. They were, in actuality, utopian subversives who ended up creating a nightmare of bloodshed and oppression of the French people that lasted for decades.

As the revolution devolved into a ruthless dictatorship, Robespierre became head of the Committee for Public Safety (a French version of the Soviet KGB or the Spartan Krypteia). His stated purpose was to protect the revolution from subversives both inside and outside of France. Although the battle cry of the revolution had been equality, liberty, and brotherhood, the revolution devolved into a mobocracy, and the guillotine became the universal symbol of the French Revolution.

Robespierre clearly had a messianic view of himself and his ability to create a utopian society. He believed that he was creating a nation of virtue in which he would determine what virtuous behavior was or was not. In essence, he acted as a "god" in the lives of his fellow Frenchmen. Any citizen who did not agree with his definition of virtuous behavior soon found himself headless.

To elevate the state and himself as a god figure, Robespierre tried to eliminate Christianity in France. Instead of Christianity, represented in France by the Catholic Church at that time, he created a short-lived "Cult of the Supreme Being." He declared a feast day to be celebrated in honor of this vaguely defined Supreme Being on June 8 each year. According to the new religion, the temple of this Being was the "universe," and "nature" was the Being's priest.[1]

In this new utopian paradise, Robespierre wrote the laws, determined who God was, and created a society that enforced his definition of virtue on its citizens through unrestricted terrorism. He and his fellow revolutionaries had the power of judge, jury, and executioner in this evolving police state.

TERRORISM USED TO PROTECT "VIRTUE"

To defend his "virtuous" nation, Robespierre justified the use of a police state by mob rule, much as did Mao in China two hundred years later. In February 1794, he gave a speech explaining why terrorism was needed to protect "virtue" and the French Revolution. According to Robespierre:

> Without, all the tyrants encircle you; within, all tyranny's friends conspire; they will conspire until hope is wrested from crime. We must smother the internal and external enemies of the Republic or perish with it; now in this situation, the first maxim of your policy ought to be to lead the people by reason and the people's enemies by terror.
>
> If the spring of popular government in time of peace is virtue, the springs of popular government in revolution are at once virtue

and terror: virtue, without which terror is fatal; terror, without which virtue is powerless. *Terror is nothing other than justice, prompt, severe, inflexible* [emphasis added]; it is therefore an emanation of virtue; it is not so much a special principle as it is a consequence of the general principle of democracy applied to our country's most urgent needs.

It has been said that terror is the principle of despotic government. Does your government therefore resemble despotism? Yes, as the sword that gleams in the hands of the heroes of liberty resembles that with which the henchmen of tyranny are armed. Let the despot govern by terror his brutalized subjects; he is right, as a despot. Subdue by terror the enemies of liberty, and you will be right, as founders of the Republic. The government of the revolution is liberty's despotism against tyranny.[2]

To "legalize" this reign of terror, in September 1793 the revolutionaries passed the Law of Suspects, which made it possible to execute people for such crimes against the state as being "unpatriotic" or for "spreading rumors." And in October, the government passed the Decree on Emergency Government. This allowed the government to suspend peacetime rights and legal safeguards. Coercion and violence were thus legalized. Of course, the revolutionaries claimed that these tough measures were only temporary until the enemies of the revolution were subdued. But no dictatorship willingly gives up power. Once it gains power, it maintains it by any means at its disposal. The French Revolution was no different from other tyrannies. It simply paved the way for a later dictator, Napoleon.

Under Robespierre, the French constitution was shelved and the working-class citizens formed armed militias to steal food and other supplies from urban citizens and to persecute suspected enemies of the revolution, thus "redistributing the wealth" by mob rule.

These mobs also set up neighborhood watch committees to spy on those they believed were traitors to the revolution. The same types of spy networks were used in the twentieth century in both the fascist and Communist versions of utopia. The purpose, of course, was to instill terror and encourage obedience.

As a result of this reign of state-sponsored terrorism, an estimated 16,594 people were executed or died in unsanitary conditions in dismal prisons. This number of deaths is small, however, compared to the half-million souls who died in the civil war that immediately followed.

The Jacobins created a police state to defend their vision of "virtue" in France, that "virtue" being the centrally planned leveling of society. The result was no different from the attempted creation of previous and later utopian states: brutality, civic enslavement, and death. Utopian tyrannies always end this way.[3]

Maximilien Robespierre's campaign of terror ended badly for him personally, as he became a victim of the revolution he had helped to foment. Robespierre was beheaded in 1794 by his fellow Jacobins, who were just as amoral and ruthless as he. The final end of this utopian experiment ended with the rise of Napoleon Bonaparte.

The brilliant British statesman Edmund Burke wrote a lengthy essay in 1790 on the French Revolution, titled "Reflections on the Revolution in France." In it, he made astonishing predictions about how it would turn out—three years before the Reign of Terror had begun in France. Burke accurately predicted that the French Revolution would result in "a ferocious dissoluteness in manners, an insolent irreligion in opinions and practices, . . . laws overturned, tribunals subverted, industry without vigor, commerce expiring . . . a church pillaged . . . civil and military anarchy . . . national bankruptcy."[4]

Burke was right, except for the true dimensions of the devastation. Robespierre left his hideous utopian mark on France, which led to a horrific cascading impact on the rest of Europe.

KARL MARX AND FRIEDRICH ENGELS

Karl Marx was by all accounts a complete failure as a husband, father, and provider for his children. It is recorded that he was arrogant, hateful, foul-mouthed, unclean, and violent. He seldom held down a real job, preferring instead to take handouts from his relatives and his wealthy benefactor, Friedrich Engels. Marx spent most of his days sitting in the

Round Room of the British Museum, studying how he could "free" the workers of the world from the evils of the rich.

Marx hated the term "utopian" to describe his brand of totalitarian socialism. He preferred to call it "scientific socialism," which he believed gave it an intellectual flair. In reality, he was indeed a utopian who burned with hatred of private enterprise and economic freedom. He became convinced that a system of social and economic justice could be designed to replace the free marketplace, which he saw as unjust.

Marx was born in Prussia in 1818. His father was a liberal thinker and a follower of the atheist Voltaire and the radical philosopher Rousseau. His father's influence is clearly evident in Karl's life.

Karl Marx earned a doctorate in philosophy at Jena University, dabbled in journalism for a time, and eventually became involved in the Communist League while living in Brussels, Belgium. He and Engels wrote the infamous *Communist Manifesto* for the League in 1848. He was expelled from Belgium in 1849 for subversive activities and landed in London, where he spent the next thirty-four years studying in the British Museum. At home, his wife and children barely survived in a squalid apartment.

According to Paul Johnson in his book *Intellectuals*, Marx fancied himself not only a brilliant scholar but a poet as well. Johnson noted, "He was fond of quoting Mephistopheles' line from Goethe's *Faust*, 'Everything that exists deserves to perish.'"[5] He certainly displayed that nihilistic, demonic philosophy in his writings.

Marx claimed to be an advocate for the poor and downtrodden, but in actuality he was an intellectual snob who wanted nothing to do with the unwashed masses. Johnson explains:

> When he and Engels organized the Communist League, and again when they formed the International, Marx made sure that working-class socialists were eliminated from any positions of influence and few sat on committees. His motive was partly intellectual snobbery, partly that men with actual experience of factory conditions tended to be anti-violence and in favor of modest, progressive improvements:

they were knowledgeably skeptical about the apocalyptic revolution he claimed was not only necessary but inevitable.[6]

Marx borrowed from the German philosopher Georg Hegel to come up with a basic Communist principle known as "dialectical materialism." This is the belief that nothing exists in the world except matter in motion—and that this matter is constantly in conflict. Atheism and a fanatical hatred of God are at the core of Marxism.

Related to this idea of matter in motion is the concept of thesis, antithesis, and synthesis. In Marxian thinking, when one thing clashes with another, it is a battle between the *thesis* and the *antithesis*. The result is something different, called the *synthesis* (between the two clashing sides). The idea of class warfare comes out of this view of the world. Workers clash with their employers and the end result is something new—and supposedly better.

Marx believed that this Communist philosophy would inevitably result in the creation of a Communist state and the establishment of what he called the "dictatorship of the proletariat." The workers would supposedly go on to rule in this utopian society, and the state itself would ultimately melt away. This is the illusion of many a utopian, but the reality is always the opposite.

Once, when Marx was asked what the objective of his life was, he replied, "To dethrone God and destroy capitalism."[7] In the *Communist Manifesto*, he clearly laid out his social objectives, listing a ten-point plan for the imposition of a Communist dictatorship on the world:

1. Abolition of property in land and application of all rents of land to public purposes.

2. A heavy progressive or graduated income tax.

3. Abolition of all right of inheritance.

4. Confiscation of the property of all emigrants and rebels.

5. Centralization of credit in the hands of the State, by means of a national bank with State capital and an exclusive monopoly.

6. Centralization of the means of communication and transport in the hands of the State.

7. Extension of factories and instruments of production owned by the State; the bringing into cultivation of wastelands, and the improvement of the soil generally in accordance with a common plan.

8. Equal liability of all to labor. Establishment of industrial armies, especially for agriculture.

9. Combination of agriculture with manufacturing industries; gradual abolition of the distinction between town and country, by a more equable distribution of the population over the country.

10. Free education for all children in public schools. Abolition of children's factory labor in its present form. Combination of education with industrial production.[8]

Self-declared "progressives" have implemented many of these goals in America during the past hundred years. The graduated income tax and the Federal Reserve Bank both came into existence during the Woodrow Wilson administration. Behind both of these was Marxist utopian Edward Mandell House, the subversive who was more than a trusted advisor to Wilson. House had become what could almost be considered Wilson's second person or alter ego.

LENIN

Marx was a theorist and not necessarily someone who could actually implement his plan to destroy capitalism and dethrone God; it was a Russian, Vladimir Lenin (formerly Ulyanov), who turned Communist theory into a terrible reality in 1917.

At the age of eighteen, Lenin began studying Karl Marx and became a fanatical follower. He organized Marxist study groups in the late 1880s and was exiled to Siberia for this activity in 1895. In 1900, he fled Russia for Western Europe, where he plotted the overthrow of the czarist government.

Sometime in 1919, J. Edgar Hoover, the legendary head of the FBI, began studying Communism when its influence began to be felt in the United States. In his book *Masters of Deceit*, Hoover devoted considerable space to describing Lenin and his philosophy of ruthless revolution and bloodshed to seize power. He wrote:

> Borrowing from the autocratic character of Marx himself, Lenin made Marxism a highly disciplined, organized, and ruthless creed. How can revolution be achieved? Not by democratic reforms, ballots, or good will but by naked, bloody violence. The sword is the weapon. Everything must be dedicated to this aim: one's time, talents, one's very life. Revolutions do not just happen. They are made. . . .
>
> Lenin conceived of the Party as a vehicle of revolution. Marx, in his philosophical abstractions, had never thought out the day-to-day composition of the Party. Lenin did. The Party must be a small, tightly controlled, deeply loyal group. Fanaticism, not members, was the key. Members must live, eat, breathe, and dream revolution. They must lie, cheat, and murder if the Party was to be served. Discipline must be rigid. No deviations could be permitted. If an individual falters, he must be ousted. Revolutions cannot be won by clean hands or in white shirts; only by blood, sweat, and the burning torch. These ideas were all inherent in Marxist thought, but they waited for Lenin to translate them into organized action."[9]

Lenin waited in exile in Western Europe for the time when he could return to Russia and seize power. His time came in March 1917, when a democratic revolution erupted in his homeland toward the end of World War I. The czarist government had been toppled by reformer Alexander Kerensky and his allies. Lenin returned quickly to begin subverting the fledging Kerensky government, which was not collectivist. He was joined by Leon Trotsky, who was in exile in New York, and Stalin, who was in exile in Siberia. Together, this troika engineered the subversion of Kerensky and ended hope for a decent future for the Russian people. After they quickly dispatched Kerensky, they introduced a Communist police state complete with slave labor camps, famine, torture, and death. It lasted for 70 years.

As Hoover noted:

> In the fall of 1917, the Bolsheviks seized power in the October Revolution. Lenin became the dictator of all Russia. Communism had made its first breach in the wall of capitalism. (The revolution occurred on October 25, 1917, according to the Eastern calendar then in use in Russia. Hence, the term "October Revolution." Under the Western calendar, later adopted by the Soviets, the date is November 7, 1917.) The Bolsheviks immediately instituted a terroristic "dictatorship of the proletariat." Marx had conceived the dictatorship of the proletariat as a transitory period for the establishment of a communist society. Lenin, however, dipped it in blood and gave it a prominence and ruthlessness that shocked the entire world. The secret police, then known as the Cheka, instituted a reign of terror; capital punishment was meted out widely. A search for enemies rocked the country.[10]

Lenin's Marxist tyranny was quite successful in rounding up and killing the enemies of the Communist Revolution, but it was a dismal failure in its economic policies from the beginning. By 1922 famine was widespread and millions of people were dying of starvation. Some estimates place the loss of human life at five million during this time. Lenin died in 1922 and an equally evil dictator, Joseph Stalin, took his place.

STALIN

In 1928, Stalin began implementing his collectivization plan, which resulted in total government control of all production in Russia. Compulsory labor increased, and private trade was abolished.

Stalin began a war on the middle class in Russia, as he attacked the successful small farmers known as the *kulaks*. In the Ukraine, which had once been known as the breadbasket of Russia, kulaks were slaughtered, and Stalin actually deliberately created a famine that resulted in the deaths of millions.

Victor Kravchenko, a Communist Party official, became an eyewitness to the Soviet-created famine in the Ukraine during the 1920s. Kravchenko eventually defected to the United States and in 1946 wrote a classic, titled *I Chose Freedom*, on his journey out of the darkness of Communism and what he saw in the Ukraine while still a Party member.

Once, while visiting a small village, Kravchenko witnessed unspeakable horrors:

> Here I saw people dying in solitude by slow degrees, dying hideously, without the excuse of sacrifice for a cause. They had been trapped and left to starve, each in his home, by a political decision made in a far-off capital around conference and banquet tables. There was not even the consolation of inevitability to relieve the horror.
>
> The most terrifying sights were the little children with skeleton limbs dangling from balloon-like abdomens. Starvation had wiped every trace of youth from their faces, turning them into tortured gargoyles . . . Everywhere we found men and women lying prone, their faces and bellies bloated, their eyes utterly expressionless.[11]

He further discovered that the peasants in these villages were actually eating manure in order to recover bits of grain for themselves. They had already eaten all of the dogs. The stench of death was everywhere.

Kravchenko was horrified by what he found, but when he entered a Soviet-controlled brick storage facility, what he discovered there was even more shocking. It was filled with the previous years' grain harvest! There was plenty of food, but it was being kept from the villagers. "These were the state reserves ordered by the government, their very existence hidden from the starving population by officialdom," he wrote. "Hundreds of men, women and children had died of undernourishment in these villages, though grain was hoarded almost outside their doors! . . . Subsequently I came to know that in many other parts of the country the government hoarded huge reserves while peasants in those very regions died of hunger. Why this was done, only Stalin's Politburo could tell—and it didn't."[12]

Between 1934 and 1938, Stalin began holding a series of purge trials, phony trials of his Bolshevik enemies—who needed to be eliminated. Stalin even brought the former head of the secret police to trial for treason against his rule.

Stalin did what every bloodthirsty tyrant does. He killed anyone who opposed him and terrorized or starved the rest of the populace into submission. Not content to simply rule the vast Russian empire, he launched into a quest for world domination. He seized Estonia, Latvia, Lithuania, and eastern Czechoslovakia, along with parts of Poland, Finland, and Romania. Then he created satellite slave states, including Yugoslavia, China, Hungary, Bulgaria, East Germany, and others. After his death in 1953, Nikita Khrushchev took over power in Russia and continued Soviet expansion throughout the world.

What was the legacy of Lenin, Stalin, and Khrushchev? Death for millions who were enslaved in Communist utopias around the world. In fact, *The Black Book of Communism* chronicles the numbers of deaths due to Communist tyrants:

- 20 million deaths in the Soviet Union

- 65 million deaths in China

- 1 million deaths in Vietnam

- 2 million deaths in North Korea

- 2 million deaths in Cambodia

- 1 million deaths in Eastern Europe

- 150,000 deaths in Latin America

- 1.7 million deaths in Africa

- 1.5 million deaths in Afghanistan

The total approaches 100 million people slaughtered for a utopian socialist system.[13]

MAO TSE-TUNG

The former Communist dictator of China rose to power in the Chinese Communist Party during the 1920s and 1930s. A biography published in 2005 shows him to be the embodiment of pure evil.

In *Mao: The Unknown Story*, authors Jung Chang and Jon Halliday reveal that Mao forced his third wife to abandon their baby son during the legendary Long March, when he led the Chinese Communist forces to a Red-controlled region in northwest China. Chang herself was a victim of Mao's "Cultural Revolution" of the 1960s and 1970s. She spent ten years researching the man and his unspeakable crimes against humanity.[14]

Before and after this Long March, Mao instigated slave labor camps, enforced starvation of the peasants, and conducted brainwashing sessions for those under his control in China. Cruel methods of torture were devised to beat his opponents into submission.

A 2012 biography, titled *Mao: The Real Story* by Professors Alexander V. Pantsov and Steven I. Levine is based on recently opened Soviet files on Mao. The 755-page book is a summary of at least fifteen volumes on Mao, including private correspondence, records of his meetings, and more.

The professors claim to be dispassionate in their view of Mao—even as they show him to be a brutal monster. They noted that the 1966 Cultural Revolution instigated by Mao resulted in at least 1 million deaths alone. "It was useless to beg for mercy," they wrote. "Terror-stricken elderly people, their arms broken, were led along the streets to the jeers and malicious shouts of the mob . . . [Mao] was the chief culprit of the senseless and merciless mass terror."

They went on to say that Mao spent his free hours "in the company of pretty 17- and 18-year-old girls," engaging in what could be described as Hugh Hefner–like sex orgies—which the professors describe as "pajama parties."[15]

Still, in light of what one writer called their "mealy-mouthed" portrayal of Mao, Pantsov and Levine have been accused of "white-washing" him.[16] Authors Jung Chang and Jon Halliday, on the other hand, provide gruesome details about Mao's ruthless dictatorship—they don't whitewash the monstrous crimes against the Chinese people. It is worth reading their biography to get a fuller understanding of Mao's hideous utopian hell.

***

It is reliably estimated that Mao caused the deaths of some 65 million Chinese both before his seizure of China in 1949 and afterward. His brutal actions make Hitler's slaughters look meager by comparison.

His disgusting personal habits and unrestrained sexual lusts have been detailed in the 1996 book *The Private Life of Chairman Mao*. He refused to bathe or brush his teeth for years at a time and used hundreds of peasant girls for his sexual pleasure, passing along numerous venereal diseases to them. He had a total disregard for human life and routinely mistreated even his most loyal followers.[17] Anyone who disagreed with Mao soon ended up dead.

In 1958 Mao decided that rodents and insects were eating too much grain, so he launched the great "Four Pests Campaign" to rid the country of every mosquito, fly, rat, and sparrow. Villagers obeyed his edict and began killing sparrows and destroying their eggs. Peasants beat pots and pans each evening to keep the sparrows from landing. Eventually, they fell from the sky from exhaustion and then were killed.

The destruction of the sparrows led to horrific results. In 1959, locusts—freed from the threat of being eaten by the birds—began ravaging the crops. A famine resulted and more than 45 million Chinese died as a result of Mao's decision to kill all the sparrows!

Finally, in 1960, Chinese scientists successfully convinced Mao that his war against the sparrow was unproductive and that sparrows actually ate more insects than grain.[18]

Zhou Xun, a professor at the University of Hong Kong, compiled a horrifying history of Mao's man-created famine in her book *The Great Famine in China: 1958–1962*. In it, Zhou recounts how starving

Chinese had to eat grass and tree bark to survive. Some of them even resorted to cannibalism to survive Mao's engineered famine. In addition, Mao destroyed family kitchens, forcing families to melt down their kitchen utensils. All food was served in canteens (common mess halls) and distributed according to how obedient the Chinese families had been to Mao's dictatorship. If you had been uncooperative, you starved. When food ran out in the canteens, villagers then had to scavenge for whatever food they could find.[19]

Mao's utopian vision for China has been an unending nightmare for the Chinese people.

POL POT

As noted in an earlier chapter, the former Cambodian dictator Pol Pot studied in Paris and became a fan of Jean-Jacques Rousseau and Karl Marx. He joined the French Communist Party and returned to Cambodia in 1953 to teach at a private school in Phnom Penh. In the mid-1960s he spent five months in China, getting training in subversive activities. He eventually became head of the Communist Khmer Rouge guerrilla force working to overthrow Cambodian king Sihanouk.

Once Sihanouk was defeated, Pol Pot began systematically killing off his enemies and implementing numerous utopian ideas: he banned money, religion, property, cities, law, and romantic marriage. This sounds like the rules Lycurgus put in place in ancient Sparta. In addition, Pol Pot took children from their parents when they were seven years old—another Spartan policy.

He killed anyone caught reading or using reading glasses because they were considered to be part of the Cambodian upper class. He also killed off skilled workers and those wearing wristwatches because they were considered to be capitalists and the enemies of his socialist state. The list of capital offenses was long and capricious.

Pol Pot hated "civilization"—much like Rousseau—and it became his goal to create a rural utopian farming society. To do this, he emptied the cities and drove city dwellers into the countryside, where they starved to death. He was determined to create a rural socialist system inspired partly by Mao's Cultural Revolution, which he had seen while in China.

Once in power, Pol Pot changed the name of Cambodia to the Democratic Republic of Kampuchea and declared "Year Zero" by purifying Cambodia of all Western influences—including capitalism, city life, and other foreign influences. He effectively took Cambodia back to the Stone Age as part of his cleansing process.

His ruthless efforts to de-Westernize his nation resulted in what became known as "the Killing Fields," with one out of five Cambodians being murdered and dumped into mass graves.

The heartless genocide of his fellow Cambodians was detailed in John Barron's exposé *Murder of a Gentle Land: The Untold Story of a Communist Genocide in Cambodia*, published in 1977.

BENITO MUSSOLINI

Benito Mussolini, the infamous Fascist dictator of Italy, was a utopian theorist and radical from his earliest years. Named after Benito Juarez, a Mexican revolutionary leader, Mussolini was reared in the home of an Italian atheist/socialist father who was an advocate of the poor taking up arms against the "rich." No wonder his son became a socialist revolutionary.

Mussolini earned a reputation early in life as a rebel, disobedient to his teachers and a bully at school. He had a few friends, but he began studying the art of revolution and honed his speaking skills for a future political career.[20] He had found his calling in life: dictator and killer.

When he was nineteen, he fled to Switzerland to avoid the military draft and became involved with numerous extremist elements in that country. Between 1902 and 1904, he was in Switzerland, studying to be a socialist politician. He built a network of like-minded radicals who based their views on such nihilistic philosophers as Friedrich Nietzsche, Georges Sorel, and Max Stirner.

Nietzsche was a German philosopher most famous for proclaiming that "God is dead." His ideas about the "superman" dominated Nazi thinking and clearly influenced the thinking of Mussolini as well.[21]

Georges Sorel was a French philosopher who popularized Marxism in France and advocated violence to accomplish Marxist objectives.[22]

Stirner was a German philosopher who denied absolutes and human reasoning. He believed rights and duties don't exist, only the might of the person's ego to justify his actions. In essence, he was advocating that every person become his own "god." His political philosophy was anarchism and rebellion against authority.[23] Mussolini gladly embraced it.

These three philosophers, who were atheists, anarchists, and Marxists, were influential in forming the philosophy that eventually became known as fascism.

Mussolini returned to Italy from his self-imposed exile in 1904 and plunged into socialist politics. He became editor of a socialist newspaper and secretary of the local socialist party.

In 1919 he helped form the Union for Struggle, or Fighting Leagues, which eventually became the Italian Fascist Party. This group included organized black-shirted young men who beat up anyone with opposing opinions. Mussolini's group was a forerunner of Hitler's Brownshirts—who engaged in the same sort of terrorist activities during the rise of Adolf Hitler in Germany.

In 1921 Mussolini won a seat in the Italian Parliament and eventually became the ruler of Italy in 1926. He dissolved Parliament and political parties, seized control of the press, and put himself in charge of the military and most of the government. He demanded absolute obedience. Those who resisted were crushed.

Before seizing complete control of Italy in 1926, he published a document that outlined his plans for a fascist state. *The Doctrine of Fascism* was actually ghostwritten by Giovanni Gentile, an Italian philosopher who followed the teachings of Georg Friedrich Hegel—the same man who had inspired Karl Marx. Gentile also wrote the "Manifesto of the Italian Fascist Intellectuals" and served as Mussolini's minister of public education. Gentile was killed in 1944 by a group of anti-Fascist partisans.

In *The Doctrine of Fascism*, Mussolini (Gentile) describes totalitarian Fascism in these glowing terms:

1. In the Fascist conception of history, man is man only by virtue of the spiritual process to which he contributes as a member of the family, the social group, the nation, and in function of history to which all nations bring their contribution.[24]

2. Anti-individualistic, the Fascist conception of life stresses the importance of the State and accepts the individual only in so far as his interests coincide with those of the State, which stands for the conscience and the universal will of man as a historic entity.[25]

3. The Fascist conception of the State is all embracing; outside of it no human or spiritual values can exist, much less have value. Thus understood, Fascism, is totalitarian, and the Fascist State—a synthesis and a unit inclusive of all values—interprets, develops, and potentates the whole life of a people.[26]

4. Fascism, in short, is not only a law-giver and a founder of institutions, but an educator and a promoter of spiritual life. It aims at refashioning not only the forms of life but their content—man, his character, and his faith. To achieve this purpose it enforces discipline and uses authority, entering into the soul and ruling with undisputed sway.[27]

5. The keystone of the Fascist doctrine is its conception of the State, of its essence, its functions, and its aims. For Fascism the State is absolute, individuals and groups relative. Individuals and groups are admissible in so far as they come within the State. Instead of directing the game and guiding the material and moral progress of the community, the liberal State restricts its activities to recording results. The Fascist State is wide awake and has a will of its own. For this reason it can be described as "ethical."[28]

Mussolini's utopian philosophy enslaved his fellow Italians and led them into disastrous defeats during World War II as Hitler's ally. He was killed in 1945 and his body was dragged through the streets and hung upside down in front of a gas station. It was a fitting end to a tyrant.

ADOLF HITLER

While Mussolini was developing his Fascist ideology in 1922, Adolf Hitler was spending time in jail for antigovernment protests. In 1923, he already had a following of Nazi thugs who were beginning to cause considerable trouble in Germany.

His goal of playing a significant role in Germany's future came about while he was serving as a soldier in World War I. Having been briefly blinded by a poison gas attack, he claimed he'd had a vision, in which he saw himself as an Aryan hero called upon by the Germanic gods to lead his country into a thousand-year reign.

Through this vision, Hitler became a utopian revolutionary who felt he was divinely called to rule over the German people.[29]

In 1920 Hitler became a member of the German Workers' Party, a Jew-hating and Communist-hating organization. The group was eventually renamed the National Socialist German Workers' Party (Nazi Party).

In 1921 Hitler was arrested and sentenced to three months in prison for violently disrupting a Bavarian League meeting in Munich. In November 1923, he engineered the famous "Beer Hall Putsch," which was an effort to seize control of the German government with his Nazi thugs. He was sentenced to five years in prison and was sent to Landsberg Prison, but served only nine months for his crime. During this time, he penned his autobiography, *Mein Kampf* ("My Struggle"), with his friend Rudolf Hess. It clearly laid out his plans for creating a Nazi dictatorship and cleansing Germany of Jews.[30]

In early 1933 Hitler was appointed chancellor of Germany and immediately began the process of converting the country into a dictatorship. He used the Reichstag fire as an excuse to issue an emergency decree giving him nearly absolute power over the German people.

Hitler, his Nazi Gestapo, and the ruthless SS began imposing a police state on Germany. Opponents of Hitler were arrested and/or killed. Eventually, he began implementing the goals he had set out in *Mein Kampf* to eliminate Jews from Germany.

The history of the slave labor and concentration camps and the wreckage he brought about in World War II hardly needs to be recounted here. Hitler's utopian goal of establishing a pure Aryan state (a racially pure empire) in Germany and of conquering the world failed—thanks to the power of the United States and its allies.

If Germans had actually carefully read *Mein Kampf* and taken Hitler seriously in the 1920s, the world might have been spared the suffering, carnage, and death that Hitler brought upon the world beginning in the late 1930s and on into the mid-1940s.

Thanks to Germany's Nazism, Italy's Fascism, and Japan's totalitarianism, more than 63 million people died—both military and civilian—during World War II.[31] Millions more were wounded and had their futures completely destroyed.

This worldwide carnage happened because one rebellious young man decided he was destined by the Germanic gods to establish a thousand-year dictatorship in Germany. Hitler's utopian dream became a bloody and cruel nightmare for the entire world.

This is the legacy of utopian thinking: people die by the millions.

5

THE CULTURAL UTOPIANS

The man who founded one of the world's greatest social service organizations, one that was focused on the Gospel, issued what can only be seen as a prophetic and fateful warning to Western civilization. It is a warning the West has failed to heed, and the results of this failure are devastating society, while giving openings to utopian thought.

William Booth, founder of the Salvation Army, lived from 1829 to 1916. As the twentieth century began, he was asked what he saw as the greatest dangers for the next hundred years. His response is chilling when taking into account the cultural and political conditions of the world through the twentieth century and into today: "In answer to your inquiry," he said, "I consider that the chief dangers which confront the coming century will be religion without the Holy Ghost, Christianity without Christ, forgiveness without repentance, salvation without regeneration, politics without God, and heaven without hell."[1]

Within a year his prophecy and warning began to play out. The first officially atheistic government, an administration without God, was founded in 1917, the year after Booth's death. The godless leaders of the Soviet Union attempted to create an earthly utopia using central planning to replace market and social forces. Citizens did not respond with their best efforts of supporting the state, so to make them comply, the Soviets used brutality. Mass arrests, reeducation camps, and murder became the primary enforcement tools to create utopian equal outcome and social justice. Tens of millions were slaughtered or deliberately starved to death, including millions of Ukrainians in the new Soviet version of utopia. Russian Jews were moved to their own "homeland" in Siberia.

Other godless governments based on central planning followed, including Chairman Mao's "Cultural Revolution" along with a murderous rampage in China by his fanatical Red Guards. In Cambodia, Pol Pot's atheistic regime killed one out of every three of its citizens in an attempt to create God's heaven here on earth, directed by atheists.

William Booth also predicted "forgiveness without repentance," in other words, a church that would not only offer forgiveness to the sinner, but excuse the sin as well, changing Jesus's words from "Go and sin no more" to "Go and sin as you please." (See John 8:1–11.)

Today in the West, including America, as government becomes more godless, the churches are also becoming Christless. Rainbow flags welcoming homosexuals adorn churches, as lesbians and homosexuals have become pastors and bishops. Many Protestant churches now promise heaven to everyone, without the threat of hell. What Booth feared would one day happen has become a reality, not just in godless governments and politics, but in churches corrupted by sin and false forgiveness.

The collapse of the family and the disintegration of the authority of the church, predicted by William Booth, have done more damage to the economy than any other factor. Government has become the head of household in a large percentage of European and American families. Government at all levels is replacing fathers, while hot lunch programs and subsidized day care are replacing mothers in the family. Worse still, these social programs are paid for not by taxes, but often by massive debt. The increased social spending is causing damage to the families of Western nations, as a permanent underclass of fatherless children continues to grow. Many of these unchurched, poorly educated, fatherless children end up living in hopelessly overcrowded jails and providing a pretext for the militarization of the police force.

There has been a purposeful drive by ruthless, unprincipled utopian fanatics who have worked relentlessly throughout the twentieth century—and continue in the twenty-first—to destroy Judeo-Christian civilization and replace it with a hedonistic society in which an all-powerful, centrally planned welfare state controls every aspect of daily life.

From the early twentieth century into the twenty-first century, the United States has suffered the damaging influence of numerous cultural utopians. These individuals—both male and female—have typically rejected our country's Judeo-Christian heritage and have worked to replace it with a humanistic morality based on such concepts as "tolerance," "sexual liberation," "fairness," and "social justice" while actually promoting a political agenda based on Marxist–Leninist ideology.

There have been dozens of amoral cultural utopians in positions of influence who have undermined religious faith and the integrity of the nuclear family, and in so doing they have damaged the social fabric of the nation over the last century. We will examine a few of them in this chapter, beginning with the early twentieth century.

SEXUAL AND MORAL ANARCHIST MARGARET SANGER

Margaret Sanger, the founder of Planned Parenthood, was a product of an openly antireligious household headed by a rather unindustrious father, Michael Higgins. He was a freethinker (atheist) and a socialist activist who mocked Christianity. By age seventeen, Margaret had developed a similar hatred for Christianity.

Margaret attended the Claverack College of the Hudson River Institute. There, she became involved in radical feminism and began to engage in unrestrained sexual license.

She eventually met and married William Sanger, who routinely attended socialist, anarchist, and Communist meetings in Greenwich Village. Margaret attended these meetings with him and was further radicalized into Marxist and sexual liberationist ideologies. She eagerly joined the Socialist Party.

Another radical Marxist, Emma Goldman, was associated with the Bolsheviks in Russia, Fabian Socialists in Russia, anarchists in Germany, and Malthusians (population control advocates) in France. Margaret Sanger soon became a fanatical follower of Goldman, reading everything she had ever written and becoming more and more radicalized into an anti-Christian, Marxist, sexual liberationist revolutionary. Sanger had found her calling: to destroy biblical morality by promoting uninhibited sexual promiscuity.

Sanger, by now estranged from her husband, eventually began publishing her own newspaper, called the *Woman Rebel*, the motto of which was "No Gods, No Masters." The first issue denounced marriage as a "degenerate institution" and attacked capitalism as "indecent exploitation" and sexual modesty as "obscene prudery."

In her second issue, she proclaimed that rebel women had the following rights: the right to be unmarried mothers, the right to be lazy, the right to destroy, and the right to love. Other articles advocated contraceptives, social revolution, and the right to engage in political assassinations!

Margaret Sanger's magazine was so controversial and borderline obscene that she was eventually served with a subpoena indicting her on three counts of publishing lewd and indecent articles. Sanger's response was to flee to England to avoid prosecution.

In England, she found fellow revolutionaries and began attending socialist lectures on moral relativism, anarchist lectures on subversive pragmatism, lectures on collectivism, and talks on Malthusian population control. George Grant, writing in *Grand Illusions: The Legacy of Planned Parenthood*, described her time in England:

> Margaret immediately got on the Malthusian bandwagon. She was not philosophically inclined, nor was she particularly adept at political, social, or economic theory, but she did recognize in the Malthusians a kindred spirit and a tremendous opportunity. She was also shrewd enough to realize that her notions of radical socialism and sexual liberation would not ever have the popular support necessary to

usher in the revolution without some appeal to altruism and intel-
lectualism. She needed somehow to capture the moral and academic
"high ground." Malthusianism, she thought, just might be the key to
that ethical and intellectual posture.

If she could argue for birth control using the scientifically veri-
fied threat of poverty, sickness, racial tension, and over-population as
its backdrop, then she would have a much better chance of making
her case.[2]

After a year in self-imposed exile in England, Sanger returned to the
United States, rallied support for her cause, and was able to have the
obscenity charges against her dropped. She then founded the American
Birth Control League and in 1922 wrote *The Pivot of Civilization*, which
became a best seller.

In *The Pivot of Civilization*, she clearly laid out her plan, based on
eugenics theory, to eliminate the "genetically inferior races," by which
she meant nonwhites and the mentally retarded. She referred to these
people as "human weeds" who needed to be sterilized. Sanger promoted
eugenics through her publication *Birth Control Review* and through
the parent organization, the American Birth Control League—the
forerunner of Planned Parenthood. The "National Council" of the
League included at least twenty-three members who were die-hard
eugenicists. Sanger was also an active, dues-paying member of the
American Eugenics Society.

The American Eugenics Society had ugly and close ties to Nazi
leaders in Germany; several top Nazi scientists served as advisors and
journal contributors.[3] Some of the Society's members even assisted
Hitler in drafting the 1933 German sterilization laws!

Margaret Sanger was promoting Hitler's racial policies years before
he came into power in Germany or began his extermination of the
"lesser races," such as the Jews and Gypsies.

In a 1921 article published in *Birth Control Review*, Sanger wrote,
"[T]he most urgent problem today is how to limit and discourage the
over-fertility of the mentally and physically defective." And, what if

women rejected her solutions? She suggested coercion: "Possibly drastic and Spartan methods may be forced upon society if it continues complacently to encourage the chance and chaotic breeding that has resulted from our stupidly cruel sentimentalism."[4]

Margaret Sanger was the image of the utopian tyrant, believing that "superior" people such as herself should see to it that lesser beings were not permitted to randomly reproduce. She was an elitist who hated poor people and was vehemently opposed to welfare systems, once writing, "Funds that should be used to raise the standard of our civilization are diverted to the maintenance of those who should never have been born."

Douglas R. Scott, author of *Bad Choices: A Look inside Planned Parenthood*, said that Sanger "preferred that government be run by an aristocracy—a privileged minority or upper class." In addition, she advocated that there should be intelligence tests for legislators and condemned Congress and state legislatures as being filled with nests of "mentally and constitutionally unfit" individuals.[5]

One of her favorite phrases, appearing often in her magazine, was "A Race of Thoroughbreds," referring to the race she believed could be created by weeding out minority races, her main target being blacks in America. To eliminate as many blacks as she could, Sanger founded the Negro Project and set up birth control clinics in minority neighborhoods. Her clear goal was to provide birth control for black women as a way of keeping the population down. Once abortion was legalized nationwide in 1973, the organization she founded, Planned Parenthood, became a minority-killing machine, relentlessly aborting minority children.[6]

From a historical vantage point, Margaret Sanger's legacy is clear. She is in large part responsible for the deaths of millions of unborn babies, the normalization of premarital sex, the creation of generations of unwed moms who spend much of their lives on welfare, and the rampant spread of venereal diseases among teens and young adults. She left death and destruction behind her—thanks to her hatred of God, her commitment to utopian collectivism, and her ideology of loveless sex.

Sanger was a longtime friend and associate of Roger Baldwin, the utopian collectivist agnostic who founded the American Civil Liberties Union (ACLU). Baldwin was never shy about clearly explaining his objectives. In his thirtieth-anniversary Harvard University class book, he wrote, "I am for Socialism, disarmament, and ultimately abolishing of the state itself as an instrument of violence and compulsion. I seek social ownership of property, the abolition of the propertied class, and sole control by those who produce wealth. Communism is the goal."[7] He was a determined destroyer of everything we hold dear in America.

The ACLU and Sanger's Planned Parenthood were natural allies ever since the forming of the two groups. Sanger, in trying to destroy sexual taboos and normalize abortion and free love, needed ruthless lawyers to defend her anti-Christian activities. The ACLU was a perfect fit.

ACLU FOUNDER ROGER BALDWIN

Baldwin's grandfather Henry earned a reputation as an "iconoclastic, and non-conforming anti-Christian crusader." Roger admitted that his grandfather, who had a hatred of all things Christian, had a profound influence on his worldview. In addition, his aunt Ruth was a member of the Socialist Party. Born a "Red diaper baby," he seemed destined to be anti-American.

Two of Baldwin's closest associates were Margaret Sanger and Emma Goldman. As mentioned earlier, Goldman was a radical Communist/anarchist who promoted the Bolshevik dictatorship in Russia for America. Baldwin was greatly inspired by Goldman and her hatred of Christianity, free enterprise, and the United States Constitution.

When Goldman was deported from what she thought was the oppressive United States and sailed away with other expelled dissidents on the "Red Ark" to the new Soviet Union, Goldman thought she was on her way to an earthly paradise. Once there, she quickly realized the error of her beliefs and wrote frantic warning letters to her Communist friends back in America, including Roger Baldwin, whom she warned not to be duped by Soviet lies. The Soviet Union, she told him, was a place of brutal prison guards and unmarked graves. This was the same woman who had once railed against the rich and whose rhetoric was so inflammatory that she was widely blamed for the assassination of President William McKinley by one of her unhinged young followers. To Goldman's great surprise, she herself was now the victim of brutal repression, having been arrested and thrown into prison for a time by authorities who viewed her and her companion anarchists and dissidents as potential troublemakers. Baldwin didn't listen to Goldman's warnings and moved forward with his radical agenda for America.

The Soviets did find useful and supported American intellectuals, such as Baldwin and other ACLU founders, who believed in the Communist experiment and could be reliable, effective propagandists in the ongoing project to change the attitudes, and eventually the whole culture, of America and the West. Although the radicals who formed the ACLU saw the role of the courts as indispensable in forcing their utopian vision on America, the majority of ACLU founders, like Baldwin himself, were not lawyers and actually had no legal background or training. They were university professors, pastors, writers, publishers, political activists, and union organizers. They all sought redistribution of wealth, totalitarian collectivist rule by an all-powerful government (run by enlightened intellectuals such as themselves), total anarchy in the area of personal morality, and the destruction of Judeo-Christian values.

In 1924, after spending time in Russia, Baldwin wrote a book called *Liberty under the Soviets*, based on his observations. If the Russians expected slick propaganda, the book was not exactly that. But it is an interesting, if frightening, look into the darkness of a totalitarian mind in pursuit of what he saw as a righteous cause. It becomes clear that Baldwin had no delusions about what he experienced in the new Soviet Union. He was well aware of the abuses of the widely feared secret police, the State Political Directorate, also known by the acronym GPU, about which he wrote:

> In most countries detailed provisions are made by law for carrying out executions, and witnesses are required to be present. . . . In Russia no

directions are given in law, and no witnesses are permitted . . . The job is usually done at night in cellar rooms, and the body is removed at once to the place of burial, which is kept secret. . . . Against all elements which the G.P.U. regards as counter-revolutionary, it conducts what is commonly characterized as a reign of terror.[8]

Why did this great "civil libertarian," the founder of the ACLU, approve of this unrestrained "reign of terror"? For one reason, he saw it as necessary to protect the government: He said, "The G.P.U. is the strong arm of the Soviet state for the protection of the Revolution and to keep the way clear of obstructions to the state's programs."[9] He simply believed, as all utopian totalitarians do, that the ends justify the means.

Further, he thought the GPU's activities were excusable because they seldom bothered with the poor workers and peasants. "The classes against which the G.P.U. directs its chief efforts are the anti-Soviet elements among the old aristocracy, the intellectuals, the students, the private traders, and the conservative priests of the old church."[10] Baldwin, just like today's modern utopians, viewed people as members of one group or other, rather than as individuals created by God.

Finally, Baldwin excused the murderous reign of the Soviet political police because, after all, how else could anyone expect a tiny, enlightened minority to govern the ignorant masses? Here is how he put it: "No dictatorship of less than one percent of a people can govern without a political police, however enlightened its policy in the interest of the masses."[11]

These statements summarize the mind-set of utopian thinkers. They are an "enlightened minority" with noble intentions to organize a perfect society for the "ignorant masses," and they are justified in using whatever means to accomplish this end.

JOHN DEWEY: "EDUCATION IS PROPAGANDA AND PROPAGANDA IS EDUCATION."

Baldwin had many like-minded associates in the ACLU who also became influential in American society. One of those was John Dewey, longtime dean of the Teachers' College at Columbia University, America's first and largest graduate school of education. A prolific writer and universally viewed as the father of modern, progressive education, Dewey shaped the direction of American public school education more than any other single person. He was also a fervent Communist who toured Russia extensively in the 1920s and wrote a book about his experiences, called *Impressions of Soviet Russia and the Revolutionary World.* As generations of education majors who have slogged through countless pages of Dewey's books can attest, he was a dry and humorless writer. Yet he was almost giddy with emotion as he wrote about his visit to Russia, along with other American educators friendly to the Soviet project.

In Russia, the new government held complete power over public education and attempted to mold citizens according to their atheistic, collectivist vision, with parental wishes not even a consideration. Dedicated Marxists such as Dewey saw this as an exciting opportunity to learn ways to conform young minds into a desired direction. He was, as stated on the Columbia University website, "best known for developing the theory of instrumentalism, which posits the value of an idea in relation to its practical consequences rather than as a transcendent truth."[12] In plain English, he believed truth is not important if a lie will further the attainment of some worthy goal.

Case in point, Dewey approvingly described Soviet "education": "In Russia the propaganda is in behalf of a burning public faith. . . . To them, the end for which propaganda is employed is not a private or even a class gain, but is the universal good of universal humanity. In consequence, propaganda is education and education is propaganda."[13]

At the time of Dewey's visit, the country had an abundance of orphans, due to the fact that so many adults had either died in World War I or been executed as enemies of the Revolution. Most of these children ran wild in feral gangs who survived by stealing and scavenging. Some orphans, though, became wards of the state and were educated in "experimental schools" run by fervent young Communist educators. These children were a collectivist utopian's dream; they had no parents, no knowledge of God, and no memory of the past. They had only the fanatical teachers hired by the state to mold them into selfless, obedient worker drones, untroubled by any original thoughts or individual differences from their group.

As Dewey explained the goal of this education, "from the communist standpoint, the problem is not only that of replacing capitalistic by collectivistic economic institutions, but also one of substituting a collective mentality for the individualistic psychology inherited from the "bourgeois" epoch—a psychology which is still ingrained in most of the peasants and most of the intellectuals, as well as in the trading class itself."[14]

At the time many Americans worried about the influence of John Dewey and others like him on public school education, but their warnings were largely ignored.

THE NEW ACLU ATTACKS AMERICA

John Dewey was an active, founding member of the ACLU and a close associate of Roger Baldwin. The ACLU began attacking American institutions from the day it was founded in 1920. That year, it defended the Industrial Workers of the World (IWW), a Communist front organization dedicated to the overthrow of the United States.

In 1925, the ACLU decided to attack organized religion in America and at the same time introduce atheism into public schools by creating a legal test case over the teaching of evolution in public school classrooms. The group advertised for a teacher who would challenge a Tennessee state law that banned the teaching of evolution. The case became known as the Scopes Monkey Trial, and the biblical view of creation was mercilessly attacked. The most strident mockery came from the famous newspaper journalist H. L. Mencken, who had actually asked the ACLU to bring the suit and engineered the circumstances of the test case. Mencken was an atheist and, like Margaret Sanger, a social Darwinist.

The ACLU has also worked for decades to ban prayer and all

symbols or expressions of religious faith from the public schools and other public places. Even today the ACLU routinely sues over Christmas displays during the holiday season. The ACLU still supports Planned Parenthood by opposing any laws that might provide protection for unborn babies. Even laws providing for the health and safety of the women who are having abortions is opposed by the ACLU.

For decades the ACLU has worked to normalize same-sex marriage and destroy the institution of marriage by attacking the sanctity of marriage between one man and one woman. Baldwin's ACLU is in the forefront of forcing schools and other institutions to allow "transsexual" men to use women's restrooms, and vice versa. The goal is the destruction of all moral norms and the establishment of a genderless, classless, and godless society.

Most recently the ACLU has routinely condemned the American military and law enforcement organizations who were attempting to protect the nation from Islamic terrorist attacks. The ACLU goal would appear to be undermining national sovereignty and placing Americans under the control of utopian international organizations to allegedly reduce world conflict.

Ironically, the ACLU has defended Islamists who seek to replace the United States Constitution with a caliphate. Because the Qur'an does not represent the type of utopian thinking of Roger Baldwin, this would seem odd; however, Islam and the ACLU share a common goal: to destroy social norms and create a state of chaos that allows radical change.

As an example, in 2005 the ACLU announced it was suing then secretary of defense Donald Rumsfeld on behalf of eight foreign nationals who said they were abused by American forces in Iraq and Afghanistan, despite the fact that the alleged abuse occurred during wartime in a war zone and not in the United States. The ACLU opposes not only the Patriot Act, but any law designed to interfere with Islamic terrorist activity. Their position is that terrorists (who wear no uniforms and represent no country) should receive the same rights as regular armed service members under the Geneva Convention.[15]

Fox News commentator Bill O'Reilly said the ACLU "is the most dangerous organization in the country and is trying to paralyze the federal government by suing over a bevy of anti-terror strategies. The ACLU is putting us all in danger by its fanatical opposition to fighting the war on terror."[16]

In 2003 ACLU leader and self-proclaimed gay activist Anthony Romero announced a conference that would promote a "new era of social justice where the principles of the United Nations Universal Declaration of Human Rights are recognized and enforced in the United States."[17] Apparently the United States Constitution isn't the kind of document that pleases Romero and his radical internationalist allies, who believe their intellect is so great as to be able to achieve a worldwide utopia under one central government.

THE "GENTLE SUBVERSIVE," RACHEL CARSON

Rachel Carson is considered the pioneer of the environmentalist movement in the United States and around the world. She was a naturalist and science writer who originally wrote about ocean life, but eventually moved on to write *Silent Spring*, which was published in 1962.

Silent Spring described a world endangered by humankind and their use of pesticides like DDT to control insect and diseases. Carson was the female version of Al Gore, with her apocalyptic vision of a world without songbirds chirping in the trees—all killed because of man's irresponsible treatment of nature.

Environmental professor Mark Hamilton Lytle wrote a gushing biography of Carson, titled *The Gentle Subversive: Rachel Carson, Silent Spring, and the Rise of the Environmental Movement.* He was right on one count: Carson was indeed a "gentle subversive" and a cultural utopian whose book spawned the dangerous, anti–free enterprise environmental movement. It also influenced the creation of the Environmental Protection Agency and the banning of DDT—one of the most effective pesticides ever invented.

According to Lytle, Carson was energized by an "anti-materialist ethic" and a "reformist impulse," which was directed at industries that produced life-saving pesticides.

Thanks to Carson's hysterical book, DDT was banned, which has since resulted in the needless deaths of an estimated 30 million people from malaria and yellow fever in tropical countries—according to Dennis Avery, a senior fellow at the Hudson Institute. Malaria has also ruined the lives of as many as a billion people who are now unable to work because of its debilitating effect on them.[18] Most of those who died because of the worldwide DDT ban are a part of Margaret Sanger's "lesser" races in Africa, which fits overall into the cultural utopianist dream.

Entomologist Dr. J. Gordon Edwards has written an essay on the lies told by Carson in *Silent Spring*. Edwards, a longtime environmentalist, said he was initially delighted when her book was published in 1962. He was working for the National Park Service in Glacier National Park at the time, and when the book hit the shelves, he eagerly read it.

Then he noticed numerous scientifically inaccurate statements. In a brief critique of her flawed work, he wrote:

> As I neared the middle of the book, the feeling grew in my mind that Rachel Carson was really playing loose with the facts and was also deliberately wording many sentences in such a way as to make them imply certain things without actually saying them. She was carefully omitting everything that failed to support her thesis that pesticides were bad, that industry was bad, and that any scientists who did not support her views were bad.
>
> I then took notice of her bibliography and realized that it was filled with references from very unscientific sources. Also, each reference was cited separately each time it appeared in the book, thus producing an impressive array of "references" even though not many different sources were actually cited. I began to lose confidence in Rachel Carson, even though I thought that as an environmentalist I really should continue to support her.[19]

Dr. Edwards then went on to write that he looked up some of

Carson's references and discovered that they didn't even support her argument. He read the book a second time with this in mind and realized that Carson wasn't interested in the truth. Dr. Edwards eventually joined the detractors of *Silent Spring* and even testified before Congress in favor of the life-saving insecticide DDT. Despite his efforts, he failed in his attempt to keep DDT from being banned—and the ultimate result, as previously mentioned, was the needless deaths of millions of poor people from malaria and yellow fever. Carson and her radical followers had succeeded in their battle against the "evil" pesticide companies, and the result was untold suffering around the globe.

In 2012, the fiftieth anniversary of the publication of *Silent Spring*, the libertarian-leaning Cato Institute published a lengthy book on *Silent Spring* to expose its falsehoods and explain the terrible legacy left by Carson. The authors of *Silent Spring at 50: Reflections on an Environmental Classic*, note that her book "encourages some of the most destructive strains with environmentalism: alarmism, technophobia, failure to consider the costs and benefits of alternatives, and the discounting of human well-being around the world."[20]

Henry I. Miller, a physician and fellow of scientific philosophy at the Hoover Institution, has written of Carson:

> Carson's proselytizing and advocacy raised substantial anxiety about DDT and led to bans in most of the world and to restrictions on other chemical pesticides. But the fears she raised were based on gross misrepresentations and scholarship so atrocious that, if Carson were an academic, she would be guilty of egregious academic misconduct. Her observations about DDT have been condemned by many scientists. In the words of Professor Robert H. White-Stevens, an agriculturist and biology professor at Rutgers University, "if man were to follow the teachings of Miss Carson, we would return to the Dark Ages, and the insects and diseases and vermin would once again inherit the earth."[21]

White-Stevens is correct. Many of Carson's current-day followers have a hatred of mankind and are working relentlessly to take the world back to the Dark Ages. They share a utopian vision of a world returned to nature, with a few small villages of humans—populated, of course, by themselves and those of like mind. If hundreds of millions die to accomplish this utopian dream, it is viewed by many radical environmental utopianists as a cost that must be paid for their view of the perfection of nature without man.

COMMUNITY ORGANIZER: SAUL ALINSKY

Saul Alinsky was a classic Marxist–Leninist cultural utopian whose work created a nationwide network of community agitators who have labored diligently to take from the "haves" to give to the "have-nots" in a quest to create a centrally planned utopia.

Alinsky began his career in social work, but eventually developed strategies and tactics in organizing individuals into activist cells determined to seize power and wealth from productive members of our society to redistribute it to a small group, himself included, who would then create a society capable of supplying all needs to all people, at least the needs he himself believed were legitimate.

Alinsky admitted that he learned many of his tactics from his friend Chicago gangster Al Capone and his brutal associates. And in the preface to his 1971 book, *Rules for Radicals*, he even tipped his hat to the devil: "Lest we forget at least an over-the-shoulder acknowledgment to the very first radical: from all our legends, mythology, and history (and who is to know where mythology leaves off and history begins—or which is which), the first radical known to man who rebelled against the establishment and did it so effectively that he at least won his own kingdom—Lucifer."[22]

Alinsky never formally joined the Communist Party USA, but his credentials as a collectivist and central planner are clearly indicated by his life and works. He believed that the free-market system deprived the poor and that redistribution of wealth was the solution to all social problems.

Two of Alinsky's star pupils who are very familiar to the American public and beloved by the political left are President Barack Hussein Obama and former senator Hillary Clinton. Clinton's college thesis was actually on Alinsky's work, and she was his intern for a while. Obama taught Alinsky's tactics as a community organizer in Chicago. Most political experts would agree that Obama ran his campaigns for the White House in both 2008 and 2012 following the rules laid out by Alinsky in *Rules for Radicals*.

A very well thought-out analysis of Alinsky's tactics is outlined in Discover the Networks:

> The goal is to foment enough public discontent, moral confusion, and outright chaos to spark the social upheaval that Marx, Engels, and Lenin predicted—a revolution whose foot soldiers view the status quo as fatally flawed and wholly unworthy of salvation. Thus, the theory goes, the people will settle for nothing less than that status quo's complete collapse—to be followed by the erection of an entirely new system upon its ruins.[23]

Alinsky portrayed himself as a hater of materialism who desired socialist revolutionaries who would "place human rights far above property rights"; who would "fight conservatives everywhere"; and who would "fight privilege and power, whether it be inherited or acquired."[24] Alinsky's tactics have been used by many leftist groups, including ACORN (Association of Community Organizations for Reform Now).

Alinsky envisioned his utopian dream coming about in much the same way as that of the anti-Christian French Revolution in 1787, through mob rule. He rightly understood that chaos and anger create the environment in which to organize masses of people to destroy free enterprise and create a centrally planned socialist welfare state! The French model is the essence of much modern conflict in Western society. Opponents of this concept of utopia are represented by the Austrian concept of liberty as described so powerfully by Friedrich Hayek in his 1960 book, *Constitution of Liberty*.

Had Saul Alinsky lived long enough to see America under President Barack Obama, he would probably have been critical of his former student. He would likely feel that the "fundamental change" in American society was not fast enough and had not gone far enough as yet because private property and "pay for value produced" still exist.

"GAY RIGHTS" FOUNDER HARRY HAY

Harry Hay was also a Marxist revolutionary who is believed to have entered into his first homosexual relationship in the early 1930s. He became the lover of Will Geer, a fellow Marxist who played Grandpa Walton on the beloved family series *The Waltons*.[25] It was Geer who recruited Hay into the Communist Party in 1934.[26] In spite of his relationship with Geer, Hay married Anna Platky, a fellow Marxist and Party member, in 1938. Common belief is that he did so because of pressures against homosexuals in the Party during that time.

In 1951 he founded the first official openly homosexual group in the United States, the Mattachine Society. He was married at the time and had two children, but was most likely bisexual. He divorced his wife, Anna, and actually convinced his own mother to become a board member of his new homosexual organization.[27]

Hay organized the Mattachine Society on the cell-based structure Lenin had designed and which was used by the Communist Party not only in the United States but worldwide. His objective was to build a nationwide homosexual network to normalize same-sex behaviors in the United States. He eventually became a supporter of pedophilia and openly supported the North American Man-Boy Love Association. Clearly, no deviant sexual behavior was too perverse for Hay.

Through his "inspiration" dozens of other homosexual groups were formed, and the movement for the legalization and normalization of homosexuality began in earnest. One of the key individuals who was energized by Hay's activities was Frank Kameny, who had been fired in 1957 from his job with the US Civil Service Commission for lewd conduct. Kameny filed a lawsuit because of his firing, and went on to later challenge the American Psychiatric Association for its listing of homosexuality as a mental disorder. He and his homosexual allies outside and inside the APA were victorious in 1973—and the floodgates of gay activism were unleashed into American culture.[28]

Hay devoted the rest of his life to promoting homosexuality through the Mattachine Society and later formed a group known as the Radical Faeries. He was later ousted from the Radical Faeries for carrying a NAMBLA (North American Man-Boy Love Association) sign in a "gay pride" parade.[29] The network he founded apparently decided sex with young children went a bit too far even for a group that promoted sodomy.

Hay died at the age of ninety in 2002, but his deviant legacy has lived on with such men as Kevin Jennings, the founder of the Gay, Lesbian and Straight Education Network (GLSEN). The group has hundreds of chapters in our nation's public schools. Jennings was also a member of ACT UP, the very aggressive activist group that terrorized pro-lifers and opponents of the homosexual agenda. Under his leadership, GLSEN recruited the very young into the homosexual lifestyle by publishing a recommended book list for teens that included stories that normalized adult-child sexual encounters.

In 2009 President Obama appointed Jennings, a very well-known homosexual advocate, to be the nation's "safe schools czar." It is impossible, in light of the White House vetting process, that the president was unaware of his past. Fortunately, Jennings resigned in disgrace after his radical past was publicly exposed.

Jennings openly expressed his admiration for cultural utopian Harry Hay—even though it was public knowledge that Hay was a NAMBLA supporter.[30] Hay left a tragic legacy of molested children, the attempted destruction of traditional marriage, and the promotion of hate crime laws aimed at banning criticism of homosexual conduct.

Hay's gay political agenda has a firm footing in Western nations, including the United States, as it is treated as a "third rail" and even sacred by the mainstream media and by politicians seeking votes from those who practice deviant sexual behavior.

LSD/DRUG CULTURE ACTIVIST TIMOTHY LEARY

Timothy Leary, born in 1902, was a rebellious young man with a very early substance abuse problem. His influential father obtained a slot for him at West Point, which soon turned sour after several episodes of drinking and failing to report. After leaving West Point without graduating, Leary went into the Army in 1943. He avoided combat by staying in the United States and working as a clinical psychologist at an Army hospital in Virginia.

Leary, who did not lack intelligence—just common sense—later earned a doctorate at the University of California, Berkeley, and went to work at the Kaiser Research Facility in Oakland, California. Behavioral change became an obsession for Leary. After obtaining a position at Harvard, he was introduced to a new drug called *Psilocybe mexicana*, taken from a mushroom found in Mexico.

After taking the drug, Leary started the Harvard Psilocybin Project and developed a program to give this experimental drug to inmates at Concord State Prison. His goal was to monitor the changes in values and recidivism rates of the inmates.

He also began giving LSD to his Harvard students and eventually spent the rest of his life promoting LSD and other mind-destroying drugs. He told teens in the early 1960s to "turn on, tune in, drop out" of school. Unfortunately, too many young people did just that in the 1960s and were referred to as the "love generation," or hippies. Countless wasted lives can be attributed to Dr. Timothy Leary's teachings.

Leary left Harvard before he was fired, but according to a slobbering biographical sketch of him in the *St. James Encyclopedia of Popular Culture*, psychedelics had become part of his utopian obsession, and he planned on using drugs as the basis of his psychedelic community. Leary and his followers returned to Mexico to start a research facility, but were kicked out within two weeks. The Dominican Republic and Antigua also evicted them. He returned to Cambridge, Massachusetts, where heiress Peggy Hitchcock volunteered her estate in upstate New York, known as Millbrook. It was an ideal locale for Leary's drug project.[31]

Leary was eventually convicted of marijuana possession and ended up in the San Luis Obispo prison, which was a minimum security facility. In 1970 the Weather Underground terrorist group, of which Barack Obama mentor Bill Ayers and his wife, Bernardine Dohrn, were a part, engineered Leary's escape from prison. He jumped the prison fence and escaped in a car the Weather Underground had waiting for him, and he escaped to Algeria on the fake passport provided for him.

In Algeria, the Black Panther Party, another violent group promoting a collectivist utopia, provided Leary with a safe house. There, he became friends with Eldridge Cleaver, then the leader of the Black Panthers. (Cleaver later joined the Mormon Church and ran for US Senate as a Republican. Sadly, his problem with addictive substances continued on and off until his death.)

Leary and his wife at some point became hostages of the Black Panthers but managed to escape to Switzerland. In 1972 Leary was arrested in Afghanistan and returned to the United States. He was released from prison in 1976 by another social utopian, Governor Jerry Brown.[32]

Timothy Leary's popularization of LSD and other mind-destroying drugs has left a trail of broken bodies, destroyed minds, and shattered futures, particularly for those young people who followed his advice to get high and drop out of school. Others under the influence of drugs also followed his guidance for many years, such as Aleister Crowley, an infamous Satanist and author of *The Book of the Law*, which included the Rule of Thelema: "Do what thou wilt shall be the whole of the Law."[33] This is actually the ultimate goal of most utopian dreamers, a society so pure in intent through collectivist thought that it requires no law. In attempting to reach this goal, tens of millions have died and hundreds of millions more have suffered.

Barbara Krantz, MD, an expert on drug addiction, published an article in *Addiction Professional* in 2008 that described a troubling trend among Baby Boomers who were turning sixty. She noted that this generation, which had been introduced to drugs during the '60s, was now having to deal with serious heroin and cocaine addictions. Krantz noted:

> As Baby Boomers age, we'll see more of them turning to illicit drugs, just as they did in their 20s. We are diagnosing more co-morbidities

such as hepatitis C in this group, as symptoms surface after decades of dormancy. In pursuit of health, youth, and happiness over a lifetime, Baby Boomers also have been widely dubbed the "Me Generation." They embrace a complex set of values, including a great belief in the quick fix for anything from rocky marriages (the divorce rate is three times higher for Baby Boomers than for their parents) to physical discomfort. "Living Well through Better Chemistry" sounds like a jest but it became a reality for many who grew up in the '60s and '70s. Many were introduced to the psychedelic age by '60s LSD guru Timothy Leary, who entreated his followers to "turn on, tune in, drop out."[34]

The introduction of drugs into our culture wasn't simply the result of Timothy Leary's LSD crusade, but he certainly played a key role in the glamorization and acceptance of drugs for an entire generation of young people in the 1960s. And we're seeing that those same Baby Boomers are now struggling with even more serious drug addictions. Leary's rebellion and his pro-drug message are still causing problems.

Thanks to Timothy Leary and his druggie friends from the '60s, America has an ongoing drug problem that has brought about social destruction in the inner cities, gang warfare over drug supplies, and border wars between American law enforcement officials and the Mexican drug cartels who continue to smuggle drugs across our porous and unprotected borders.

Leary's utopian dream of "living well through better chemistry" has been a continuing nightmare for law enforcement and for families that have been torn apart by drug-addicted family members.

SHADOW GOVERNMENT LEADER: GEORGE SOROS

George Soros is a billionaire atheist who has openly admitted that he has a "god-complex" about his role in refashioning the world in his own image. He is the living and breathing embodiment of the utopian who believes all others can live better lives by living as he intends them to live.

Soros admits that he sees himself as "some kind of god, the creator of everything." In his 1991 book, *Underwriting Democracy*, he said, "If truth be known, I carried some rather potent messianic fantasies with me from childhood."[35] He's pursued his utopian vision with a vast financial empire ever since.

Soros openly despises Christianity and the free enterprise system, even though he has made billions of dollars during his life through capitalist ventures. He once nearly collapsed the economy of the United Kingdom while making futures plays on that nation's currency. As of this writing he has an estimated $13 billion personal fortune. In obtaining that fortune he was once convicted of insider trading.

Soros was born in Hungary in 1930. He worked as a teenage assistant to an official in the fascist government whose job it was to confiscate the property of Jews. Somehow he survived the war and ended up in England at the London School of Economics, where he learned to be an advocate of one-world government and became a utopian visionary who believed that he could perfect humanity through social engineering.

In 1993 Soros founded the Open Society Institute (OSI), an organization dedicated to creating what he believes will be a utopian society in his image.

Soros put human rights activist Aryeh Neier in charge of OSI. That name isn't familiar to most Americans, but it should be. Neier was the founder of the Students for a Democratic Society (SDS) in the 1960s, a radical Marxist student group, the stated goal of which was the violent overthrow of the United States and the creation of a dictatorship of the proletariat. One of the many spin-off groups from the SDS was the Weather Underground. Ayers and Dohrn are, to this day, unrepentant about their participation in various bombings during the 1970s aimed at destabilizing government.

Neier also worked fifteen years as a leader in the American Civil Liberties Union and twelve years as executive director of Human Rights Watch, an organization that targets the United States and Israel as the greatest human rights abusers on the planet.[36]

This radical Marxist and lifelong subversive was trusted by Soros to run his flagship organization promoting "equality" while living the life of an aristocrat in multimillion-dollar homes. This may seem atypical, but it is not. Often those who seek utopia believe that its designers and overseers should be rewarded to a greater extent than those who are supposed to "equally benefit" from it. This has been true since the first documented attempt in Sparta.

The Open Society Institute funds dozens of organizations that are dedicated to Soros's objectives, mainly: legalizing drug use; undermining national sovereignty by creating a borderless world; legalizing homosexual marriages; destroying conservative media outlets; protecting the abortion industry; defending voter fraud; and similar goals.

Almost every project Soros funds is specifically designed to injure America's Judeo-Christian heritage, the republican form of government, and the free enterprise system, while attempting to create a perfect, selfless society.

Soros has said that capitalism "is today a greater threat than any totalitarian ideology." He has expressed a desire to redistribute the wealth of the United States to poorer nations through the UN Millennium Goals. This is a scheme designed to siphon off American gross national product (GDP) to promote the economic welfare of poorer nations. Most often this would become a welfare program for nations that are suffering economic ruin because they've chosen socialism as their economic model! Soros wants the evil capitalist America to bail them out![37]

When Soros was asked in 2008 if he wanted European-style socialism for America, he replied, "That is exactly what we need now. I am against market fundamentalism. I think this propaganda that government involvement is always bad has been very successful—but also very harmful to our society."[38]

Unfortunately, George Soros is not the only American billionaire who, perhaps out of guilt about wealth, finances schemes to redistribute wealth from hardworking members of society to the "less fortunate." Far too many billionaires, rather than using their wealth to invest and thereby create jobs, have begun to promote causes such as "social justice," which demands an impossible "equal outcome"—something that exists only in utopian dreams.

6

THE COLLECTIVIST ROAD TO POVERTY

AND SLAVERY

I n 1931 a young man from Vienna, Austria, who would later have significant influence in the political and economic thinking of President Ronald Reagan and British Prime Minister Margaret Thatcher, traveled to London to give four lectures at the London School of Economics, an institute that advocated Fabian Socialist policies. Friedrich A. Hayek stayed at the London School until after World War II. His views on economics and human freedom were clearly at odds with the prevailing worldview at this socialist-leaning school.

Hayek gave a significant lecture on what was known as the German Historical School of economic theorists at the London School on March 1, 1933. Hayek, at the time, was a member of the Austrian School of Economics, which included such notables as Ludwig von Mises. This school of thought clashed with the goals of the socialist planners prevalent at that time because it promoted free markets and individual freedom. It was von Mises's writings on the devastating impact of socialism that turned Hayek toward a lifetime of defending free enterprise and personal liberty.

Hayek's lecture was given just a day after the infamous Reichstag fire in Berlin, which was used by the recently appointed chancellor of Germany, Adolf Hitler, as an excuse to persecute his perceived enemies. Hitler imposed martial law on the country and shut down opposition newspapers. His seemingly endless reign of terror to bring about a Germanic utopia had begun.

Hitler's actions confirmed Hayek's views on the destructive effects of central planning, socialist or otherwise, on a country. He spent his time in England warning the West about the dangers of socialism and fascism to individual liberty.

Hayek eventually wrote a book based on his lecture series that has become a classic among both libertarians and conservatives: *The Road to Serfdom*, which was published in 1944 while World War II was still raging. One key feature of this work was the revelation that socialist central planning in Germany before the rise of Adolf Hitler provided the institutions that allowed him to suppress the people of that nation so quickly.

Hayek also later wrote *Law, Legislation and Liberty*, which described how Western democracies were increasingly circumventing constitutionalism by passing coercive legislation in order to achieve misguided notions of "social justice." Hayek held that the practice of social justice—which is in fact attempting to determine market outcome in advance—would contribute to the erosion of personal liberties. He held that this was a step toward totalitarianism, which has proven to be the case.

Even before Milton Friedman, whom we'll look at later, Hayek in *The Road to Serfdom* made the point that, without economic freedom, personal freedom and political freedom were not possible: "We have progressively abandoned that freedom in economic affairs without which personal and political freedom has never existed in the past. Although we had been warned by some of the greatest political thinkers of the nineteenth century, by Tocqueville and Lord Acton, that socialism means slavery, we have steadily moved in the direction of socialism."[1]

He continued:

How sharp a break not only with the recent past but with the whole evolution of Western civilization the modern trend toward socialism means becomes clear if we consider it not merely against the background of the nineteenth century but in a longer historical perspective? We are rapidly abandoning not the views merely of Cobden and Bright, of Adam Smith and Hume, or even of Locke and Milton, but one of the salient characteristics of Western civilisation as it has grown from the foundations laid by Christianity and the Greeks and Romans. Not merely nineteenth- and eighteenth-century liberalism [modern day conservatism], but the basic individualism inherited by us from Erasmus and Montaigne, from Cicero and Tacitus, Pericles and Thucydides, is progressively relinquished.[2]

Hayek pointed out that socialism had been spreading throughout Europe since the 1870s, but it was in Germany where many of the socialist ideals were transformed into reality before Hitler, with tragic consequences for the entire world. He also noted that Alexis de Tocqueville, the French philosopher and student of the American democratic experience, was correct in his assessment of the loss of freedom under socialist ideology: "Democracy extends the sphere of individual freedom [he said in 1848], socialism restricts it. Democracy attaches all possible value to each man; socialism makes each man a mere agent, a mere number. Democracy and socialism have nothing in common but one word: equality. But notice the difference: while democracy seeks equality in liberty, socialism seeks equality in restraint and servitude."[3]

Socialism demands the destruction of private enterprise and the creation of a "planned economy," where all economic decisions are in the hands of one tyrant or an army of unaccountable bureaucrats who make decisions based on what they believe is the common good for the population without deference to a free marketplace. This results inevitably in controlling all aspects of an individual's life.

Hayek noted that in Britain in the 1940s, it was becoming more and more evident among bureaucrats that, in order to achieve their goals for the so-called common good, they had to be free of democratic procedures. They had to rule without restraint.

This reflects the view of President Barack Obama's declaration that he cannot wait for the democratically elected Congress to act upon his plans for "social justice." Instead, he said, "I can use that pen to sign executive orders and take executive actions and administrative actions that move the ball forward in helping to make sure our kids are getting the best education possible and making sure that our businesses are getting the kind of support and help they need to grow and advance to make sure that people are getting the skills that they need to get those jobs that our businesses are creating."[4]

Much of what President Obama wanted to accomplish, as well as others who pursue utopian solutions, is equal outcome rather that equal opportunity. While working toward the goal, the president worked around using the collectivist "From each according to his ability and to each according to his need" mantra, but he still came close. During one campaign stop he said, "Should we settle for an economy where a few people do really well and then a growing number are struggling to get by? Or do we build an economy . . . where everybody gets a fair shot, and everybody does their fair share."[5]

The president was referring to a new freedom: the freedom from necessity. It is this same concept that drove him to create Obamacare, the idea that medical care is a right, a necessity that the government should, even through coercion, provide. Hayek had an answer to this new concept of freedom in his chapter titled "The Great Utopia" in *The Road to Serfdom*:

> To the great apostles of political freedom the word [*freedom*] had meant freedom from coercion, freedom from the arbitrary power of other men, release from the ties which left the individual no choice but obedience to the orders of a supervisor to whom he was attached. The new freedom promised, however, was to be freedom from necessity, release from the compulsion of the circumstances which inevitably limit the range of choice of all of us, although for some very much more than for others. Before man could be truly free, the "despotism

of physical want" had to be broken, the "restraints of the economic system" relaxed . . . The demand for the new freedom was thus only another name for the old demand for an equal distribution of wealth.[6]

Moving forward with social plans that benefit certain groups always has a negative effect on other groups or individuals. Rarely can this "taking" from one group to benefit another be accomplished without central planning outside the democratic process.

Hayek pointed out that this central planning inevitably leads to dictatorship because that form of government is the most efficient in coercing the population to abide by rules that interfere with free markets of both ideas and products. Because these concepts of social justice pick winners and losers, the government must operate in an arbitrary manner in dealing with individuals and groups. Laws are not applied equally. The liberty of the individual, the freedom of choice, cannot long exist in a system that is designed by central planners.

According to Hayek, a state that values freedom—both individual and economic—must be governed by what is known as the Rule of Law. He explained:

> Stripped of all technicalities, this means that government in all its actions is bound by rules fixed and announced beforehand—rules which make it possible to foresee with fair certainty how the authority will use its coercive powers in given circumstances and to plan one's individual affairs on the basis of this knowledge. Though this ideal can never be perfectly achieved, since legislators as well as those to whom the administration of the law is entrusted are fallible men, the essential point, that the discretion left to the executive organs wielding coercive power should be reduced as much as possible, is clear enough.[7]

In a free-market system, for example, the government confines itself to fixed rules that determine the conditions under which available resources can be used—leaving all other decisions to individuals. Under a socialist form of government, the central planners direct the means of production to accomplish a desired outcome. "The difference between the two kinds of rules is the same as that between laying down a Rule of the Road, as in the Highway Code, and ordering people where to go," he explained, "or, better still, between providing signposts and commanding people which road to take."[8]

With central planning the state determines most or all aspects of an economy; it also must plan how individuals are to behave inside that economy. To achieve the desired market outcome, freedom of choice in the market must be restricted. The recent debacle with Obamacare could easily be used as an example. The law forces some but not all Americans to buy a product they may not want or cannot afford. Many of the aspects of the law are arbitrary, such as how it affects different sizes of businesses.

This example of central planning that manipulates markets exemplifies Hayek's point in that, for the first time in the United States, the power of the federal government is used to coerce citizens to buy a product. With this precedent set, the government could move to force the purchase or perhaps the sale of other products at prices set not by the market but by the central planners. Currently the coercion to purchase the health insurance demanded by Obamacare is massive fines; however, as past regimes remind us, this could well become prison time later.

With the federal government effectively taking over the health care of individuals, it will also have to determine who gets what treatment, how much doctors will be paid, and who ends up with or without lifesaving procedures. Decisions of life and death move to the hands of faceless bureaucrats rather than doctors and their patients.

As Hayek noted back in 1944: "There can be no doubt that planning necessarily involves deliberate discrimination between particular needs of different people, and allowing one man to do what another must be prevented from doing. It must lay down by a legal rule how well off particular people shall be and what different people are to be allowed to have and do."[9]

From these examples you can see that the totalitarian nature of government does not suddenly appear in a democracy. First there must be social acceptance among the elite, who then persuade the rest of society to go along with them. Hayek noted this progress in his 1944 essay "The Intellectuals and Socialism":

> The political development of the Western World during the last hundred years furnishes the clearest demonstration. Socialism has never and nowhere been at first a working-class movement. It is by no means an obvious remedy for the obvious evil which the interests of that class will necessarily demand. It is a construction of theorists, deriving from certain tendencies of abstract thought with which for a long time only the intellectuals were familiar; and it required long efforts by the intellectuals before the working classes could be per- suaded to adopt it as their program.[10]

TYRANNY THROUGH THE BALLOT BOX

Hayek reminded us that socialist tyrannies can come through legal means in the democratic process just as easily as through abrupt totalitarianism. Adolf Hitler, for example, was elected to office, unlike Cambodia's Pol Pot, who seized power. Thus, democracies aren't nec- essarily a protection against utopian central planners taking away the liberties of individuals.

Quite often, democratically elected representatives can delegate authority to bureaucrats who have the authority to impose the draco- nian policies on an unwilling populace. Hayek wrote, "By giving the government unlimited powers, the most arbitrary rule can be made legal; and in this way a democracy may set up the most complete despotism imaginable."[11]

Hayek isn't the only philosopher or economist to warn about the dangers of tyranny being imposed through the democratic process. Alexis de Tocqueville, the famous French philosopher who visited the United States in the mid-1800s to study the democratic system and culture, warned that democratic systems could become despotic.

In *Democracy in America*, in his classic chapter "What Sort of Despotism Democratic Nations Have to Fear" (volume 2), Tocqueville accurately predicted the rise of bureaucratic czars and webs of legislation that would stifle human freedom and productivity. It is as if he were writing prophetically about the Environmental Protection Agency, which has imposed so many irrational rules on industry that our nation is in danger of losing its ability to compete in many industries, such as energy.

Tocqueville compared the ancient tyrannies of the past and noted that Roman emperors had tremendous power over the lives of their subjects who were scattered throughout the world, but that the "details of social life and private occupations lay for the most part beyond his control." However, Tocqueville warned:

> It would seem that if despotism were to be established amongst the democratic nations of our days, it might assume a different character; it would be more extensive and more mild; it would degrade men without tormenting them. I do not question, that in an age of instruction and equality like our own, sovereigns might more easily succeed in collecting all political power into their own hands, and might interfere more habitually and decidedly within the circle of private interests, than any sovereign of antiquity could ever do. But this same principle of equality which facilitates despotism, tempers its rigour.[12]

He continued: "I think then that the species of oppression by which democratic nations are menaced is unlike anything which ever before existed in the world: our contemporaries will find no prototype of it in their memories. I am trying myself to choose an expression which will accurately convey the whole of the idea I have formed of it, but in vain; the old words 'despotism' and 'tyranny' are inappropriate: the thing itself is new; and since I cannot name it, I must attempt to define it."[13]

According to Tocqueville, this kind of democratic oppression is

> absolute, minute, regular, provident, and mild. It would be like the authority of a parent, if, like that authority, its object was to prepare men for manhood; but it seeks on the contrary to keep them in perpetual childhood: it is well content that the people should rejoice, provided they think of nothing but rejoicing. For their happiness such

a government willingly labors, but it chooses to be the sole agent and the only arbiter of that happiness: it provides for their security, foresees and supplies their necessities, facilitates their pleasures, manages their principal concerns, directs their industry, regulates the descent of property, and subdivides their inheritances—what remains, but to spare them all the care of thinking and all the trouble of living? Thus it every day renders the exercise of the free agency of man less useful and less frequent; it circumscribes the will within a narrower range, and gradually robs a man of all the uses of himself.[14]

America's schoolchildren today are educated under policies of "no tolerance" that demand they become automatons. Showing various emotions, such as anger or love, can lead to expulsion from school, or worse. Children have been arrested for pointing a finger and saying, "Bang!" and suspended from classes for sharing a hug in the hallways. Currently, some high school students, thanks to legislation promoted by First Lady Michelle Obama, are not allowed to eat more than 750 calories for lunch, even boys on the football team, who require upwards of 3,000 calories a day. This is exactly the type of democratic oppression that both Tocqueville and Hayek discussed, and it continues to spread in Western nations.

Tocqueville described what happens to citizens when they're slowly enslaved by an all-powerful central government:

It [the statist] covers the surface of society with a network of small complicated rules, minute and uniform, through which the most original minds and the most energetic characters cannot penetrate, to rise above the crowd. The will of man is not shattered, but softened, bent, and guided: men are seldom forced by it to act, but they are constantly restrained from acting: such a power does not destroy, but it prevents existence; it does not tyrannize, but it compresses, enervates, extinguishes, and stupefies a people, till each nation is reduced to be nothing better than a flock of timid and industrious animals, of which the government is the shepherd.

I have always thought that servitude of the regular, quiet, and gentle kind which I have just described, might be combined more easily than is commonly believed with some of the outward forms of freedom; and that it might even establish itself under the wing of the sovereignty of the people.[15]

Like a frog placed in cold water, and then the temperature is increased slowly until the frog is cooked, the populace do not notice the melting away of individual liberty. For instance, the American people were placed in the cold water of a "small" income tax imposed by President Woodrow Wilson that has become today almost total control of the economy by the central government. Hayek and Tocqueville both described accurately the destruction of individual liberty, not only through absolute dictatorships, but by democratic totalitarianism as well.

THE END OF TRUTH

Hayek devoted a full chapter in *The Road to Serfdom* to the function of propaganda in a socialist welfare state. He pointed out that in such a totalitarian system, it isn't enough just to force everyone to work for the end desired; they must also be convinced that those ends are actually theirs and that they are obtainable. Thus, the propagandist must be able to brainwash the populace into believing that the central planners are benevolent and that their goals are actually those of the people.

As Hayek observed, "The skilful propagandist then has power to mold their minds in any direction he chooses, and even the most intelligent and independent people cannot entirely escape that influence if they are long isolated from all other sources of information."[16]

According to Hayek, the moral consequence of totalitarian propaganda is that it undermines the sense of and respect for the truth. In fact, the totalitarian propagandist isn't concerned with the truth. He only wants to convince the populace that the rulers are acting in the best interest of the enslaved citizens, to achieve their utopian dreams. Lying becomes the standard of utopian governments.

FRÉDÉRIC BASTIAT'S WARNINGS AGAINST SOCIALIST UTOPIANISM

French economist and politician Frédéric Bastiat's writings aren't well known in the United States these days, but they certainly should be. Bastiat was the deputy to the Legislative Assembly in France during the mid-1800s, when that nation was rapidly turning into a socialist state.

Alarmed by the trend, Bastiat spent his time and energies debunking all of the excuses that were used to impose statism on the French people. His classic, *The Law*, was published in 1850 and followed some of the similar lines of logic as did Hayek's later work. It was his desire to convince his fellow Frenchmen that socialism would inevitably lead to slavery and Communism. Regrettably, his warnings were mostly ignored, but his prophetic writings against socialism are very timely, as our own nation's leaders play with totalitarian ideas about how to turn us into dependent serfs.

Bastiat began *The Law* by clearly asserting that God gave us life, including physical, intellectual, and moral life. In addition, God gave each person the ability to use resources to create value and to own property. He further asserted, "Each of us has a natural right—from God—to defend his person, his liberty, and his property. These are the three basic requirements of life, and the preservation of any one of them is completely dependent upon the preservation of the other two. For what are our faculties but the extension of our individuality? And what is property but an extension of our faculties?"[17]

He defined law as the "organization of the natural right of lawful defense. It is the substitution of a common force for individual forces. And this common force is to do only what the individual forces have a natural and lawful right to do: to protect persons, liberties, and properties; to maintain the right of each, and to cause justice to reign over us all."[18]

But what happens when the state uses the law to destroy freedom? It is engaging in what Bastiat rightly called "lawful plunder."

When a state legalizes plunder, wrote Bastiat, one of the first effects is to erase "from everyone's conscience the distinction between justice and injustice. No society can exist unless the laws are respected to a certain degree. The safest way to make laws respected is to make them respectable. When law and morality contradict each other, the citizen has the cruel alternative of either losing his moral sense or losing his respect for the law."[19]

When legalized plunder becomes commonplace in a socialist government, noted Bastiat, every group in society will want to get their share of it. Everyone will begin plundering from everyone else: "Under the pretense of organization, regulation, protection, or encouragement, the law takes property from one person and gives it to another; the law takes the wealth of all and gives it to a few, whether farmers, manufacturers, ship owners, artists, or comedians. Under these circumstances, then certainly every class will aspire to grasp the law, and logically so."[20]

Bastiat clearly shows us how we can determine if a law is actually legalized plunder. His definition perfectly fits much of the transfer of wealth that occurs in Western nations today, including in the United States.

> See if the law takes from some persons what belongs to them, and gives it to other persons to whom it does not belong. See if the law benefits one citizen at the expense of another by doing what the citizen himself cannot do without committing a crime.
>
> Then abolish this law without delay, for it is not only an evil itself, but also it is a fertile source for further evils because it invites reprisals. If such a law—which may be an isolated case—is not abolished immediately, it will spread, multiply, and develop into a system.[21]

Sadly, when Woodrow Wilson introduced the income tax, the people had the opportunity to stop just such an evil, but out of the promise that it would benefit the many at the expense of the few rich of the time, a constitutional amendment was approved to allow the theft of the income of those who produce value through labor or investment. The result is massive government today, which takes from virtually everyone's earnings to some degree.

Bastiat continued: "Socialists desire to practice legal plunder, not *illegal* plunder. Socialists, like all other monopolists, desire to make the law their own weapon. And when once the law is on the side of socialism, how can it be used against socialism? For when plunder is abetted by the law, it does not fear your courts, your gendarmes, and your prisons. Rather, it may call upon them for help."[22]

Augustine of Hippo made a similar statement regarding government plundering in the fifth century:

> Justice being taken away, then, what are kingdoms but great robberies? For what are robberies themselves, but little kingdoms? The band itself is made up of men; it is ruled by the authority of a prince, it is knit together by the pact of the confederacy; the booty is divided by the law agreed on. If, by the admittance of abandoned men, this evil increases to such a degree that it holds places, fixes abodes, takes possession of cities, and subdues peoples, it assumes the more plainly the name of a kingdom, because the reality is now manifestly conferred on it, not by the removal of covetousness, but by the addition of impunity.[23]

Following a road to serfdom as described by Hayek inevitably leads to what might be called a benign authoritarian system, where everyone is brainwashed into docile obedience, or to a brutal dictatorship that includes a police state, a reign of terror, and gulags to keep the populace under control. Authors George Orwell and Aldous Huxley have described these two kinds of societies, but the result is the same in both: freedom of the individual is destroyed and the state rules from cradle to the grave.

ORWELL'S TOTALITARIAN FUTURE

Although we will discuss major works of fiction that had a profound effect on the United States in the next chapter, a review of British author George Orwell's dystopian science fiction novel *1984* will demonstrate that his work exemplifies the same "road to serfdom" that F. A. Hayek described. Orwell's book was written between 1947 and 1948 during a time of far less surveillance technology than today.

The novel *1984* describes a future world where three superstates exist that are perpetually at war with one another. All three are police states in which freedom as we understand it has ceased to exist and the individual is a slave to the state, as represented by Big Brother. Those who fail to obey are brainwashed and tortured until they once again worship Big Brother. If they still refuse, they become "unpersons," which is the politically correct word for death.

The main character is Winston Smith, a member of "the Party," who works in the Ministry of Truth, which is of course the propaganda arm of the dictatorship that is tasked with lying to the public. His job is to document that the current Party Line agrees with history, not by changing the Party Line, but by changing history, rewriting it, and altering photographs to achieve his task.

The homes of Party members in Oceania, including Smith's, are equipped with "telescreens," which permit members of the Thought Police to view every action and every conversation. No one can escape the all-seeing eye of the secret police. Any criticism of Big Brother or the totalitarian system as a whole is considered a thought crime and will be severely punished.

This may seem totally alien to a free society with democratic leaders, but in many Western nations it is very much against the law to have the "wrong" thoughts without ever acting upon them. These are often referred to as "hate crimes" or even as violations of "hate speech laws." In 2014 Darren Conway of Gainsborough in the United Kingdom was sentenced to a year in jail for placing a placard in his front window that was, according to the court, "anti-Islamic hate literature."[24]

A member of the Dutch parliament, Geert Wilders, was prosecuted for remarks he made about the Qur'an, and a French actress who is an animal activist has been fined numerous times for being critical of the way animals are slaughtered in Islamic sacrifice rituals. Often people are arrested for the most innocuous comments for "racial hatred" in the United Kingdom. These same laws exist in the United States, but for now must be associated with an actual crime. As an example, if there is a bar fight and someone is injured, and as a result there is an assault conviction, the sentence may be a year in jail. However, if racial epithets were used, the sentence may be ten years.

In *1984* Winston Smith lives a hopeless and dreary life in a one-room flat, where he keeps a diary about his hatred of the system. He thinks he's been successful in keeping his secrets from the Thought Police, but he hasn't been, and the result is predictable.

During Smith's torture sessions he is told:

> There will be no loyalty, except loyalty towards the Party. There will be no love, except the love of Big Brother. There will be no laughter, except the laugh of triumph over a defeated enemy. There will be no art, no literature, no science. When we are omnipotent we shall have no more need of science. There will be no distinction between beauty and ugliness. There will be no curiosity, no enjoyment of the process of life.
>
> All competing pleasures will be destroyed. But always—do not forget this, Winston—always there will be the intoxication of power, constantly increasing and constantly growing subtler. Always, at every moment, there will be the thrill of victory, the sensation of trampling on an enemy who is helpless. *If you want a picture of the future, imagine a boot stamping on a human face—forever* [emphasis added].[25]

Winston's future and everyone else's is described to him during his torture: "The espionage, the betrayals, the arrests, the tortures, the executions, the disappearances will never cease. It will be a world of terror as much as a world of triumph. The more the Party is powerful, the less it will be tolerant: the weaker the opposition, the tighter the despotism."[26]

At the time, the author, Orwell, had his inspiration from the Stalin-era Soviet Union, but his description aptly fits all totalitarian utopias, such as Sparta in ancient Greece or Nazi Germany under Hitler. He could also be describing democratic totalitarian governments to come.

BRAVE NEW WORLD

Aldous Huxley wrote his dystopian novel *Brave New World* in 1931, just two years before Adolf Hitler came to power in Germany and plunged the entire world into more than a decade of horror, building his thousand-year Germanic utopian Third Reich.

Huxley's book describes a future society that is a utopian tyrant's dream. Everything is planned from the moment of birth to the moment of death. Free will is abolished, and the slave population, which is everyone except the rulers, is kept docile by the use of drugs.

Children are bred in test tubes for specific futures; some are actually genetically manipulated to be mentally challenged. The population is divided into several categories: Alphas, who hold leadership positions; Betas, who have high intelligence; Gammas and Deltas who have lesser intelligence, and the Epsilons (Semi-Morons), who are created to do menial labor.

This brave new world created by Huxley is based on Henry Ford's invention of mass auto production back in the 1920s. In fact, the calendar has been changed to reflect the importance of Ford to this totalitarian state. The book's events take place in the year A.F. 623—A.F. meaning "After Ford"—which would be AD 2532.

This utopian tyranny is run by the World State, whose motto is: "Community, Identity, Stability." The story begins inside the "Bottling Room," where babies are bred in test tubes. Once the eggs are fertilized, they're bottled, labeled, and sent to the Social Predestination Room. It is in this room that the Predestinator bureaucrats decide what sort of child they want and how many they want. Each child's future is determined by these social engineers. Once these children are born, they are sent to various parts of the world to fulfill whatever quotas are needed in those areas.

Children of all classes are taught a particular set of values by the World State rulers. Among them is the idea of uncommitted sexual activity. According to one critique of *Brave New World*, "The sexual license encouraged by the World State also eliminates emotional tension which may engender creative or destructive impulses. By removing tension and anxiety, the World State can better control its citizens."[27]

The World State rulers also control the population through the use of a drug called "Soma," which is used in a mockery of Christian communion. Citizens in the *Brave New World* attend a "Solitary Service" where they take Soma and a liquid around a common table. Once the drug takes effect, they engage in indiscriminate sex. Soma becomes the substitute for religion in this utopian tyranny.

In 1958 Aldous Huxley wrote a follow-up book to *Brave New World*, called *Brave New World Revisited*. In it, he noted:

> I feel a good deal less optimistic than I did when I was writing *Brave New World*. The prophecies in 1931 are coming true much sooner than I thought they would. The blessed interval between too little order and the nightmare of too much has not begun and shows no signs of beginning. In the West, it is true, individual men and women still enjoy a large measure of freedom. But even in those countries that have a tradition of democratic government, this freedom and even the desire for freedom seem to be on the wane. In the rest of the world freedom for individuals has already gone, or is manifestly about to go. The nightmare of total organization, which I had situated in the seventh century After Ford, has emerged from the safe, remote future and is now awaiting us, just around the next corner.[28]

Huxley compared the dismal future in his book to *1984*, noting that in Orwell's novel the society is controlled almost exclusively by punishment and the fear of punishment. In his, the nearly perfect control of humans is accomplished by psychological manipulation, conditioning, and genetic engineering.

He predicted that within twenty years of his writing *Brave New World Revisited*, most of the overpopulated and undeveloped nations of the world would be under Communist rule. What he didn't foresee was the collapse of the modern model of the failed utopian state, the Soviet Union, or the rise of Islam, which is becoming the dominant totalitarian system in the world today.

Both Huxley and Orwell described future worlds where individual freedom had been extinguished in favor of a serf-like existence under all-powerful central governments. These rulers would keep the populations in check with police state terrorism, psychological conditioning, sex, and drugs.

WE'RE HURTLING DOWN THE NEW ROAD TO SERFDOM

Daniel Hannan is a member of the European Parliament who loves America and doesn't want her to copy the failing utopian policies of the European Union. In fact, he's written what amounts to a love letter to Americans, warning them not to go down the road to serfdom and off the cliff into totalitarian failure.

In *The New Road To Serfdom: A Letter of Warning to America*, Hannan clearly lays out the reasons why socialism is failing in Europe and why a republican system of government in the United States is the best available to preserve personal and economic freedom. Hannan's comments are those of a modern-day Alexis de Tocqueville. Both traveled throughout the United States to study our institutions—and both left in wonder at the system that the Fathers created. Hannan observed:

> The diverse Euro-woes identified in this chapter gush from a single spout. All of them are caused, or at least exacerbated, by the phenomenon of large and remote government. Other things being equal, big and centralized states are likelier than small and devolved states to: be sclerotic; have more bureaucrats and higher taxes; have soulless and inefficient welfare systems; crowd out non-state actors, from churches to families; and have fatalistic and cynical electorates.
>
> To put it the other way around, the devolution of power stimulates growth, makes administration more democratic, connects citizens to their nation, and allows a flourishing private sphere: the attribute that Tocqueville most admired about America.[29]

After listing all of the reasons why European socialism is failing and reminding Americans of their rich heritage of freedom, he ended his book with a plea:

> The eyes of all people are upon you. And if they see you repudiate

your past, abandon that which has brought you to greatness, become just another country, they, too, will have lost something.

So let me close with a heartfelt imprecation, from a Briton who loves his country to Americans who still believe in theirs. Honor the genius of your founders. Respect the most sublime constitution devised by human intelligence. Keep faith with the design that has made you independent. Preserve the freedom of the nation to which, by good fortune and God's grace, you are privileged to belong.[30]

He clearly articulated the importance of defending the vision of the Fathers who authored a Constitution with checks and balances, a limited federal government, and freedom for the states and for individuals.

If we value individual and economic liberty, which are intricately linked, we must get off the road to serfdom and get back on the highway of free enterprise, constitutional government, a greatly reduced federal government, and a judiciary that is filled with individuals who interpret rather than create laws. The alternative is a state of serfdom.

7

TWENTIETH-CENTURY UTOPIAN FICTION

Very few people today know who "Colonel" Edward Mandell House was, but he played a key role in Woodrow Wilson's administration—especially in foreign policy during and after World War I. (His title, "Colonel," was purely honorary.)

Nor do most Americans have any knowledge of Edward Bellamy, the socialist utopian who wrote *Looking Backward* in 1887. Both House and Bellamy had an enormous and historically disastrous long-lasting impact on our world.

Colonel House was a political operative from Texas who was educated at a New England prep school and later studied at Cornell University in 1877. He was forced to quit his studies when his father died, and he returned to Texas to run his father's cotton plantations and banking interests.

In Texas, House used his natural ability to manipulate people to help several Democrats win gubernatorial races in his home state. He never sought political office or government appointments for himself; rather, he was the Karl Rove of his day, preferring to work secretly behind the scenes, to place people whom he could influence in positions of power. In fact, he spent his entire life using other people to accomplish his goals.

Edward House became a very wealthy man, thanks to his inheritance and skills. According to Robert Higgs, PhD, a senior fellow in political economy at the Independent Institute, House's father was an English-born blockade-runner who made a fortune during the Civil War. He died in 1880, leaving his five children a fortune estimated at $500,000 in today's currency.[1]

House maintained a mansion in Austin but bought an apartment in New York City in 1902. In 1912, he anonymously published a utopian novel called *Philip Dru: Administrator: A Novel of Tomorrow, 1920–1935*. It is an awful work of literature, but it clearly lays out House's utopian vision of a "benevolent" dictator who wisely rules America.

While living in New York, House spent his summers on the seashore near Boston or in Europe. He hobnobbed with the rich and famous, including authors Henry James, Edith Wharton, and Rudyard Kipling. Among his friends was millionaire J. P. Morgan. During this period, House was making nearly half a million dollars a year in today's currency.

According to Dr. Higgs, House spotted a political opportunity to advance his utopian dreams in 1911. The opportunity appeared in the person of Woodrow Wilson, who had been elected governor of New Jersey the year before. House became a power player for Wilson and deserves major credit for Wilson being nominated and later elected president of the United States in 1912.

Wilson was so appreciative of House that he offered him any cabinet post he wanted—except the post of secretary of state, which he had promised to William Jennings Bryan. House, however, refused any cabinet post, preferring to work in the shadows, manipulating players and policies. It was House, for example, who lobbied for and was ulti-mately rewarded for his efforts by the creation of the Federal Reserve System. He was also involved in the formation of both the graduated income tax and, in 1921, the Council on Foreign Relations (CFR). The CFR has been referred to as an "invisible government," and its members have played key roles in numerous administrations since its formation.

Higgs wrote of House:

As war clouds began to gather over Europe, House, with Wilson's approval, undertook to head off hostilities by bringing about an understanding among the United States, Great Britain, and Germany, making them jointly the guarantors of world peace. He met with Kaiser Wilhelm II and separately with British foreign secretary Sir Edward Grey, among others, to work up interest in the plan, but this attempt at preemptive reconciliation obviously never came to fruition.

During the war, House actively engaged in efforts to bring the fighting to an end. He shared Wilson's view that the most desirable outcome would be one that left the postwar world drastically reshaped in a way that eliminated or greatly diminished militarism, promoted national self-determination, spread democracy, left the United States standing astride the international political system, and brought about the recognition of Wilson as the world's savior.[2]

Later, House began pushing for an end to America's neutrality in the war that was raging in Europe. As part of this process, he began preaching "preparedness," which included building up our Army and Navy.

In 1916, Wilson won reelection with the campaign slogan "He kept us out of war," but behind the scenes, House was pushing for war. The colonel's efforts were successful, and shortly after his election to a second term, Wilson asked Congress for a declaration of war. House bragged in one of his daily diary entries: "I began with him before he became President and I have never relaxed my efforts. At every turn, I have stirred his ambition to become the great liberal leader of the world."[3]

As the war was coming to a close, House was engineering a way for Wilson to take a key role in the peace process. Once again, House succeeded in manipulating Wilson.

President Wilson accepted House's proposal to assemble a group of foreign policy experts who worked on what was called the Inquiry. This became the basis for Wilson's Fourteen Points and for his proposals for the Versailles peace conference. (One of those fourteen points was the establishment of a League of Nations.) House served as Wilson's chief negotiator during the peace negotiations between 1917 and 1919.

According to the *Columbia Encyclopedia*, "He helped to draft the Treaty of Versailles and the Covenant of the League of Nations. More conciliatory and realistic than Wilson at the peace conference, his friendship with Wilson ended in 1919 because of conflict on the conduct of the negotiations."[4]

House was a strong advocate for the League of Nations as well as the World Court, known as the Permanent Court of International Justice. He was perfectly willing to submerge American sovereignty under the authority of the League and the World Court. Fortunately, the US Senate refused to ratify the Treaty of Versailles or to permit the United States to become part of the League of Nations. Our nation's sovereignty was protected, to the regret of Edward Mandell House.

The Treaty of Versailles included numerous provisions dealing with disarmament and was harsh in its treatment of Germany. It took 13.5 percent of Germany's 1914 territory and all of its overseas possessions. It limited the German army and banned the use of heavy artillery, gas, tanks, and aircraft. The German navy was also diminished and restricted.

The reparations demanded of Germany were astronomical and actually led to hyperinflation in Germany and the rise of Adolf Hitler, and eventually to World War II. The treaty demanded that Germany pay back (in today's figures) $400 billion for the damages it caused during the war. In fact, Germany did not pay off its last installment of the reparations until 2010!

According to World War I historian Gerd Krumeich at the University of Düsseldorf, "Nothing played a greater role in Nazi propaganda than the refusal of Versailles and the promise to go back on the treaty. It gave rise to a campaign of propaganda and hatred."

Carl-Ludwig Holtfrerich of Berlin's Free University agrees. "Without the Treaty of Versailles, the course of German history would have been quite different."[5]

In 1935 House published an article that showed his support for

Mussolini's Fascist objectives in Africa. He wrote: "The tension in Europe will lead to new disasters unless the imperial urge of Mussolini has the opportunity to spend itself on African soil. The legions of Mussolini marching into Africa may lay the foundation for a new Roman Empire great enough to give the Italian people a chance to breathe. If Mussolini succeeds, Italy will expand in Africa without exploding in Europe."[6]

House died in 1938 before the full fury of the Nazi machine was unleashed in Germany and throughout the world. He is partially responsible for the ruthless Versailles treaty and the ultimate rise of Adolf Hitler.

David M. Esposito, a history professor at Pennsylvania State University, has studied House's character and political policies and has concluded that he was a dishonest and self-promoting master manipulator. "A careful review of House's writings, assembled in the House collection at Yale University, discloses habitual dissimulation and calculated mendacity on a previously unrecognized scale," he wrote. "Sometimes he lied for the historical record and sometimes he seems only to have fooled himself."[7]

From 1912 through 1926, House kept a diary of his actions and manipulations as a shadowy figure in Wilson's administration and later on. Esposito noted that the diary was designed to show his brilliance in directing US foreign and domestic policies and recorded every compliment ever paid to him by foreign leaders.

What is even more significant in House's diary is the emphasis he placed on his real-life actions as a fulfillment of Philip Dru's totalitarian goals in his novel. For example, in one entry in March of 1917, while writing about the probability of a declaration of war against Germany, House noted, "Philip Dru expresses my thoughts and aspirations. . . . Perhaps the most valuable work I have done in that direction has been in influencing the president."[8]

Esposito gives example after example of House puffing himself in his diary and lying both to Wilson and to British and French allies before, during, and after the war. His lies eventually caught up with him, and he was fired by Wilson in 1919. Says Esposito:

> House had his own imagined agenda. He repeatedly undermined Wilson, sometimes unintentionally, but sometimes by design. His sycophancy, pseudo-fascist fiction, glad-handing, self-delusions, and daydreams of blood and revenge, although truly peculiar, do not seem to have visibly damaged American diplomacy, as House never had as much power and prestige as he imagined. However, the misleading, misquoted, and mistaken reports that he gave Wilson jeopardized Wilson's credibility with foreign leaders and undermined the President's initiatives.[9]

COLONEL HOUSE'S ALTER EGO: PHILIP DRU

In his utopian book, House described the life and totalitarian philosophy of the fictional Philip Dru, a West Point graduate who has a disdain for the free enterprise system; gives lectures to his girlfriend, Gloria, about the corruption of our political system; and preaches about the importance of the rich helping the poor.

Dru is portrayed as an idealistic young man who doesn't really have any desire to fight in a war, but who feels compelled to serve his country in some noble fashion.

His first assignment as a young Army officer is at Fort Magruder in Texas, where his life changes dramatically. As he and Gloria ride through the desert one day, they become lost and nearly die of heat stroke. During this ordeal, Dru goes blind and must be led out of the desert. He is then put on medical leave. His eyesight eventually returns to him; however, he has decided to leave the military to pursue a nobler calling—getting rich people to help the poor. "The strong will help the weak, the rich will share with the poor, and it will not be called charity, but it will be known as justice," he enthusiastically tells Gloria. "And the man or woman who fails to do his duty, not as he sees it, but as society at large sees it, will be held up to the contempt of mankind. A generation or two ago, Gloria, this mad unreasoning scramble for wealth began. Men have fought, struggled and died, lured by the gleam of gold, and to what end? The so-called fortunate few that succeed in obtaining it, use it in divers ways."[10]

As the story moves forward, Dru moves to New York, and later goes on to take part in a War Department contest that calls on members of the military to come up with a defensive solution to an imaginary attack on the United States. Dru writes up his proposed solution and submits it to the War Department for their consideration. When he wins, he is catapulted into the national spotlight.

Eventually, Dru is offered the opportunity to write newspaper columns for two major newspapers, both of which syndicate their articles throughout the country.

In one of his columns, Philip Dru pontificates that

> our civilization was fundamentally wrong inasmuch as among other things, it restricted efficiency; that if society were properly organized, there would be none who were not sufficiently clothed and fed; that the laws, habits and ethical training in vogue were alike responsible for the inequalities in opportunity and the consequent wide difference between the few and the many; that the result of such conditions was to render inefficient a large part of the population, the percentage differing in each country in the ratio that education and enlightened and unselfish laws bore to ignorance, bigotry and selfish laws.[11]

Of course, every hero in a novel needs a nemesis, and Dru has one in Senator Selwyn, an evil rich man who works behind the scenes to make certain that no one is elected to federal office who isn't in the wealthy businessman's pocket. Selwyn has created a cabal of one thousand multimillionaires who each contribute $10,000 to a fund that is used to mislead, and to debauch the political process.

Selwyn operates in the shadows, much as House did in real life, to manipulate people into positions of power. He would make and control whomever he wished.

Selwyn's chief ally in this fictional cabal is John Thor, a banker who controls vast business holdings. Together, they pick a list of millionaires to help them manipulate the political system to their advantage.

Selwyn has a plan to win the presidency and to control the House, Senate, and Supreme Court. He targets Governor James R. Rockland to become the nominee for president of the United States. Rockland agrees to the plan and Selwyn engineers his victory. Later, Rockland tries to become independent of Selwyn, but he is easily put back under the businessman's control after Selwyn uses his vast media contacts to launch nationwide smears against him. Eventually, the whole Thor/Selwyn plan is exposed to the public and a national crisis emerges.

The nation splits into two warring camps, with Dru on one side and Selwyn and his wicked millionaires on the other. Both sides organize huge armies and begin fighting against each other. Dru, of course, wins the final battle and seizes total power over the United States government as a "benevolent" dictator. He issues a proclamation to the military, naming himself "Administrator of the Republic." Today, we'd call him an unelected czar.

Once in office and protected by his vast military might, Dru begins to fundamentally change America into his image. During this process, his old foe, Senator Selwyn, becomes his friend and confidant, and together they work to reshape American government and its institutions.

One of Dru's first acts is to meet with all the leaders who had helped him overthrow the federal government and to give them an inspiring speech:

> My fellow countrymen:—I feel sure that however much we may differ as to methods, there is no one within the sound of my voice that does not wish me well, and none, I believe, mistrusts either my honesty of purpose, my patriotism, or my ultimate desire to restore as soon as possible to our distracted land a constitutional government.
>
> We all agreed that a change had to be brought about even though it meant revolution, for otherwise the cruel hand of avarice would have crushed out from us, and from our children, every semblance of freedom. If our late masters had been more moderate in their greed we would have been content to struggle for yet another period, hoping

that in time we might again have justice and equality before the law. But even so we would have had a defective Government, defective in machinery and defective in its constitution and laws. To have righted it, a century of public education would have been necessary. The present opportunity has been bought at fearful cost. . . .

For a long time I have known that this hour would come, and that there would be those of you who would stand affrighted at the momentous change from constitutional government to despotism, no matter how pure and exalted you might believe my intentions to be.

But in the long watches of the night, in the solitude of my tent, I conceived a plan of government which, by the grace of God, I hope to be able to give to the American people. My life is consecrated to our cause, and, hateful as is the thought of assuming supreme power, I can see no other way clearly, and I would be recreant to my trust if I faltered in my duty. Therefore, with the aid I know each one of you will give me, there shall, in God's good time, be wrought "a government of the people, by the people and for the people." [12]

After this meeting, Dru begins reshaping America and tossing out the US Constitution with its systems of checks and balances.

One of Dru's most significant acts is to bring together "five great lawyers" who have no "objectionable" corporate or private practices, and he gives them the authority to define the powers of all courts—both state and federal! They have the sole power to abolish or create courts as they see fit—and to fashion their own rules of what is permitted for prosecutors and defenders to argue before these courts.

Dru directs his five lawyers to limit the power of the courts and to decree that judges are to be appointed for life—with a mandatory retirement age of seventy. They are also to "reform legal procedure" and reduce the number of existing laws—both federal and state—eliminating whichever ones they think are unneeded.

On the issue of taxation, the Administrator of the Republic decides to find the best men he can—not in America, but in England, France, and Germany. He then instructs his new tax board to create a "graduated income tax" that will exempt no one.

Interestingly, the graduated income tax was part of Karl Marx's Communist Manifesto plan for destroying the "rich" and centralizing power in government. And as stated earlier, Edward Mandell House himself was involved in pushing for a graduated income tax when he was working for Woodrow Wilson. It was during his first year in office that Wilson oversaw passage of the Sixteenth Amendment, which created the progressive income tax. In addition, the Federal Reserve System was codified into federal law at the end of 1913.

In the novel, Philip Dru decides that the US Constitution is obsolete and needs to be streamlined. His plan involves centralizing all power in the federal government and essentially abolishing states' rights. According to House, Dru has realized that "the National Government [has] to take upon itself some of the functions heretofore exclusively within the jurisdiction of the States. Up to the time of the Revolution a state of chaos had existed. For instance, laws relating to divorces, franchises, interstate commerce, sanitation and many other things were different in each State, and nearly all were inefficient and not conducive to the general welfare."[13]

In addition to centralizing all power in the federal government—and erasing state sovereignty—Dru "also proposed making corporations share with the Government and States a certain part of their net earnings, public service corporations to a greater extent than others."[14] This is fascism!

In justifying his power grab over every aspect of American government and the economy, Dru as Administrator issues the following address to his subjects:

It is my purpose not to give to you any radical or ill-digested laws. I wish rather to cull that which is best from the other nations of the earth, and let you have the benefit of their thought and experience. One of the most enlightened foreign students of our Government has rightly said that "America is the most undemocratic of democratic countries." We have been living under a Government of negation, a Government with an executive with more power than any monarch, a

Government having a Supreme Court, clothed with greater authority than any similar body on earth; therefore, we have lagged behind other nations in democracy. Our Government is, perhaps, less responsive to the will of the people than that of almost any of the civilized nations. Our Constitution and our laws served us well for the first hundred years of our existence, but under the conditions of to-day they are not only obsolete, but even grotesque. It is nearly impossible for the desires of our people to find expression into law.[15]

Dru also proposes that the federal government establish employment bureaus in every part of the country to provide places for men and women to sign up for work. But if "no work is to be had," he promises, "I shall arrange that every indigent person that is honest and industrious shall be given employment by the Federal, State, County or Municipal Government as the case may be."

It would seem that Roosevelt's Works Progress Administration (WPA) boondoggles and Obama's "stimulus" plans and the dumping of billions into wasteful public works projects were foreseen in House's utopian novel.

Amazingly, Philip Dru has his own version of Obamacare as well. He creates a board consisting of two physicians, a scientist, and an educator to formulate a plan to rid medical colleges and the medical profession of incompetent doctors. He believes there are too many doctors in the United States, so he plans on reducing their numbers. In essence, he takes control of the medical profession and puts it in the hands of unelected bureaucrats.

In foreign affairs, Dru engineers the blending of Canada and the United States as one superstate. He also negotiates a deal with Japan, giving them authority over the Philippines. Both Japan and China are to have influence over all of Eastern Asia. "Thus," says House, "Dru had formulated and put in motion an international policy, which, if adhered to in good faith, would bring about the comity of nations, a lasting and beneficent peace, and the acceptance of the principle of the brotherhood of man."[16] This sounds suspiciously like Rodney King's "can't we all just get along?"

Dru also creates a new constitution for the federal government and a model constitution for each state. In essence, he wipes out our original Constitution and state sovereignty, and places power in the hands of the central government.

At the end of the book, after ruling as a dictator for seven years, Dru finally decides that his work is done, and he and Gloria board a ship in San Francisco and sail off into the sunset. Yet in real life, utopian dictators never give up power until they die or are driven from office by angry citizens. No megalomaniacs, like Lycurgus, Muhammad, Hitler, Mussolini, Lenin, Stalin, or modern-day tyrants such as the late King Abdullah of Saudi Arabia, willingly hand over the power they have acquired. Dictators have a messianic belief that they are to rule over people for life, telling them how they are to live and who is to die. These ego-driven despots recognize no power higher than themselves and will kill anyone who challenges their authority or their goals.

PHILIP DRU AND SENATOR SELWYN = EDWARD MANDELL HOUSE

In reality, the characters of Dru and Selwyn express the totalitarian views of Edward M. House himself, who called his work "a semi-political novel showing how a dictator seized the government of the United States and anticipated Mussolini by a number of years."[17] So what was portrayed as fiction was really a political tract and an outline of how House wished to govern the United States and the world in the future. He partially implemented his plan through his close association with Woodrow Wilson.

House based his political viewpoint on the totalitarianism of Karl Marx and foreshadowed the ideology of fascism—by which the government controls, but doesn't directly own—corporations. It was a system of governing that House, in later years, admitted he admired.

In a 1998 reissue of *Philip Dru*, author William Norman Grigg details House's fascist and Marxist agenda. He demonstrates that, though President Wilson didn't accomplish everything House wanted, Franklin D. Roosevelt had considerable success in creating an America in the form desired by House (who served as an advisor to Roosevelt in the early years of the administration).

Even so, Woodrow Wilson was deeply influenced by the *Philip Dru* novel. Immediately after his election as president of the United States, he spent time in Bermuda, meditating on Dru's dictatorial domestic and foreign policy proposals. Historian Arthur Walworth, who edited House's diaries for the Yale University Press, has pointed out that Wilson's 1913 book *The New Freedom: A Call for the Emancipation of the Generous Energies of the American People,* was based in large part on *Philip Dru.*

Wilson, it can easily be argued, was a socialist when he was elected to office, so he and House were in total accord about the need to transform the United States into a utopian socialist state.

Political analyst Westbrook Pegler, who studied House's machinations during the Wilson administration, described him this way: "Wilson's Rasputin, the most influential private citizen in America and indeed one of the most powerful human beings in all the world, copyrighted Fascism." He went on to lament that "even today few citizens have heard of [*Philip Dru*] and hardly one in a million has read it. . . . And, of course the press will still ignore it diligently. . . . Practically all our historians and our teaching professors either know nothing about all this or refuse to teach this historical information to their students. One of the most important political documents of our age has been blacked out."[18]

In 1922, House wrote about his contempt for the US Constitution:

> For a long time it had seemed to me that our Government was too complicated in its machinery and that we had outgrown our Constitution. It has been my constant wonder that our people were willing to go along without protest with such an inefficient machine. . . . The negative character of our Government and its lack of responsiveness to the will of the people makes it less efficient than it should be. . . . One of the purposes in writing "Philip Dru" was a desire to bring to our people a realization of this.[19]

At this point I do hope I am not confusing readers with the terms "fascist" and "socialist." Both are forms of utopianism and are based on central planning by a few elitist individuals. The only true difference is in the ownership of production. In the classic socialist or Marxist state, the government not only directs but owns the means of production. In the fascist state—sometimes referred to as "national socialist" —the central planners still direct the means of production, but ownership or part ownership remains with individuals. Under this definition, the current single-party economic model of China is "national socialist" or "fascist" rather than Communist. While Bellamy, whom we'll discuss next, wrote favorably of socialism and Communism in general, he leaned toward the national socialist model. Thus Bellamy's version of utopia as described in his works is generally the fascist utopian model.

EDWARD BELLAMY'S UTOPIAN NOVEL: *LOOKING BACKWARD*
Edward Bellamy isn't well known today, but in the late 1800s and early twentieth century, he was a powerful influence for an American form of fascism that he called "nationalism."

Bellamy's utopian book, *Looking Backward: 2000–1887*, outlines his vision of an America that has adopted a totalitarian fascist society in which the government is everything and the individual is a virtual slave. In 1897 he published a sequel, *Equality*, with the same character narrating the story. Both novels advocate totalitarian government.

Bellamy was reared in the New England home of his Baptist minister father and Calvinist mother. He later rejected his Christian upbringing and turned instead to the philosophies of European socialists for his world-view. Bellamy attended law school but worked only briefly as a lawyer.

He became a writer and initially worked in the newspaper industry, but then left editorial work and started writing essays, short stories, and novels to promote his utopian concept of an American society free of capitalism, poverty, and war.

In *Looking Backward*, set in 1887, the main character is Julian West, a young man living in Boston. West has trouble sleeping, so he has a special vault created in his basement to serve as his bedroom. He then has a mesmerist put him to sleep.

While he's asleep, West's house burns down and everyone assumes he has been killed in the fire. Eventually, a new home is built over the top of his vault. Meanwhile, he remains blissfully asleep for more than a century.

Julian West's vault remains undetected until the year 2000, when he is discovered and awakened by the homeowner, Dr. Leete. The doctor serves as his host and shows him around the modern world in which he now lives. (Spoiler alert: at the end of the book, we learn that West has only had a dream and that he's still in 1887—but he has a whole new outlook on the evils of capitalism and the possibility of a new world without competition, where all people are equal and have no fear of poverty or war.)

The twenty-first-century world that West discovers is one where individual liberty has disappeared. The all-powerful government rules the life of each citizen from the moment of birth to death. Every man and woman becomes part of a militarized industrial army—much like the civilian army proposed by Barack Obama during his 2008 campaign. And speaking of armies, journalist Heywood Broun, a well-known Soviet apologist in the 1920s and 1930s, wrote an enthusiastic introduction for the 1926 edition of *Looking Backward*, in which he noted:

> Much which is now established in Soviet Russia bears at least a likeness to the industrial army visioned in this prophetic book. However, Communism can scarcely claim Bellamy as its own, for he emphasizes repeatedly the non-violent features of the revolution, which he imagined. Indeed, at one point he argues that the left-wingers of his own day impeded change by the very excesses of their technical philosophy. There is in his book no acceptance of a transitional stage of class dictatorship. He sees the change coming through a general recognition of the failings of the capitalist system. Indeed, he sees a point in economic development where capitalism may not even be good enough for the capitalist.[20]

In West's utopian world, everyone must work. Citizens eat in public kitchens; clothing is washed in public laundries; medical care is free (socialized); and if anyone fails to do his or her job properly, the individual is put on bread and water.

The central government has taken over all industries and manages everything, supposedly for the common good. Dr. Leete tells West:

> Early in the last century the evolution was completed by the final consolidation of the entire capital of the nation. The industry and commerce of the country, ceasing to be conducted by a set of irresponsible corporations and syndicates of private persons at their caprice and for their profit, were entrusted to a single syndicate representing the people, to be conducted in the common interest for the common profit. The nation, that is to say, organized as the one great business corporation in which all other corporations were absorbed; it became the one capitalist in the place of all other capitalists, the sole employer, the final monopoly in which all previous and lesser monopolies were swallowed up, a monopoly in the profits and economies of which all citizens shared.[21]

Money has been abolished in West's new world and replaced by a global cashless card system. This has supposedly done away with most property theft crime. Because all citizens are taken care of from the moment they are born, they have no need to covet the goods of others. Furthermore, citizens no longer eat meat but are vegetarians, and they drive electric cars instead of those running on fossil fuel. (One can only wonder where the electricity comes from in this totalitarian system. In our world, most electric energy to fuel "nonpolluting" electric cars comes from fossil fuels.)

The profit motive, seen as an evil by Bellamy, has been replaced in 2000 by a patriotic desire of citizens to serve their government, a concept that was tried and failed during the barbaric Communist era of the twentieth century. Political parties, banks, labor unions, prisons, and retail stores have all been eliminated in this dreamworld as no one has a personal or corporate agenda outside that of the utopian leadership. Everyone is living in harmony and serves the all-powerful government, which has become the sole employer. The concept of personal liberty is gone.

According to Leete, "When the nation became the sole employer, all the citizens, by virtue of their citizenship, became employees, to be distributed according to the needs of industry."[22] This of course is the classic utopianist mantra "From each according to his ability, to each according to his need," which was actually in common socialist usage well before Karl Marx's *Das Kapital*. The actual quote from Marx in an 1875 letter to German socialists is astoundingly similar to this novel:

> In a higher phase of communist society, after the enslaving subordination of the individual to the division of labor, and therewith also the antithesis between mental and physical labor, has vanished; after labor has become not only a means of life but life's prime want; after the productive forces have also increased with the all-around development of the individual, and all the springs of co-operative wealth flow more abundantly—only then can the narrow horizon of bourgeois right be crossed in its entirety and society inscribe on its banners: From each according to his ability, to each according to his needs.[23]

In the influential novel, culture is designed in such an authoritarian way that no one can escape it. According to Leete, "Our entire social order is so wholly based upon and deduced from it that if it were conceivable that a man could escape it, he would be left with no possible way to provide for his existence. He would have excluded himself from the world, cut himself off from his kind, in a word, committed suicide."

The future is described as a society that does away with cash or gold or other precious metals as a medium of exchange. Anyone outside of the cashless system faces starvation. He can neither buy nor sell without the approved credit card Bellamy envisioned.[24] In his economy, Bellamy has cleverly mimicked the biblical era described in the book of Revelation, leaving out only the "mark of the beast" (see Revelation 13:15–16).

As mentioned previously, every able-bodied man and woman is

conscripted into an industrial army, to serve for twenty-four years, after which the person can still be called back into service if there's a national emergency.

The rulers of this fictitious society are supposedly free of corruption because the lust for money is no longer meaningful in this utopian world. Bellamy completely ignores the reality that power corrupts and absolute power corrupts absolutely.

Commerce and *profit* are dirty words in the America of 2000. "According to our ideas," Leete tells his student, "buying and selling is essentially anti-social in all its tendencies. It is an education in self-seeking at the expense of others, and no society whose citizens are trained in such a school can possibly rise above a very low grade of civilization."[25]

With great pride, Leete goes on to say:

> The coarser motives, which no longer move us, have been replaced by higher motives wholly unknown to the mere wage earners of your age. Now that industry of whatever sort is no longer self-service, but service of the nation, patriotism, passion for humanity, impel the worker as in your day they did the soldier. The army of industry is an army, not alone by virtue of its perfect organization, but by reason also of the ardor of self-devotion which animates its members.[26]

Leete has critical words for the men of West's century. "Selfishness was their only science," he says, "and in industrial production selfishness is suicide. Competition, which is the instinct of selfishness, is another word for dissipation of energy, while combination is the secret of efficient production; and not till the idea of increasing the individual hoard gives place to the idea of increasing the common stock can industrial combination be realized, and the acquisition of wealth really begin."[27]

Ironically, this notion played out in the Soviet era as a poison pill to innovation. As the traditional steel mills of the twentieth century were no longer needed in an advancing Western economy, steel production for the "common good" continued to rise in the Soviet Union. Often mills had hundreds of tons, much of it rusting on mill grounds because of impurities, unusable by other overburdened state industries.

In the novel, twenty-first-century America has also done away with retail stores. People shop in huge warehouses where they order what they want from clerks who swipe their cards and give them their products. Edith, West's love interest in the novel, takes him shopping at one of these warehouses.

"The goods are the nation's," she tells him. "They are here for those who want them, and it is the business of the clerks to wait on people and take their orders; but it is not the interest of the clerk or the nation to dispose of a yard or a pound of anything to anybody who does not want it." Smiling, she adds, "How exceedingly odd it must have seemed to have clerks trying to induce one to take what one did not want, or was doubtful about!"[28]

Edith goes on to inform West that the warehouses are all within walking distance of most neighborhoods, and every warehouse carries the same products. It's like living in a world where everyone must shop at Sam's Club, except that only one brand is offered for each product, just one brand of government-approved toothpaste is available, and other products are available only outside of the government-run warehouse system.

State governments have been eliminated, and there are no jury system and no attorneys. Legal decisions are made by judges, who are appointed by the president. The president himself is not elected, because democratically elected government is considered obsolete in the utopian world of 2000. Instead, he is chosen by a small group of elitists.

"The President of the nation appoints the necessary judges year by year from the class reaching that age," Leete says. "The number appointed is, of course, exceedingly few, and the honor so high that it is held an offset to the additional term of service which follows, and though a judge's appointment may be declined, it rarely is. The term is five years, without eligibility to reappointment. The members of the Supreme Court, which is the guardian of the constitution, are selected from among the lower judges."[29]

This may seem impossible for the real future of the United States, but virtually every law passed by Congress and state legislators is now challenged and often changed in courts by appointed judges. Same-sex marriage, as an example, as of 2014 had been approved only by court order, not by the people, who have rejected it in vote after vote. Unelected bureaucrats in the EPA send men and women to jail sometimes for decades for breaking rules written by the agency, not a law written by Congress. All federal agencies have their own police forces and most have SWAT teams.

In the novel, European nations, Australia, Mexico, and parts of South America are also organized along fascist lines and comprise a "loose form" of federal union (a mini one-world government) although each nation supposedly enjoys autonomy within its own borders.

In the strange new world in which West has found himself, he learns that, other than the industrial army, the government has no military. It also has no departments of state or treasury, no excise or revenue services, and no taxes or tax collectors. "The only function proper of government, as known to you, which still remains, is the judiciary and police system," Leete tells him. "I have already explained to you how simple is our judicial system as compared with your huge and complex machine. Of course the same absence of crime and temptation to it, which make the duties of judges so light, reduces the number and duties of the police to a minimum."[30]

As science writer Martin Gardner puts it:

> [The book's] most spectacular hit is not its vision of America in 2000, but its description of a command economy that strongly resembles the Soviet Union under Lenin and Stalin, especially their dream of the Communist state they believed would follow a temporary but necessary "dictatorship of the proletariat." It's as if West awoke not in Boston but in Lenin's Moscow![31]

Edward Bellamy didn't like to use the word *socialism* to describe his political philosophy. He called his ideology *nationalism*, and established more than 150 "Nationalist Clubs" across the United States to promote his essentially fascist ideas. He also began publishing the *New Nation* to promote his ideology.

Bellamy developed utopian fascist views early in life while traveling through Germany in 1868. During those travels he began reading the writings of German socialists and was later influenced by Albert Brisbane, a socialist who followed the ideology of totalitarian French philosopher Charles Fourier. Bellamy actually adapted some of Brisbane's ideas in *Looking Backward.*[32]

Bellamy did, however, express his sympathy with Communism while he worked for the *New York Post*. While on staff, he reviewed novelist Charles Nordhoff's book titled *The Communistic Societies of the United States*, and concluded:

> The words socialist and communist fall unpleasantly on American ears, being generally taken as implying atheistic or superstitious beliefs and practices and abnormal sex relations. This prejudice, largely a mistaken one, has prevented anything like a general under-standing of the nature and results of the communistic experiments in the country. . . . These societies have no less than seventy-two communes . . . number 5000 persons, own over 750,000 acres of land, and hold over $2,000,000 of property.[33]

Bellamy also wrote an introduction to *Fabian Essays in Socialism*, in which he stated, "Socialism may be said to be the application of the democratic method to the economic administration of a people. It aims by substituting public management of industry and commerce in the common interest, for private management in diverse personal interests, to more nearly equalize the distribution of wealth, while at the same time increasing the volume of wealth produced for distribution."[34]

Bellamy's writings were immensely influential among America's elitists at the time. His fascist novels even inspired radical Communist Elizabeth Gurley Flynn.

Flynn read *Looking Backward* when she was just fifteen. The book sparked her interest in socialism and authoritarian governments, and she began giving speeches on socialism that same year. At sixteen, she was reading Karl Marx and Friedrich Engels.

Flynn soon became an agitator for the Industrial Workers of the World (IWW), and in 1938 was elected to the Communist Party USA national committee. She was also a founder of the American Civil Liberties Union, an organization that has undermined traditional family values, Judeo-Christian beliefs, and the free enterprise system in America since the 1920s. She spent her entire life attempting to establish a Soviet-style government in the United States.

Flynn died in Russia in 1964 and was given full honors at her funeral by her Soviet benefactors. She had served them well throughout her life.[35]

Marxist journalist Heywood Broun admitted "I am among those who first became interested in Socialism through reading 'Looking Backward' when I was a freshman in college."[36] He then spent his life fighting for the destruction of free enterprise and Christian morality in America. He was also involved in fighting on behalf of Margaret Sanger, the founder of Planned Parenthood; for John Scopes, the teacher who taught evolution and was at the center of the Scopes trial in Tennessee; and for D. H. Lawrence, for publishing obscenity.[37]

In short, Broun became an enemy of traditional values, Christian morality, and the free enterprise system, thanks to the inspiration he received from Edward Bellamy's novel.

Bellamy's promotion of fascist utopianism inspired others, too, including Norman Thomas, the lifelong socialist; Upton Sinclair, whose novels promoted government regulation; John Dewey, the socialist educator who brought totalitarian thinking into education; Jack London, author of *The War of the Classes*; historian Charles Beard, a harsh critic of the Founding Fathers; Carl Sandburg, a onetime member of the Social Democratic Party (a branch of the Socialist Party of America); Erich Fromm, who rejected Western capitalism; and others. All of these individuals worked to promote utopian socialism in America.

Bellamy's ideology had a pernicious and long-lasting influence in

Franklin Roosevelt's New Deal. Among those who pushed his utopian concepts was Arthur Morgan, who ran the Tennessee Valley Authority under President Roosevelt and wrote the first biography on Bellamy. Another Bellamy zealot was Adolf Berle Jr., who was one of Roosevelt's key strategists in crafting the New Deal—a series of policies that brought our nation closer and closer to Bellamy's ideal society. According to Morgan, "Striking parallels may be drawn between *Looking Backward* and various important aspects of New Deal public policy. It may be said with considerable force that to understand the long range implication of the New Deal one must read *Looking Backward*."[38]

Adolf Berle's father was a friend of Edward Bellamy and was one of his disciples. Berle became a member of Franklin Roosevelt's "Brain Trust," whose members operated as modern-day czars in the federal government.

Berle was a law school professor who had authored a controversial book in 1932, titled *The Modern Corporation and Private Property.* In it Berle argued that large business corporations no longer serve the public interest and that they should be taken over by the federal government.

In 1932 Berle sent a memo to Roosevelt to say that nineteenth-century competition and individualism were anachronistic. He became assistant secretary of state in 1938 and influenced New Deal policies on banking, securities, railroads, and other economic matters.[39]

The head of Roosevelt's so-called Brain Trust was Raymond Moley, a professor of political science at Columbia University. Moley opposed the free enterprise system and favored the utopian fascist model, in which central government *controlled* businesses without owning them outright. He advocated the federal government controlling all land in the United States. According to Moley, "We have depended too long on the hope that private ownership and control would operate somehow for the benefit of society as a whole." Moley had visited the Soviet Union in the 1920s and had returned to America to sing the praises of collectivism. He helped create Roosevelt's National Industrial Recovery Act and the Agricultural Adjustment Act. Edward Bellamy would have been pleased by Moley's utopian influence in the Roosevelt administration.[40]

Roosevelt's Brain Trust also included another student of Bellamy, Rexford Guy Tugwell. He also favored a national socialist form of government. According to Tugwell, "Planning will become a function of the federal government; either that or the planning agency will supersede the government, which is why, of course, such a scheme will be assimilated to the State."[41]

In 1947 Tugwell was part of a project to draft a "World Constitution" to create a one-world government. And in 1974, he authored *The Emerging Constitution,* which stated that the US Constitution is a "living document" that must be redefined for modern times. Tugwell was a utopian who desired to radically transform our economic system into a near-Soviet-style planned economy.

During Roosevelt's first hundred days in office, the Brain Trust pushed through numerous policy changes that were ostensibly designed to end the Great Depression. All of these policies would have been encouraging to Edward Bellamy and Edward Mandell House because they pushed America away from free enterprise and toward a fascist/socialist model of government.

Roosevelt and his Brain Trust created the Civilian Conservation Corps, the industrial army envisioned by Bellamy in *Looking Backward.* Next was a plan for the Federal Emergency Relief Administration, which became the Works Progress Administration (WPA). Bellamy's vision of the federal government "creating" jobs became a reality—all at taxpayer expense, of course.

John T. Flynn, writing in *The Roosevelt Myth,* listed dozens of other federal takeovers of private enterprise and business institutions. "Still the reforms, the projects, the adventures in social reconstruction followed 'treading on each other's heels, so fast they came'—bills to supervise the traffic in investment securities, to prevent the foreclosure of farm mortgages, with one to save the owners of city homes from the mortgage incubus, bills to regulate the railroads, bills for federal action in the oil industry."[42]

The utopian fiction of Edward Mandell House and Edward Bellamy became models for real-life policies within the administrations of Woodrow Wilson and Franklin D. Roosevelt. These collectivist ideas were transformed into federal institutions that transformed our society from a free market–based economic system to the more controlled model we have today.

Collectivist planners have done considerable damage to the free-market system in the United States by building government regulation to the point of near-absolute control of industry. Clyde Wayne Crews at the Competitive Enterprise Institute calculated the annual cost of government regulation at $1.863 trillion just in federal compliance costs for 2013. To put that in perspective, that is equal to the entire gross national product of the tenth-largest economy in the world.[43]

The central planners, such as Woodrow Wilson, Franklin Roosevelt, and Barack Obama, used the Bellamy and House utopian models to bring about a more powerful central government, which can only mean a reduction in the size of the sphere of liberty that Friedrich Hayek and Milton Friedman stated is the key to political as well as economic freedom.

The understanding of the role of fictional utopias on the actual thinking of political leaders cannot be underestimated. It is important that those who love liberty be aware of these major works and the influence they have had and continue to have.

8

AMERICAN UTOPIANS IN GOVERNMENT

PROGRESSIVES: ENEMIES OF FREEDOM AND CONSTITUTIONAL GOVERNMENT
Progress should be defined as a cumulative growth of knowledge.[1]

Throughout the nineteenth and twentieth centuries, the fascists, Communists, and other central planners, who limited or totally eradicated freedom of the individual, disguised their evil as "progress" and referred to themselves as "Progressives." Often these Progressives stopped progress by limiting the collective growth of knowledge. The extreme example was Pol Pot of Cambodia, who killed any citizen who spoke a foreign language or had traveled out of the nation. Virtually all intellectuals and educated citizens were eradicated in the name of progress. Similarly all advances in industry other than military were halted in the Soviet Union.

In the United States the Progressive movement to limit true liberty in the name of economic freedom or other purpose began in the nineteenth century but did not become politically popular until the twentieth century. To understand the Progressive mind-set, we must look at their self-definition.

Self-defined Progressives are those who embrace centralized planning of economic and social activities for what they believe is the benefit of all. While there have been fascist versions of the Progressive move-ment, Progressives in the United States have leaned toward Marxism–Leninism, while claiming their goal can be accomplished without the Stalinist slave labor camps and endless bloodshed. American Progressives have so far been able to bring about change within the government non-violently. As we have seen in other nations, many utopian planners did not at first envision the level of violence that would be required to force submission to their utopian plans, yet executions and imprisonment on a massive scale were the result of their central planning schemes, in addition to deaths by starvation and societal collapse.

Progressives for the most part honestly believe that they have "evolved" and have greater intelligence and knowledge than the prole-tariat, and thus have the self-authority to tell the masses how they should live for their betterment. They profess to know how the vast majority should think and what they should do, down to what foods should be consumed, and they are willing to create laws to enforce those beliefs. You know you have met a Progressive if he wants to outlaw the large soda you want to buy at McDonald's.

Jonah Goldberg, author of *Liberal Fascism*, traces the beginning of the Progressive movement back to 1888 when Edward Bellamy's uto-pian novel *Looking Backward* was published, as mentioned in chapter 7 of this work.

Presidents Woodrow Wilson and Franklin Roosevelt were both self-described Progressives. Wilson openly called for a rejection of our Constitution and Bill of Rights as being too outdated to have much relevance for Americans living in the early 1900s.

Associate professor of politics Ronald J. Pestritto at Hillsdale College describes Progressives this way:

> Progressives sought to enlarge vastly the scope of the national govern-ment for the purpose of responding to a set of economic and social conditions that, it was contended, could not have been envisioned during the founding era, and for which the Founders' limited, consti-tutional government was inadequate. While the Founders had posited

what they held to be a permanent understanding of just government, based upon a fixed account of human nature, the Progressives countered that the ends and scope of government were to be defined anew in each historical epoch. They coupled this perspective of historical contingency with a deep faith in historical progress; they believed that government was becoming less of a danger to the governed due to historical evolution, and was also becoming more capable of solving the great array of problems besetting the human race.[2]

In 1912 Woodrow Wilson gave a speech entitled "What Is Progress?" and laid out his view that the US Constitution was a "living" or "evolving" document that had to be reinterpreted for modern times. Wilson also claimed that the federal government was a living organism that shouldn't be restricted by a static document like the Constitution. This concept of a living document rather than a static guarantee of rights is still professed today by figures such as Barack Obama and Hillary Clinton. A static guarantee of rights such as the Constitution of the United States is anonymous, granting the same rights to all. Progressives, on the other hand, want laws that are directed at certain groups and individuals for the purpose of obtaining "equality" and thus the need for a "living" Constitution.

According to Woodrow Wilson, the first president in the Progressive camp:

> Living political constitutions must be Darwinian in structure and in practice. Society is a living organism and must obey the laws of life, not of mechanics; it must develop. All that progressives ask or desire is permission—in an era when "development," "evolution," is the scientific word—to interpret the Constitution according to the Darwinian principle; all they ask is recognition of the fact that a nation is a living thing and not a machine.[3]

In 1908 while Wilson was president of Princeton University, he wrote an essay titled "Constitutional Government in the United States." In this essay, he clearly rejected the inalienable rights of Americans under the Constitution and the Bill of Rights. He observed:

Government is a part of life, and, with life, it must change, alike in its objects and in its practices; only this principle must remain unaltered—this principle of liberty, that there must be the freest right and opportunity of adjustment. Political liberty consists in the best practicable adjustment between the power of the government and the privilege of the individual; and the freedom to alter the adjustment is as important as the adjustment itself for the ease and progress of affairs and the contentment of the citizen.[4]

Note that Wilson used the term "privilege," not inalienable right, to describe how the individual interacts with the government. He believed that government has the freedom to alter the relationship between free Americans and the federal government! He rejected the idea that our rights come from God and are inalienable.

Wilson's views perfectly reflect those of Edward Mandell House, his closest advisor, who leaned more toward being a fascist utopian. As you saw in the previous chapter, House outlined his utopian views of government in his novel *Philip Dru: Administrator*. The "Administrator" represented, of course, the model of a Progressive president of the United States.

According to Wilson, the president of the United States was essentially endowed with unlimited power: "The President is at liberty, both in law and in conscience, to be as big a man as he can. His capacity will set the limit; and if Congress is overborne by him, it will be no fault of the makers of the Constitution . . . but only because the President has the nation behind him and Congress has not."[5]

(This same self-defined Progressive mind-set was apparent in the remarks of President Barack Obama when he felt Congress was not moving forward with the legislation he wanted. Just before a cabinet meeting in 2014, he warned, "One of the things that I'll be emphasizing in this meeting is the fact that we are not just going to be waiting for legislation in order to make sure that we're providing Americans the kind of help that they need. I've got a pen and I've got a phone."[6])

Mark Levin, writing in *Ameritopia*, described Wilson's totalitarian views: "Wilson's objective was to centralize and consolidate power in the federal government and redefine the relationship between it and the individual. His assignation of human characteristics to the federal government was an argument for maximalist federal power where the central government has unrestrained flexibility and freedom to operate, and where the rights of actual human beings are diminished and their pursuits restricted."[7]

Franklin D. Roosevelt was inspired by Wilson's views on the need to restrict individual liberty. Like Wilson, he, too, felt that the Constitution was a barrier to government action, and believed that the solution was an all-powerful central government. Roosevelt surrounded himself with "Brain Trust" utopians who viewed the federal government as "god" in the lives of the American people.

Among those Brain Trust advisors was Rexford Guy Tugwell, whom we met in the last chapter. Tugwell was a self-styled intellectual who believed—like Wilson—that the Constitution was an "emerging" document that could be redefined to adjust to Progressive ideas about the importance of a planned economy and a strong centralized government.

Tugwell admired totalitarian systems. He once said of Mussolini's Fascist government: "It's the cleanest, neatest, most efficiently operating piece of social machinery I've ever seen. It makes me envious."[8]

Tugwell became assistant secretary of agriculture under Henry Wallace, also a radical Progressive, who later served as Roosevelt's vice president between 1940 and 1944. (Wallace was actually recruited by the Communists in 1948 to run as a third-party presidential candidate on the Progressive Party ticket. At the time the Communists had seized the name Progressive as their own.)

Immediately on taking office in 1932, Roosevelt and his Progressive advisors began to refashion American government into a powerful, far-reaching giant by creating a myriad of boards and agencies to control the American economy. He called this massive buildup of government agencies his "New Deal." The New Deal led to the expansion of the federal government and the diminishing of the liberties for those engaged in both business and labor.

Jonah Goldberg, in *Liberal Fascism*, noted that there existed "many common features among New Deal liberalism, Italian Fascism, and German National Socialism, all of which shared many of the same historical and intellectual forebears." That's not surprising, given the ideological views of Roosevelt and his Brain Trust.[9]

Just as utopians in other nations saw established conservative governments as impediments to progress, so Roosevelt saw that certain aspects of the US government would have to be altered in order for his New Deal to proceed. Foremost, the Supreme Court, which at the time upheld the rights granted citizens and the states according to a strict interpretation of the Constitution, had to be altered.

During his second term in office, beginning in January 1937, Roosevelt spoke to one of his speechwriters and told him, "When the Chief Justice read me the oath and came to the words 'support the Constitution of the United States,' I felt like saying: 'Yes, but it's the Constitution as I understand it, flexible enough to meet any new problem of democracy—not the kind of Constitution your court has raised up as a barrier to progress and democracy.'"[10]

Only two weeks after his inauguration to a second term, he sent a message to the Congress that he wanted them to draft a bill that would give him the power to appoint a new Supreme Court justice for every member of the Court who had reached the age of seventy—and who was refusing to retire. If this had been accomplished, he could have appointed six additional judges who viewed the Constitution as he did—outdated and irrelevant to modern society.

Roosevelt had been angered at the Supreme Court for its previous decisions that ruled against his National Recovery Act and the Agricultural Adjustment Act, as well as other New Deal laws. His Court-packing plan failed, but he eventually got a Supreme Court that would validate his socialist schemes. During the whole Court-packing incident, an intimidated Justice Owen Roberts started voting with four liberal members of the Court instead of with the four conservatives. Then, a vacancy occurred on the Court, and Roosevelt filled the post with Hugo

Black, a former Ku Klux Klan member. Another Roosevelt replacement on the Court was Stanley Reed, who had worked for various federal agencies under Hoover and Roosevelt. He later got Felix Frankfurter, William O. Douglas, and Frank Murphy on the Supreme Court—all radical liberals and enemies of the Constitution as a static document.[11]

A SECOND BILL OF RIGHTS?

Roosevelt disagreed with the first Bill of Rights in the Constitution, as it dealt primarily with individual liberty, so he contrived a Second Bill of Rights that would justify his utopian totalitarian agenda of controlling every aspect of our society. He proposed that his Second Bill of Rights would be based on "security and prosperity." His proposal included:

> the right to a useful and remunerative job in the industries or shops or farms or mines of the Nation; to earn enough to provide adequate food and clothing and recreation; of every farmer to raise and sell his products at a return which will give him and his family a decent living; of every businessman, large and small, to trade in an atmosphere of freedom from unfair competition and domination by monopolies at home or abroad; of every family to a decent home; to adequate medical care and the opportunity to achieve and enjoy good health; to adequate protection from the economic fears of old age, sickness, accident, and unemployment; to a good education.[12]

The Progressives' concept of "liberty" or "freedom" shares virtually nothing in common with the vision of the Founders in the Constitution. The utopian socialist agenda living on today in the Democratic Party—and to some degree in the Republican Party—defines privileges as rights and social guarantees as liberties. In the mind-set of those such as Barack Obama, Hillary Clinton, Nancy Pelosi, and Harry Reid, people have a "right" to privileges such as medical care or guaranteed employment, but not a right to freedom of speech.

Both presidents Lyndon Johnson and Barack Obama attempted to fulfill the part of Roosevelt's Second Bill of Rights that promised "adequate medical care and the opportunity to achieve and enjoy good health; to adequate protection from the economic fears of old age, sickness, accident, and unemployment; to a good education," not only through legislation but by directive and abuse of agency powers. Even before becoming president, Lyndon Johnson as a senator worked to reduce freedom of speech by muzzling clergy. As president, he created the first government media mouthpiece, the Public Broadcasting Service (PBS).

LYNDON JOHNSON'S WAR ON LIBERTY DISGUISED AS A "WAR ON POVERTY"
The year 2014 was the fiftieth anniversary of Lyndon Johnson's infamous "War on Poverty" that resulted in the institutionalization of the welfare state and Big Government in America.

Most who desire to achieve the utopian state honestly believe, if misguidedly, that this can be accomplished. Lenin believed it, as did Mao; however, there are those such as President Lyndon Johnson who have used the promise of a utopian state simply to gain power. The first step of Johnson's climb to power was accomplished by cheating during the 1948 Senate race in Texas, when he "miraculously" won the election by only eighty-seven votes.

Johnson's dishonesty and ruthlessness were chronicled in 1964 by J. Evetts Haley in his book *A Texan Looks at Lyndon* as Johnson was facing Barry Goldwater in the upcoming presidential election in November of that year. Haley's book was roundly trashed by liberals, who claimed he had gotten his facts all wrong, but decades later, after all the damage was already done to our culture, liberal historians like Robert Caro confirmed that Johnson did indeed steal his 1948 election by having his operatives stuff Ballot Box 13 with fake votes. He was called "Landslide Lyndon" for having "won" the election by only eighty-seven votes.[13]

While in the Senate and running for reelection in 1954, Johnson faced criticism from two anti-Communist nonprofit groups that were educating the public about his liberal views. In retaliation for this attack, Johnson managed to insert language into the IRS Code that prohibits nonprofits, including churches, from endorsing or opposing candidates for political office. In effect, this corrupt man used the power of the IRS to silence his opposition. From that time forward and to the detriment of American society, the churches became less involved in public life and were too often unwilling to speak out on moral issues. Johnson would not be the last to use the IRS to silence opponents. President Obama's operatives used the IRS to silence opposition at a level that could make an opportunist like Lyndon Johnson blush.

Johnson amassed considerable influence in the Senate as a shrewd politician who would do whatever it took to attain power and further his agenda. In 1957 it became clear that Johnson was formulating a plan to move the black population, which voted Republican and had been repressed in some Southern elections, including those in Texas, to forge a permanent voting bloc for the Democratic Party and his Big Government programs.

According to historian Doris Kearns Goodwin in *Lyndon Johnson and the American Dream*, Johnson was discussing the Civil Rights Act of 1957 with Senator Richard Russell of Georgia when Johnson told him, "These Negroes, they're getting pretty uppity these days and that's a problem for us since they've got something now they never had before, the political pull to back up their uppityness. Now we've got to do something about this, we've got to give them a little something, just enough to quiet them down, not enough to make a difference."[14]

Johnson's power in the Senate and on the national scene increased, until he attained the office of vice president under John F. Kennedy in 1960. He was now just a heartbeat away from imposing his collectivist New Deal philosophy on the nation. Johnson was a longtime liberal who was a follower of Franklin D. Roosevelt. In fact, Roosevelt actually mentored him. As Jonah Goldberg explains in *Liberal Fascism*:

> Amazingly, Johnson was the only full-fledged New Dealer to serve as president save FDR himself. Indeed, in many respects LBJ was the ultimate company man of the modern welfare state, the personification of everything the New Deal represented. Despite his large personality, he was in reality the personification of the system he helped

to create. From the beginning, FDR took a shine to LBJ. He told Harold Ickes that Johnson might well be the first southern president of the postwar generation. Johnson was a fanatically loyal FDR man.[15]

That presidential prediction of FDR's became a reality on a fateful November day in Dallas, when Johnson was sworn in as president after John Kennedy's assassination. The nation would soon learn that "FDR was Johnson's 'political Daddy,' in Johnson's own words, and more than any other elected official LBJ mastered the art of working the New Deal."[16]

The new president's even more grandiose version of the New Deal would be called the "Great Society" and would impose the federal government into every aspect of American life. Johnson knew that, for his Progressive vision of the "Great Society" to become a reality, he needed to consolidate power for his party and himself. He found a convenient avenue for this in the Civil Rights Act of 1964, even though he himself clearly exhibited racism. Numerous Johnson biographers have now revealed that he was indeed a racist who only used the black population for his own political purposes. For instance, when Johnson was discussing the Civil Rights Act of 1964 with two governors, he told them, "I'll have them n***ers voting Democratic for two hundred years."[17]

The Civil Rights Act of 1964 was passed during the first year Johnson was in office, and it did provide justice in that it ended segregation of the schools and expanded voting rights for Southern blacks; however, like all projects conceived by Progressive utopians, it went too far and took away too much liberty. It created the Equal Employment Opportunity Commission which, in addition to protecting racial minorities, called for an end to gender discrimination in employment, and eventually to nondiscrimination against sexual preferences of job applicants. It led to affirmative action to help racial minorities and women in their pursuit of jobs and college admissions, and became just as unfair and unjust as segregated schooling had been.

School desegregation paved the way for court-ordered busing, which broke apart communities, weakened parents' ability to be involved in their children's education, and enabled the government to appropriate for itself more of the parental role.

In addition to the Civil Rights legislation, Johnson planned to appeal to black voters through the "War on Poverty," and he got this massive welfare legislation passed during his first year in office, creating many government entitlements and agencies that are still with us today. His entire political career was based on fraud, and his utopian vision for a "War on Poverty" turned out to be a fraud as well. His "War on Poverty" actually became a war on the black family and on independence and self-reliance.

In early 2014 black conservatives with the Project 21 Leadership Network issued a stinging rebuke of Johnson's "War on Poverty" as a failure and as a government program that resulted in the destruction of the black family in America:

> "Five decades after President Johnson initiated the 'war' on poverty, America remains at around the same percentage of people still living in poverty as it did back then. In 1964, the poverty rate was approximately 19 percent. Today, it's around 15 percent," said Project 21 spokesman Derryck Green. "Statistics such as these demonstrate the War on Poverty was a continually-mismanaged disaster. That isn't to say there haven't been people helped by it. All things considered, however, it's been a tragedy."
>
> Green added: "The disastrous effects of the government's management of anti-poverty initiatives are recognizable across racial lines, but the destruction is particularly evident in the black community. It effectively subsidized the dissolution of the black family by rendering the black man's role as a husband and a father irrelevant, invisible and—more specifically—disposable. The result has been several generations of blacks born into broken homes and broken communities experiencing social, moral and economic chaos. It fosters an inescapable dependency that primarily, and oftentimes solely, relies on government to sustain livelihoods."[18]

President George H. W. Bush, in his own 1992 State of the Union Address, pointed out: "Welfare was never meant to be a lifestyle; it was never meant to be a habit; it was never supposed to be passed on from generation to generation like a legacy." Bush's comment echoed a statement by President Franklin D. Roosevelt, who, long before the War on Poverty even began, warned government assistance could be like a "narcotic."

"The War on Poverty has arguably destroyed the black nuclear family," said Project 21's Christopher Arps. "Roughly 75 percent of black children were born to a married two-parent family when the 'war' began in 1964. By 2008, the percentage of black babies born out of wedlock numbered over 72 percent. Today, the rate of unwed motherhood in the black community is more than twice as high as among whites—and almost three times higher than before big government's grand intervention. And all this comes at a steep financial cost. The federal government has spent an estimated $15 trillion dollars to end poverty. Government reportedly spent $20,610 on every poor individual and $61,830 per poor family in 2012."[19]

These are the words of black leaders who have not sold out for handouts from the central planners, and who have the facts to show how Johnson's utopian government programs produced more poverty, more family breakups, and dependence on the federal government—just as all such programs have throughout history.

By the time the eventful year of 1964 came to an end, conservative Americans were worried about all the Progressive changes being made and the speed with which Congress and the president were moving. They had no time to catch a breath, though, for on January 4, 1965, President Johnson came before the nation with his State of the Union Address, in which he asked for War on Poverty spending to be doubled, and furthermore he unfolded his truly breathtaking plan for the Great Society. It was a plan that touched on virtually every area of life. "Our concern and interest, compassion and vigilance, extend to every corner of a dwindling planet," said LBJ.

The Great Society plan he laid out was to educate every child through direct aid to school districts, eradicate diseases, beautify America, preserve the environment (Environmental Protection Agency), prevent crime, create a National Foundation on the Arts, seek full employment opportunities for every American, greatly extend the minimum wage, "improve" unemployment compensation, provide hospital care under Social Security (Medicare would come along two years later), end country-of-origin quotas and open the floodgates for immigrants, launch Head Start, provide student loans, begin a new Department of Housing and Urban Development, and much more.

When Ronald Reagan was campaigning for Barry Goldwater during the 1964 election, he gave an amazing speech on freedom, entitled "A Time for Choosing." In it, he clearly outlined the difference between Goldwater's conservative view of government and Lyndon Johnson's utopian totalitarian views on governing. The difference is stark and prophetic of the times we're living in.

Reagan noted:

> You and I are told we must choose between a left or right, but I suggest there is no such thing as a left or right. There is only an up or down. Up to man's age-old dream—the maximum of individual freedom consistent with order—or down to the ant heap of totalitarianism. Regardless of their sincerity, their humanitarian motives, those who would sacrifice freedom for security have embarked on this downward path. Plutarch warned, "The real destroyer of the liberties of the people is he who spreads among them bounties, donations and benefits."
>
> The Founding Fathers knew a government can't control the economy without controlling people. And they knew when a government sets out to do that, it must use force and coercion to achieve its purpose. So we have come to a time for choosing. . . .
>
> You and I have a rendezvous with destiny. We will preserve for our children this, the last best hope of man on earth, or we will sentence them to take the first step into a thousand years of darkness. If we fail, at least let our children and our children's children say of us we justified our brief moment here. We did all that could be done.[20]

Unfortunately, voters in 1964 picked Lyndon Johnson instead of Barry Goldwater, and our nation was subjected to his "Great Society" socialist boondoggles and a no-win war in Vietnam that resulted in the needless deaths of more than fifty-eight thousand American soldiers, sailors, and Marines.

Johnson managed to greatly expand the welfare state, but ultimately, Ronald Reagan was proven right. When he became president of the United States in 1981, he set about to fix our economy that had been destroyed by Obama's clone Jimmy Carter; he successfully defeated the Soviet Union—bringing freedom to millions in Soviet slave-states, and he restored America's optimism in the future.

For eight years, Reagan held off the utopian tyrants from regaining power to destroy our freedoms. Every generation must fight to preserve the freedoms we have in this wonderful country. Will the next generation do so? That remains to be seen.

Johnson's social engineering to control millions of Americans has squandered billions of taxpayer dollars over the decades and brought misery to countless individuals who are now locked in intergenerational poverty. For many, the "safety net" provided by liberals to help the poor has become a hammock for the unmotivated in our ever-growing entitlement society. What's the liberal solution to this ongoing culture of misery? Why, more government programs and more wasted taxpayer dollars, of course.

As usual, utopian programs by Big Government advocates like Lyndon Johnson inevitably end up bringing misery, family destruction, more poverty, and more dependence on the central government, which is all too ready to "manage" the lives of its subjects. But, of course, that's what they want. Government programs breed dependence and provide central planners with reliable voters who will continue to vote for any program that will give them more "free stuff," which they actually pay for with their freedom. But someone has to pay; nothing is free, and the value has to be produced by someone.

Utopians find themselves forced to pick winners and losers to pay for their centrally planned society; in this case, enslavement to welfare makes those in the black community the losers. Even those who consider themselves winners pay a heavy price for dependence on the central planners. Johnson's War on Poverty resulted in the genocide of black babies to abortion, the incarceration of one out of every five black men, and the destruction of the black family.

This tragic result of central planning has not, however, slowed the march of American Progressives and their assault on the Constitution, free speech, free enterprise, and religious freedom. The Obama administration became a who's who of Progressive utopians bent on collectivism and central planning.

REGULATORY UTOPIANS

CASS SUNSTEIN

Cass Sunstein was the Edward Mandell House/Rexford Tugwell character in the Obama administration. He was appointed to run Obama's White House Office of Information and Regulatory Affairs in 2009. He left the administration in 2011 to return to Harvard, where he continues to brainwash his students into supporting his anti-Constitutional and totalitarian beliefs.

Sunstein is the consummate Progressive and utopian tyrant. He believes that the Constitution is a "living document"—code words for liberal judges having the power to interpret the Constitution and law in general to support the latest leftist political agenda.

Writing in *The Partial Constitution* (Harvard University Press, 1993), Sunstein pushed the idea of a "First Amendment New Deal," which would create a government panel of experts to ensure a "diversity of views" on the airwaves. Imagine a panel of presidential appointees determining what constitutes diversity on TV and radio.

Sunstein also believes hunting should be banned, that animals should have the same rights as humans, and that lawyers should be empowered to file lawsuits on behalf of animals. Despite being against the killing of rabbits or deer, he is, like all Progressives, perfectly agreeable to destroying unborn humans at any stage of pregnancy.

In 2004 he published *A Second Bill of Rights: FDR's Unfinished Revolution and Why We Need It More Than Ever*. In it, he proposed a series of "rights" for individuals that would inevitably result in greatly expanding the power of the federal government over every aspect of our lives.

According to Sunstein, "Much of the time, the United States seems to have embraced a confused and pernicious form of individualism. This approach endorses rights of private property and freedom of contract, and respects political liberty, but claims to distrust 'government intervention' and insists that people must fend for themselves. This form of so-called individualism is incoherent, a tangle of confusions."[21]

Sunstein's views sound like those of Benito Mussolini or Philip Dru in the utopian novel.

JOHN HOLDREN

President Obama appointed John Holdren to run the White House Office of Science and Technology Policy and to cochair the President's Council of Advisors on Science and Technology.

Holdren sounds like a very dangerous tyrant in his written statements on population control and other issues. In 1977 he coauthored a book with Paul R. and Anne H. Ehrlich, titled *Ecoscience: Population, Resources, Environment* (W. H. Freeman, 1978), which seriously proposed, among other things, that women should be forced to abort their children; that populations should be sterilized by dropping drugs into the water supply; that people who "contribute to social deterioration" should be forcibly sterilized or forced to abort their children; that a "Planetary Regime" should assume total control of the global economy; and that an international police force should be used to dictate how all of us are to live our lives.

Because this was a White House office, the Senate did not have the authority to stop the appointment; however, some senators should have come forward and pointed out on the record that Holdren's suggestions were very much the same as those of fascist utopian Adolf Hitler.

Holdren openly condemns the free enterprise system as the enemy of the people and a threat to the environment. Writing in his 1973 book, *Human Ecology: Problems and Solutions*, also cowritten with the Ehrlichs, he called for a "massive campaign . . . to de-develop the United States" and other Western nations.

According to Holdren, the "mad czar" of science and technology:

> De-development means bringing our economic system (especially patterns of consumption) into line with the realities of ecology and the global resource situation. . . . The need for de-development presents our economists with a major challenge. They must design a stable, low-consumption economy in which there is a much more equitable distribution of wealth than in the present one. Redistribution of wealth both within and among nations is absolutely essential if a decent life is to be provided for every human being.[22]

Elsewhere, he wrote, "By de-development, we mean lower per-capita energy consumption, fewer gadgets, and the abolition of planned obsolescence."[23]

The Soviet Union successfully did away with "planned obsolescence" by eliminating innovation. As no new cars were designed for decades, vehicles like the unsafe Lada lived on unchanged for decades. Like many Progressives who believe jobs should be "preserved" as a right, Holdren does not understand that artificially preserving outdated industries and nonproductive jobs results in a failure for new industries to come into existence.

DR. DONALD BERWICK

Dr. Berwick was picked by President Obama to run the Center for Medicare and Medicaid Services. Knowing that Berwick's views were so radical, Obama used a recess appointment to get him into this position so he wouldn't have to undergo Senate scrutiny. Once his recess gig expired, he simply resigned to avoid having to answer questions under oath before a Senate committee.

Berwick has an open love affair with the British National Health Service (NHS). In his own words, "I'm romantic about the National

Health Service. I love it!" In fact, he loves it so much that he says it is an "example for the whole world—an example . . . that the United States needs now." Why? Because he considers America's health care system to be "immoral" and an example of the "darkness of private enterprise." And in typical utopian-tyrant fashion, he believes that only government-enforced "collective action" can override "individual self-interest."

He was, however, a bit more honest than his boss, President Obama. He openly admitted that under Obamacare, "the decision is not whether or not we will ration care, the decision is whether we will ration with our eyes open." Conservatives always find this a terrifying thing about central planners—their willingness, even eagerness, to assume the role of making life-and-death decisions about the fate of other individuals.

So, how is the love of his socialist life working for British citizens, keeping in mind that this is the same system he wanted to bring to the United States? The *Boston Globe* shares some quotes from UK newspapers:

> "Overstretched maternity units mean mothers face a 100-mile journey to have baby."

> "Hundreds of patients died needlessly at NHS hospital due to appalling care."

> "Cash-strapped NHS trust introduces rationing for common children's conditions."

> "Standard of care in some wards 'would shame a third world country.'"

> "Stafford Hospital caused 'unimaginable suffering.'"

And to top it all off, in Britain 36 percent of patients wait more than four months for nonemergency surgery. In America, only 5 percent do.[24]

According to Berwick, "Any healthcare funding plan that is just, equitable, civilized and humane, must redistribute wealth from the richer among us to the poorer and the less fortunate. Excellent health-care is by definition distributional."[25]

That sounds familiar, doesn't it? From Woodrow Wilson, Franklin Delano Roosevelt, and Lyndon Johnson to Barack Obama, there's a clear socialist utopian model in play that results in the control of Americans' lives through rationed medical care.

These are only three of the most high-profile utopian totalitarians to serve in the Obama administration, but they are typical of those whom the president picked to assist in an Imperial Presidency in which central planning of society has become the goal.

FOOD UTOPIANS

First Lady Michelle Obama and former New York City mayor Michael Bloomberg are what could be politely referred to as the "Food Police" by the vast majority of Americans who prefer to choose their own foods. A more accurate description would be Food Nazis, because they both desire to dictate to Americans what they will eat, how much they will eat, and what size portions they will be served at restaurants.

Mrs. Obama's mind-set about Americans may be defined by her husband's definition of her during pre–White House years as his "bitter half." Apparently even President Obama knew that his wife was not capable of seeing a glass half full; how, then, could she possibly see that a hamburger with lettuce and tomato was actually a balanced meal?

Michelle Obama decided early on that she would seize the issues of "childhood obesity" and "food deserts" as her crusade while inhabiting the White House. She and her utopian handlers created the "Let's Move" campaign to force restaurants, schools, and parents to feed children more "nutritious" meals. Initially she wanted a mere $400 million from taxpayers for her program.

Without any real evidence, Mrs. Obama has claimed that poor Americans are trapped in what she calls "food deserts," where they must apparently trudge for miles outside of their dismal neighborhoods to buy a piece of fruit or some celery sticks. According to Mrs. Obama, a food desert is an inner city without a grocery store. She envisioned spending millions of federal dollars to plant grocery stores in those blighted areas so the "poor" won't have to buy food at mini-marts.

Secretary of Housing and Urban Development Shaun Donovan actually attended Al Sharpton's National Action Network annual convention in April 2012. There he told an absurd story about how Barack Obama, who attended Harvard University, knows what "it's like to take a subway or a bus just to find a fresh piece of fruit in a grocery store." No fruit at Harvard?

The story may be ridiculous, but Michelle Obama was dead serious about extorting $400 million from American taxpayers to solve the nonexistent problem of food deserts.[26]

In reality there are no such things as food deserts. Researcher Roland Sturm at the Rand Corporation studied food desert claims and found that individuals in urban areas can get any kind of food they want within a couple of miles. He suggested we call these areas "food swamps," rather than food deserts.

In addition, researcher Helen Lee at the Public Policy Institute in California found that in poor neighborhoods, citizens had twice as many fast-food restaurants and convenience stores as wealthier neighborhoods had, and more than three times as many corner stores. These areas had twice as many supermarkets and large-scale grocery stores as wealthier neighborhoods.[27]

The truth was exactly the opposite of Mrs. Obama's claim, but hers satisfied the mind-set of the utopians, who believe they alone could solve problems that never existed. Mrs. Obama later began a second crusade to force restaurants and schools to serve "healthy" foods, ban "junk food," and bully restaurants into serving smaller portions.

Michelle Obama worked in 2010 to get Congress to pass a nutrition bill that would give the Department of Agriculture new powers to regulate school lunches. The bill was passed in December of that year, and now that the regulations have gone into effect, it is having a devastating impact on students and their angry parents.

Under Department of Agriculture edicts, cinnamon rolls and chili are banned. School bands and groups can't sell candy bars for fund-raising. The government is now mandating portion sizes, including how many tomatoes must go into a salad!

Children are permitted to refuse three items on a tray, but not fruits and vegetables. Of course, the Food Police can't yet force them to eat their veggies, but it's not far-fetched to think they might someday. After all, the Obamas have rammed through legislation that initially demanded that nuns buy insurance coverage for contraception and pregnancy. Fortunately the Supreme Court ended that requirement in 2014.

The new federal guidelines, thanks to Michelle Obama, now limit caloric intake to between 750 and 850 a day for schoolchildren. Teenagers require between 2,000 and 3,000 calories a day to be healthy and grow, and high school athletes need up to 5,000 calories per day. In short, the First Lady is responsible for malnourishing kids through the school lunch program.[28]

In 2006 the three-term mayor of New York City, Michael Bloomberg, decided to add the title "Food Police Chief" to his list of duties in the Big Apple. That year, he banished trans fats from city restaurants and, in 2010, forced food manufacturers to alter their recipes to include less sodium. He failed, however, to remove salt shakers from the tables. Patrons who receive a dish of food at a New York restaurant that they deem not salty enough may still simply add salt.

In spring 2012 Bloomberg decided that New Yorkers had to be protected even more from themselves, so he issued an edict banning soft drinks larger than sixteen ounces. The ban applied to restaurants, movie theaters, stadiums, and arenas.[29]

In August 2012 Bloomberg banned the distribution of baby formula in city hospitals unless it is medically necessary because he, a man, had decided that new mothers should always breast-feed regardless of their weight, professions, or other personal details. Free formula provided to mothers was also eliminated. Bloomberg determined that breast-feeding is best for children and that new mothers should not have a voice in the decision regardless of their circumstances. But Bloomberg did want women to have freedom of choice to kill their young before they are born. He was willing to give moms the option to abort their unborn babies, but not to feed formula to those who are living.[30]

What is next for those like Obama and Bloomberg? Mandated calisthenics each morning at six? Currently the United States seems to be incubating and hatching utopian tyrants at an alarming rate.

WATERMELONS (THE GREEN UTOPIANS)

America is threatened not only by the Food Nazis, but by the Watermelon Utopians, who are working to destroy our industrialized civilization and bring us back to an agrarian society in the name of the environment.

These are the Watermelons. They're Red (Marxist-Leninist) on the inside, but are using the Green movement on the outside to promote totalitarian central-planned government.

VAN JONES

The poster child for this Watermelon movement is Van Jones, a Marxist with a nice smile who hates free enterprise just a bit less than nuclear power and fossil fuels.

In March 2009 President Obama picked Jones to be his "Green Jobs Czar." In September 2009 Jones resigned after television host Glenn Beck exposed the fact that Jones was a militant Marxist radical.

After his departure from the Obama administration, Jones went to work at the Center for American Progress, a socialist group funded by one-worlder George Soros. Jones also began teaching at Princeton University at the African American Studies and Woodrow Wilson School of Public and International Affairs. He is a "senior fellow" at the Center for American Progress and is an advisor for the extremist group Green for All, which he founded in 2007.

In an unsurprising way, Van Jones symbolizes the support Barack Obama received from the left that helped him win two terms. Jones also highlights the vast portion of the US population who do want the government to take care of all their needs and are willing to allow government to be the god of their lives in return.

Jones openly said he became a Communist shortly after the 1992 Rodney King riots and the trial. According to Jones, "I was a rowdy nationalist on April 28th" and "by August, I was a communist."[31]

In 1993 he moved to San Francisco and helped found the Bay Area Police Watch, which demonized the police in that city. In 1996 he founded the Ella Baker Center for Human Rights, designed to undermine the criminal justice system, which he saw as unjust to minorities. The Baker Center received more than $1 million from George Soros's Open Society Institute.

As Jones's commitment to Marxist-type central planning grew in the late '90s, he became a leader of the group called STORM (Standing Together to Organize a Revolutionary Movement).

Then in 2006 Jones endorsed an antipolice day held by the Maoist Revolutionary Communist Party. Jones considers all American prisons to be racist and nothing more than "slave ships on dry land."

As a green activist, Jones demanded that America "build a pipeline from the prison economy to the green economy." He wants the federal government to hire ex-felons to work in "green jobs" to do weather-stripping for energy efficiency in homes and offices. He did not mention if the home and business owners would be informed of workers' felony convictions.

According to Jones, in an interview on Uprising Radio in Los Angeles, "The green economy will start off as a small subset" of a "complete revolution" against what he calls "gray capitalism." The goal is the "redistribution of all wealth."[32]

Part of this anticapitalist effort is being accomplished through Green for All, funded in part by George Soros and our incredibly wealthy former vice president Al Gore—a true multimillionaire of the people. The organization's alleged purpose is "building an inclusive green economy strong enough to lift people out of poverty."[33] In reality the plan would use taxpayer dollars to fund centrally planned government-run boondoggles in the inner cities.

Jones has openly admitted that his green agenda is designed to destroy capitalism. "We are going to push it and push it until it becomes the engine for transforming the whole society," he said.[34]

DR. JAMES HANSEN

Political green activist James Hansen is one of the most vocal watermelon activists in the globalist movement. Hansen is a longtime liberal media darling. An Al Gore adviser and former John Kerry campaigner, he runs the Goddard Institute for Space Studies under NASA and rakes in millions of dollars from environmental groups as well as George Soros's Open Society Institute.

Hansen expresses a deep hatred of capitalism as well as the fossil fuel industry and is working—at taxpayer expense—to destroy the very system from which he benefits.

Christopher Horner, author of *The Politically Incorrect Guide to Climate Change (and Global Warming)* has been a longtime critic of Dr. Hansen. In fact, his organization, the American Tradition Institute, has sued NASA under the Freedom of Information Act for data on Hansen's financial arrangements with green activist groups. According to Horner, "Hansen's office appears to be somewhat of a rogue operation. It's clearly a taxpayer-funded global warming advocacy organization."[35]

The American Tradition Institute's Environmental Law Center received 2010 financial disclosures on Hansen. The data revealed that Hansen got between $236,000 and $1,232,500 in extra income outside his job as a federal employee. He got between $150,000 and $1.1 million in prizes and $60,000 for travel expenses.

In 2010 Hansen won the Blue Planet Prize for "having predicted global warming in the early stage" and calling on "the governments and the public to take immediate action to reduce and mitigate the impact of climate change."[36] He also won the Sophie Prize, "for his clear communication of the threat posed by climate change and for his genuine commitment to future generations." According to the Sophie Prize website, "Hansen strongly believes that we need to phase out our coal mining and let fossil reserves stay in the ground. If all reserves of oil, gas and coal that still exist on this planet are used and the emissions are let out into the atmosphere it will be the end of our civilization. Still 'some see it as their God-given right to harvest and burn all fossil fuels that are within their territories,' states Hansen."[37]

The Sophie Prize Internet site is clearly anti–free enterprise and pro–centralized government. It states: "Today's economic system is at odds with the limits set by nature. Too many decisions are based on short-term profit for a few select groups rather than a moral and fair distribution of the world's resources. . . ."

"For as long as the means allow," reads the mission statement, "The Sophie Prize will be awarded to an individual or an organization that, in a pioneering or a particularly creative way, has pointed to alternatives to the present development and put such alternatives into practice."[38] Note that no mention is made of who decides what would be a "moral and fair distribution of the world's resources," nor if they will be democratically chosen, which, of course, they will not be. Democracy is poison to central planners.

Hansen is a hero to Sophie Prize.

Hansen clearly opposes the use of fossil fuels and also believes that nations have no right to their own resources. Clearly, then, he is opposed to the concept of national sovereignty. He has the record of a militant Watermelon Utopian who uses cushy taxpayer-funded posts to lobby for the destruction of free enterprise under the guise of protecting the environment.

CONCLUSION

We've briefly surveyed the history of Progressive thinking and its impact on our nation over the decades; we've also detailed real-life examples of how utopians in government are working to destroy freedom of speech, national sovereignty, free enterprise, freedom of choice, and even freedom to eat what we choose.

These individuals and organizations often see the Constitution and its Bill of Rights as well as the free enterprise system as impediments to creating a centrally planned, collectivist society that in their view would be prosperous and lack conflict caused by the profit motive. Their efforts have in fact been a drain on society both economically and socially.

9

THE UTOPIAN NATIONS (UN)—

A THREAT TO AMERICA'S SOVEREIGNTY

The United Nations' building in New York City and its related organizations around the world are filled with utopian central planners who are working feverishly day in and day out to destroy the sovereignty of the United States and every other nation on the earth.

That is a strong statement, I know, but it's the truth. Everything the utopians in the UN are doing is ostensibly designed to promote "global peace and prosperity," but in reality, the goal is the consolidation of total power over all resources and all people on planet Earth. Their visions of the perfect world may vary, but utopians of many persuasions, Communists, environmentalists, Islamic extremists, and others, have all seen the enormous potential in the United Nations for forcing their will upon all the peoples of the earth.

Anyone who takes the time to read through the rather boring United Nations reports and their various published agendas will realize that this international organization is engaged in what can be called an open conspiracy against human freedom, free enterprise, human dignity, religious liberty, private property, parental rights, and other God-given liberties that Americans, in particular, hold dear.

A LOOK AT THE FOUNDING OF THE UN

One of the most detailed—and probably the most reliable—histories of the United Nations was written by G. Edward Griffin in 1964. His book *The Fearful Master: A Second Look at the United Nations* reveals that the United Nations was a longtime goal of the international Communist movement to consolidate power into one organization that could be used to socialize the economies of all nations as an incremental step toward total Communist control of the world.

Stalin laid out his plan in 1942 for incremental world conquest in *Marxism and the National Question*. His plan was to confuse, disorganize, and neutralize the forces of capitalism around the world; bring all nations into a single world economic system; force advanced nations to send millions in aid to underdeveloped countries; and divide the world into regional groups of nations that would eventually be brought into a one-world system.[1]

In 1944, during the planning stages of the United Nations, Earl Browder, a leader of the Communist Party USA at the time, wrote, "The American Communists worked energetically and tirelessly to lay the foundations for the United Nations, which we were sure would come into existence."[2]

Soviet general Pantelei Bondarenko had given a speech supportive of the UN to students at the Frunze Military Academy in Moscow. He told the future soldiers, "From the rostrum of the United Nations, we shall convince the colonial and semi-colonial people to liberate themselves and to spread the Communist theory all over the world. We recognize the UN has no authority over the Soviet Union, but the United Nations serves to deflect the capitalists and warmongers in the Western World."[3]

The Soviet Union no longer exists, but that certainly doesn't mean that the current central planners with Marxist ties have retreated from their goal of a single world government in control of all aspects of people's lives.

Clearly, the leaders of the Soviet Union and Communist subversives in America in the 1940s wanted the UN for their goal of world conquest. G. Edward Griffin revealed that more than a dozen Americans in our government who were involved in creating the United Nations were actually secret Communist agents!

In 1950 the US State Department published a document entitled "Post-War Foreign Policy Preparation, 1939–1945," which listed several key men who helped create the United Nations. Among them were:

All of these men worked inside the State Department and Treasury

1.	Dean Acheson	10.	Abraham George Silverman
2.	Solomon Adler	11.	Nathan Gregory Silvermaster
3.	Virginius Frank Coe	12.	William Taylor
4.	Laurence Duggan	13.	William L. Ullman
5.	Noel Field	14.	John Carter Vincent
6.	Harold Glasser	15.	Henry Julian Wadleigh
7.	Alger Hiss	16.	David Weintraub
8.	Irving Kaplan	17.	Harry Dexter White
9.	Victor Perlo		

Department in forming the UN. And all were associated with the Communist movement—with the exception of Acheson, who was a far-left liberal.

Alger Hiss is probably the most infamous Communist spy and traitor among the group. He was the chief planner of the San Francisco conference where the UN was brought to life. He was also the UN's first acting secretary general.[4]

Hiss was eventually convicted of perjury for lying about being a Soviet spy, but served only a few years of his sentence. He was ninety-two when he died in 1996, but he had done immeasurable damage to the United States by leading in the creation of the UN.

It is probably no coincidence that the wording of the Soviet Constitution and the United Nations Declaration on Human Rights is nearly identical. In section after section, both documents "grant" rights from government, but typically include phrases that erase those "rights" at the convenience of the totalitarian state. In both documents, rights are neither from God nor inalienable. They are handed out by the state and can be canceled at any time for whatever reason.

In both the Soviet Constitution and the UN Declaration on Human Rights, all "human rights" are granted by the government, but are subject to "such limitations as are prescribed by law," or "otherwise provided by law." The Declaration, for example, guarantees freedom of opinion, but then cancels out that freedom by noting that it will be limited "as provided by law."

As Griffin has observed, "There are a great many . . . similarities between the Soviet Constitution and the United Nations Declaration on Human Rights. . . . The basic concept embodied in both of these documents is that the government has full responsibility for the welfare of the people and, in order to discharge this responsibility, must assume control of all their activities. How different this is from the traditional concept of limited government."[5]

The United Nations was designed by Communists from the beginning of its existence to be a tool used by the Soviets to create a one-world government, where every person on earth was to be enslaved by Marxist dictators. The "Soviet Union" may be gone, but the collectivists are still actively working for a dictatorship. But now, they often refer to themselves as "environmentalists."

WATERMELON MARXISTS: AGENDA 21

Central planners are alive and well at the United Nations, but they are no longer red; they're green. They are using environmentalism, "global warming," "climate change," and "sustainable development" as ways of destroying the sovereignty of independent nations. Their main target is the United States because it is considered the worst polluter on the planet and is supposedly using up all of the world's natural resources for our industrialized civilization. Their hope is to destroy the American economic and military might and return the world to an agrarian age with a smaller population.

The UN Watermelons operate primarily within the Intergovernmental Panel on Climate Change (IPCC), but they're also scattered among all UN organizations; for instance, many work in UNESCO.

James Delingpole, author of *Watermelons: The Green Movement's True Colors*, describes in detail how totalitarians are using the UN as a weapon against sovereign nations. One of the primary ways they are working to destroy independent nations is through Agenda 21, a plan endorsed by 179 nations at the Earth Summit in Rio back in 1992. "Agenda 21 effectively puts an end to national sovereignty, abolishes private property, elevates Nature above man, and places a host of restrictions on what we've come to accept as our most basic freedoms—everything from how, when and where we travel to what we eat," Delingpole wrote.[6]

Who is behind Agenda 21—and how could this plan destroy American sovereignty? The man behind this sustainable development action plan is Maurice Strong, who chaired the first UN Conference on the Human Environment in 1972. Strong, who was a key official at the UN for many years, had close ties with the Communist Chinese during all that time. In fact, he served as an advisor to Communist China on issues of climate change and carbon trading.[7]

As a Communist sympathizer, Strong stands against the concept of national sovereignty, which he calls "an immutable, indeed sacred, principle of international relations. It is a principle which will yield only slowly and reluctantly to the new imperatives of global environmental cooperation," he says. "It is simply not feasible for sovereignty to be exercised unilaterally by individual nation states, however powerful. The global community must be assured of environmental security."[8]

In short, all nations must give up their sovereignty in order to assure "environmental security."

Ron Taylor, author of *Agenda 21: An Expose of the United Nations' Sustainable Development Initiative and the Forfeiture of American Sovereignty and Liberties*, has studied numerous UN documents on

Agenda 21 as well as American initiatives under Hillary Clinton and Barack Obama to implement UN plans. "Originally devised to regulate the global environment, the United Nations' Agenda 21 initiative, also known as Sustainable Development, has evolved into a political objective, calling for the complete subjugation of the world's population," he warned, "including the people of the United States, through massive relocation of entire cities, depopulation, and the expansive cordoning of land into nature preserves."[9]

The UN document outlining the goals of Agenda 21 is 351 pages long. Its preamble, according to Taylor, "sets forth the vision of the sustained development initiative as a global partnership, where all nations must cooperate to eradicate hunger, poverty, illiteracy, and ill-health. As you can see, in the first paragraph of this document, the United Nations has expanded the vision of climate and environment control to include the health, safety, and education of the world's population. It is this type of 'mission creep' that is dangerous, as bureaucracies are created to implement the Agenda 21 vision, and each bureaucracy expands its reach, budget, and goals."[10]

In the foreword to the UN's 1992 Agenda 21: Programme of Action for Sustainable Development, Maurice Strong wrote:

> The economic gulfs which lie within and among the world's peoples and nations not only remain, but are daily deepening. Hunger and poverty which are both a cause and an effect of global environmental degradation—are still appallingly pervasive in the developing world, where population growth compounds the problems of alleviating them. Industrial countries continue to be addicted to the patterns of production and consumption which have so largely produced the major risks to the global environment.[11]

Notice Strong's use of the word "addicted" to describe countries such as the United States, which are industrial powers. The industrial nations are the culprits in creating pollution, hunger, and poverty, according to Strong.

According to the introduction of this document, no nation can work alone to manage the alleged deterioration of the environment. There must be a "global partnership for sustainable development," which will be implemented through the UN Commission on Sustainable Development.

Agenda 21 describes twenty-seven principles that must guide nations in implementing its plan for global domination. Principle 1 states that humans are entitled to healthy and productive lives in harmony with nature. What in the world does that mean? Does it mean that totalitarian governments should shut down McDonald's restaurants or forbid the building of new home developments on forested lands?

Although romanticized by comfortable modern utopians, primitive cultures that "live in harmony with nature" are in reality victimized by nature's brutality. Modern cultures conquer nature and use the resources it provides to create civilizations and better lives for those living in those nations. Contrast those who live "in harmony with nature" but are dying at early ages with no medical care, to the people living in advanced societies. The gap couldn't be more obvious.

The difference between the collectivism that is proposed as the solution and the free-market experience is also dramatic. A satellite photo of North and South Korea at night shows that contrast. North Korea is dark while South Korea is filled with millions of lights—symbols of a productive, free enterprise–oriented society in which the individual has liberty.

Principle 3 says that nations have the "right to development," as long as any developments "equitably meet" the "developmental and environmental needs of present and future generations." And, of course, it will be UN bureaucrats who get to decide what is "equitable."

Principle 5 says that all nations must work to eradicate poverty in order to "decrease the disparities in standards of living" and "better meet the needs of the majority of the people of the world." In other words, productive free enterprise–oriented nations must give away billions to unproductive socialist countries to erase "disparities" in living conditions. Those welfare payments, however, will not make poorer nations productive. By whatever name, this is just a Marx/Wilson/Stalin/

Roosevelt/Obama redistribution of income plan.

Principle 6 says that the least developed countries should receive the highest priority.

Principles 20 and 21 say that women and youth are important in forging a "global partnership" in fighting for sustainable development.

Principle 24 says that "warfare" is harmful to the environment and that nations must protect the environment while they're engaged in war.

In essence, what these principles propose is total control over the environments, resources, and people in every country on the planet. Principle 8, for example, says that governments should "reduce and eliminate unsustainable patterns of production and consumption and promote appropriate demographic policies." In other words, they should *take control* of production and consumption. Does this mean closing down Walmart stores to reduce the amount of spending by American citizens? Who knows? It is up to UN bureaucrats and their one-world allies in the various governments around the globe to define these policies for their citizens.

And what does "promote appropriate demographic policies" mean? Forbidding citizens to have more than one or two children? Would abortions be forced, as they have been in Communist China? Or, does it mean moving populations from one part of a country or the world to another by force? Cambodian tyrant Pol Pot may have thought he was using "appropriate demographic policies" when he emptied out Cambodian cities and forced city dwellers into the country to farm (and eventually starve to death). Perhaps Principle 8 could provide justification for John Holdren's proposal that sterilization drugs be put into the water supply to "promote appropriate demographic policies."

Principle 9 states that developed nations such as the United States have an obligation to willingly transfer scientific and technical knowledge to nations that do not have it. This would eliminate patents and stifle innovation, since no profit motive would exist. Thomas Edison, after all, would have had no desire to create the lightbulb, phonograph, or movie projector had he been forced to immediately hand over the technology to other manufacturers around the world. Principle 9 removes liberty from individuals by taking away their intellectual property.

Agenda 21 is another example of utopian tyranny. Under the guise of "saving the planet," the totalitarians pushing this UN nightmare may ultimately enslave all of us.

WORLD HERITAGE AND BIOSPHERE ZONES

The United Nations is engaged in a subtle landgrab all over the globe through the United Nations Educational, Scientific, and Cultural Organization (UNESCO). This land confiscation scheme came out of the World Heritage Convention, which was created in 1972. The goal of the Convention is to list sites around the world that are considered so valuable that they must be protected by the United Nations. Of course, that includes just about anything. For example, in the United States, such sites as the Statue of Liberty, Independence Hall, and Jefferson's home at Monticello are listed as "World Heritage" sites by UNESCO.

Since the United States signed this convention, it is now obligated to run these designated sites by UN rather than American standards. Since 1972, UNESCO has designated at least twenty-two sites in the United States as "World Heritage" sites. Among those was Yellowstone National Park, which was named as a protected site in 1995.

The violation of our national sovereignty over this park by UN bureaucrats was evident in 1995 after New World Mining Corporation began to conduct a mining operation three miles from the park. Environmentalists rallied against the mining operation, which would have brought an estimated $650 million in gold and other materials out of the ground and provided employment for at least 280 workers in the area. The Clinton administration allowed the UN to enforce a 12 million–acre "buffer zone" around the 2.3 million–acre park in order to "protect" it.

Eventually, the federal government paid $65 million in buyout and cleanup costs for the mine and it was closed down. Instead of infusing millions into our economy, the Clinton/UN coalition cost taxpayers $65 million and destroyed potential jobs.[12]

UNESCO keeps adding new lands to its list of "World Heritage" sites—and nations that signed the treaty continue to have their sovereignty usurped by UN bureaucrats.

Not only does UNESCO have its World Heritage landgrab scheme, but even more territory is being declared off-limits to development of any kind by establishing "biosphere reserves." These UN-created reserves began spreading around the world in 1976.

According to the *Environmental Encyclopedia*, a Biosphere Reserve is designed to

> preserve islands of the world's living resources from logging, mining, urbanization, and other environmentally destructive human activities. The term derives from the ecological word "biosphere," which refers to the zone of air, land, and water at the surface of the earth that is occupied by living organisms. Growing concern over the survival of individual species in the 1970s and 1980s led increasingly to the recognition that endangered species could not be preserved in isolation. Rather, entire ecosystems, extensive communities of interdependent animals and plants, are needed for threatened species to survive.[13]

In July 2012 UNESCO announced the addition of twenty new biosphere reserves—bringing the total at that point up to 598 reserves in 117 countries. Many of these have been used by environmental activists to shut down logging operations and significant oil-drilling developments throughout the world. The radical Ecuadorian environmental group known as Amazon Watch, for example, has been fighting against development of an oil reserve that amounts to one-fifth of all of the country's known reserves. The oil, however, is beneath one of the UN-designated biosphere reserves.[14] As a result, the rather poor nation of Ecuador cannot develop this vast and rich resource for the benefit of its citizens.

In Spain environmental extremists have been fighting against oil drilling off the coast of the Spanish Canary Islands because they were declared a UNESCO biosphere reserve in 1993. The oil found off the coast could provide one-tenth of the oil used in Spain, but the Spanish are not allowed to touch those millions of barrels. Yet, the Canary Islands are allowed to have windmills, which kill thousands of birds a year, including many threatened species, since the islands are a "renewable energy paradise" due to their supposed potential for wind farms.[15]

Using the UN as a tool, radical environmentalists who want to reduce the global population to a small number of agricultural villages to "protect" the environment have shut off millions of square miles of land and ocean from energy development!

THE INTERNATIONAL CRIMINAL COURT (ICC)

The UN's International Criminal Court is a primary tool being used to undermine national sovereignty around the globe. Fortunately, our country has not yet entered into an agreement to come under its authority because there are still enough rational men and women in the Senate to reject ratification of any agreement giving it power over us.

President Barack Obama and former secretary of state Hillary Clinton, however, made it clear that they wanted America to be subjugated to this court. In 2009 Secretary Clinton said that it was her "great regret" that we were not yet a signatory" to the Rome Statute, the document that founded the ICC in June 1998. Former president Clinton did sign it; however, there were never enough votes in the Senate to ratify it. Fortunately, former president George W. Bush unsigned the Rome Statute. He also signed one hundred separate agreements with other nations to protect American citizens from being brought before the ICC.

President Barack Obama has been an open advocate of placing American interests under international law. He endeavored to submit American foreign policy to the dictates of UN and "coalition partners."

Former UN ambassador John Bolton, in *How Barack Obama Is Endangering Our National Sovereignty*, wrote that "Barack Obama is our first post-American president—someone who sees his role in foreign policy less as an advocate for America's 'parochial' interests and more as a 'citizen of the world,' in his own phrase. He broadly embodies many European social democratic values, including those regarding sovereignty, so it was not surprising that an ecstatic student said after hearing him on one of his first overseas trips, 'He sounds like a European.' Indeed he does."[16]

Should the United States Senate ever ratify the Rome Statute, American citizens will be subject to the International Criminal Court—and we will have lost our national sovereignty to the United Nations—a collection of anti-American nations the majority of which are ruled by dictators and monarchs. They view the United States as a giant ATM to bail them out of the socialist disasters they have created for themselves, and they could very well use the ICC as a means to that end.

LAW OF THE SEA TREATY

The utopian nations' totalitarians don't just want to control how all the land on earth is used; they also want control of the resources available in the world's oceans. They plan to seize control of the open waters through the Law of the Sea Treaty (LOST).

According to this treaty, which has never been ratified by the Senate, the UN controls 71 percent of the earth's surface, which contains 97 percent of the world's water![17] One in every six jobs in America is related in some way to the oceans, and a third of our nation's GNP originates in coastal areas. Oceans are important to America for commercial transportation, recreation, food production, and energy production—including vast reserves of oil off our shores. In addition, our nation's national security is dependent on our Navy and its ability to move freely around the oceans of the world.

Not only would the treaty give the UN control of the resources of the ocean just a few miles from the coast of the United States, but control of all the sources of water that flow into it. In other words the UN would have some jurisdiction over every little stream in the United States that is in some way connected to a river whose waters eventually flow into the ocean.

This is a very unique problem to the United States, because we have the only Constitution in the world that requires government to comply with all aspects of a treaty; this was a grave error made by our Founders in attempting to show that the American Revolution would not isolate us from the world.

The UN's Division of Ocean Affairs and Law of the Sea (DOALOS) described what LOST would cover:

> The United Nations Convention on the Law of the Sea . . . is perhaps one of the most significant but less recognized twentieth century accomplishments in the arena of international law. . . . Its scope is vast: it covers all ocean space, with all its uses, including navigation and overflight; all uses of all its resources, living and nonliving, on the high seas, on the ocean floor and beneath, on the continental shelf and in the territorial seas; the protection of the marine environment; and basic law and order. . . . The Convention is widely recognized by the international community as the legal framework within which all activities in the oceans and the seas must be carried out.[18]

LOST would give the UN totalitarians control not only of all ocean space and resources, but of who gets to fly over the oceans!

Senator James Inhofe (R-OK) has been an outspoken opponent of ratifying LOST. He noted:

> LOST would trade in our Constitution for a vague two hundred-page compact drafted by foreign diplomats. It would swap our Founding Fathers for the United Nations, and we the people for the foreign secretaries we've never heard of and didn't elect.
>
> This desire to substitute the received wisdom of international committees, led by nations like Sudan and Russia, for the electoral judgment of the American people is the motivation behind LOST and every other sovereignty-peddling treaty making the rounds.[19]

Frank Gaffney, a national security expert who is president of the Center for Security Policy, is also an opponent of LOST. According to Gaffney, LOST "would constitute the most egregious transfer of American sovereignty, wealth and power to the U.N. since the founding of that world body. . . . Never before in the history of the world has any nation voluntarily engaged in such a sweeping transfer to anyone."[20]

Gaffney also noted that LOST will actually dictate rules for how undersea intelligence gathering is conducted! Do we really want the UN telling the US Navy how they can gather intelligence in the oceans of the world? Signing this treaty would be a death warrant to America's naval power. The UN utopians, who want a one-world government with them in control, are eager to start by controlling all the resources on the planet!

BLASPHEMY LAWS AND RELIGIOUS FREEDOM

The utopian tyrants of the UN are also eager to destroy the Bill of Rights, starting with the right to religious freedom and the right to freedom of speech. Almost one-third of the UN member nations are repressive Islamic states. These nations are leading the charge, along with the cowardly secularists of Europe, to criminalize worldwide any criticism of Islam.

As an example, after a YouTube video called "Innocence of Muslims" supposedly inspired Muslim outrage around the world, UN Secretary General Ban Ki-Moon warned that "when some people use this freedom of expression to provoke or humiliate some others' values and beliefs, then this cannot be protected."[21]

Ban's statement is very clear: free speech must be suppressed if someone else's values or beliefs are offended or humiliated—and especially if such speech offends the delicate sensibilities of Muslims, who riot against Western civilization for any perceived offense. There is now apparently a "human right" not to be offended. Islam, of course, is the favorite religion in the UN, and its "rights" will be aggressively defended by the utopian tyrants who inhabit the United Nations building in New York City.

The criminalization of criticism of Islam is being spearheaded by the Organization of Islamic Cooperation (OIC), made up principally of dictators and monarchs along with the Muslim Brotherhood. Currently the OIC consists of fifty-six Islamic nations and the Palestinian Authority, all working together to impose sharia law on every non-Muslim on the earth. Sharia strictly forbids criticism of Islam. It is considered blasphemy even for non-Muslims to speak ill of Muhammad or of any part of the Islamic sociopolitical system disguised as a religion.

Every year, without fail, the OIC offers a resolution at the UN that proposes to ban "blasphemy" against Islam. It recently added other religions to protected status in order to get approval, but the real purpose is to impose censorship of free speech on anyone who dares tell the truth about the most ruthless sociopolitical system on earth.

President Barack Obama and his leftist minions at the UN did support passage of a resolution in the Human Rights Council that would create an international standard that would restrict some forms of "anti-religious speech." Its title is: "Combating Intolerance, Negative Stereotyping and Stigmatization of, and Discrimination, Incitement to Violence and Violence Against, Persons Based on Religion or Belief." Naturally, Egypt's UN ambassador, at the time that nation was controlled by the Muslim Brotherhood, hailed the resolution and noted that freedom of speech has been "sometimes misused" to insult Islam.[22]

This resolution was passed, and it calls on governments to make a "strong effort to counter religious profiling, which is understood to be the invidious use of religion as a criterion in conducting questions, searches and other law enforcement investigative procedures."

The resolution also urges countries "to take effective measures to ensure that public functionaries in the conduct of their public duties do not discriminate against an individual on the basis of religion or belief."

In addition, the resolution calls for the criminalization of anti-religious speech or actions that may cause "incitement or imminent violence." Is burning a Qur'an an incitement to violence? Probably. Is publishing an anti-Islamic cartoon? Undoubtedly. In short, any activity or statement that might cause Muslims to riot in the streets is considered criminal behavior and must be prohibited by law.

In fact, the OIC has adopted UN language on "hatred" in the International Covenant on Civil and Political Rights (ICCPR), Article

20.2, which says that any advocacy of hatred that "constitutes incitement to discrimination, hostility, or violence shall be prohibited by law." This article was ratified by the United States in 1992, but with the stipulation that it "does not authorize or require legislation or other action by the United States that would restrict the right of free speech and associated protected by the Constitution and the laws of the United States."

Other countries, however, don't have the Bill of Rights that we do. Any action or statement that could be considered "hatred" of Islam can be criminalized in countries that have ratified this resolution.[23]

Muslims are constantly outraged over some perceived insult to their sociopolitical system that they refer to as a religion. They respond against cartoons, pictures, articles, and speeches against Islam by rioting, burning down buildings, and beheading or shooting their critics. There is no concept within Islam of free speech or tolerance for viewpoints of other religions. They believe it is their duty—as commanded by Muhammad— to slaughter the infidels if they "blaspheme" Allah or Islam. There are no officially Islamic nations where a Christian or Jew may freely speak of his religious beliefs in public. In Saudi Arabia Christian guest workers have been arrested and tortured for praying even in private.

David Horowitz and Robert Spencer noted in *Islamophobia: Thought Crime of the Totalitarian Future* that "a religion that recognizes no principle of separation from governmental authority, whose prescriptions dictate what is proper for every aspect of private life is the very definition of totalitarian rule. Where Islam becomes the religion of the state, violations of Islamic doctrine and heretical thoughts are inevitably seen as crimes against the state."[24]

Spencer and Horowitz say that the OIC is currently the largest voting bloc in the UN since the Soviet Union collapsed. In fact, it has managed to get more than two hundred resolutions passed that condemn Israel! And the OIC continues to wage a relentless war against free speech, particularly freedom of religious speech at the UN and around the world.

The leader of the anti–free speech movement in the United States is the Council on American-Islamic Relations (CAIR), a Muslim Brotherhood front group. CAIR was created as a spin-off group of the Hamas front group known as the Islamic Association for Palestine.

Unfortunately, CAIR seems to be winning the battle against free speech in the United States. Whenever someone makes a statement of fact that is critical of Islam or Muslim activities, CAIR is there to condemn the statement and demand that it be censored. CAIR, of course, is a darling of the hard left in America, and leftists in the mainstream media rush to CAIR spokesmen to smear honest critics of Islam and Islamic terrorism. CAIR's goal is to intimidate and discredit people into silence over Islam and, if possible, obtain passage of laws protecting Islam from critics.

"The demagogue Huey Long once said that if totalitarianism came to the United States, it would come calling itself anti-totalitarianism—or tolerance," Spencer and Horowitz wrote. "Islamophobia is the perfect totalitarian doctrine as it is the first step in outlawing freedom of speech— and therefore freedom itself—in the name of religious tolerance."[25]

If the OIC manages to impose its anti–free speech ban on the nations who are members of the UN, it is likely that, at some point in the future, critics of Islam could be tried in the International Criminal Court for blaspheming Islam. The criminalization of criticism of Islam is already occurring in European nations—so this isn't a delusional statement. Islamic critic Oriana Fallaci, for example, faced prosecution in France for daring to criticize Islam. Spencer and Horowitz tell her story: "In the end, Fallaci escaped prosecution only because she fled Europe and took refuge in America, where the Bill of Rights still prevailed. Shortly before she died of cancer in 2006, she predicted that when the case came to trial, she would be found guilty."[26]

The utopian tyrants—including Islamists—inside the UN want to protect Islam by violating our God-given right to freedom of speech as guaranteed in our Bill of Rights.

Clearly, they want to make anti-Islamist statements an Orwellian Thought Crime, punishable by prison time! These brutal haters of freedom are determined to control even our speech.

VIOLATING PARENTAL RIGHTS

The UN utopians not only want to control everyone's speech; they want to control everyone's children too. They hope to accomplish this through American ratification of the UN Convention on the Rights of the Child (UNCRC).

During the first year of the Obama administration, President Obama and UN ambassador Susan Rice expressed support for ratification of this convention. The UNCRC would have had devastating effects on the rights of American parents. Homeschooling leader and lawyer Michael P. Farris explained how dangerous this convention will be if ratified:

> There are two core reasons that Americans should oppose ratification. First, the UNCRC would replace domestic law with international law, effectively overriding most American family statutes. Second, the substance of this treaty places government in a position to overrule parents' decisions in key areas affecting their children. . . .
>
> Virtually all American law governing the parent-child relationship is currently controlled by state statutes, not federal law. But if the treaty is ratified, states will no longer have primary jurisdiction, and Congress will have the duty to implement the international legal standards contained in the convention. Moreover, judges would be able to enforce many of its provisions directly. Both federalism and American self-government would be severely damaged. . . .
>
> [Under UNCRC], parents are supplanted not only by social workers, but also by the whims of their own children. The UNCRC guarantees that children have the legal authority to make their own decisions in areas that have previously been left to the discretion of their parents.

In other words, children could choose their own religion; they would have a UN-guaranteed "right" to leisure; parents could not administer spankings to their children; they would be prohibited from removing their children from sex education classes; and children would have the "right" to abortion services without parental consent or knowledge, and much more.[27]

Children would, in effect, become the property of the United Nations. Parents would simply be caretakers of children and would only have those "rights" that the UN grants them.

This all sounds eerily similar to how children were treated in the utopias of ancient Sparta, Nazi Germany, and the Soviet Union. In those utopian dictatorships, children were possessions of the state, and they were raised to worship and serve the state. Parents were obliged to make sure their children were taught absolute obedience to the central government.

THE INTERGOVERNMENTAL PANEL ON CLIMATE CHANGE (IPCC)

The United Nations' IPCC is a hotbed of Watermelon Marxist ideologues who use their "scientific" standing to push for the end to national sovereignty and for a one-world government.

For anyone wondering about the inner workings of the Intergovernmental Panel on Climate Change, there is a book that thoroughly examines this insidious organization. Investigative journalist Donna Laframboise took two years to research and write *The Delinquent Teenager Who Was Mistaken for the World's Top Climate Expert*. She has done an amazing job of exposing the ongoing corruption inside the IPCC.

While the title may be a bit unwieldy, the content is excellent. The "climate expert" she is referring to, of course, is the United Nations Intergovernmental Panel on Climate Change (IPCC), the golden child of the radical environmentalist movement.

The IPCC is the panel that produces all sorts of reports on "global warming" and "climate change" for the governments of the world. It is considered by radical greens as the fountain of all truth when it comes to all-things-climate. And, of course, the EPA relies on the IPCC for much of its information on climate change. Here we have liars relying on other liars to produce policies that are designed to destroy the free enterprise system.

As Laframboise has documented, the IPCC is a fraud from top to bottom. It is not a scientific body at all, but a gaggle of hard-left green activists who use their immense influence to push for a one-world government and the destruction of thriving capitalistic societies—primarily the United States.

The compliant media consider the information provided by the IPCC to governments around the world to be objective, science-based, and thoroughly researched by IPCC scientists.

None of this is true, as Laframboise discovered in her two-year research project. In her quest for the truth about the IPCC, she discovered some disturbing facts, including these:

- IPCC authors are frequently not reputable scientists at all, but graduate students.

- Sources cited in IPCC documents are frequently from radical green groups, not objective scientists.

- The IPCC routinely censors scientists who do not agree with the current global warming hysteria about greenhouse gases.

- The IPCC is pursuing a leftist, globalist political agenda, not a scientific one.

- The "peer review" process used in determining what articles get published by the IPCC is a charade. Only radical green viewpoints get favorable treatment.

- The IPCC seeks out articles with predetermined conclusions to fit the IPCC agenda.

Is there any chance that the IPCC can be reformed? Not according to Laframboise: "For years we have been told the IPCC is a reputable and professional organization—a grownup in a pinstripe suit. In reality, it's a rule-breaking, not-to-be-trusted, delinquent teenager."[28]

Surely climate activists and climate skeptics can agree on this one thing: The future of the planet is too important to be left in hands such as these. Governments should suspend funding immediately. The IPCC must be disbanded.

Laframboise is right. The IPCC is so hopelessly compromised it can't simply be reformed. It must be shut down—for the safety of sovereign nations and the future of free markets everywhere. Its reports are worthless, its "scientists" are radical Watermelons, and its conclusions are destructive of self-government and capitalism. In short, the IPCC is the perfect UN agency to help impose a one-world government on us.

LEGALIZING HOMOSEXUALITY WORLDWIDE—AND SUPPRESSING OPPOSITION

The current crop of utopians, including those in the Obama White House and at the United Nations, seems to believe that as long as individuals can be involved in any type of sex act, publicly or otherwise, and abort their children, that is all the freedom they need.

The push to legalize same-sex marriage has little to do with the institution of marriage and very much to do with the attack on Judeo-Christianity by the utopian movement. Freedom of speech and freedom of religion must be controlled in a centrally planned utopian society, but sex, as in *Brave New World*, is abundant. For Progressives, sex, drugs, and rock 'n' roll are about all human beings need beyond the basics a collective society is able to produce. With this in mind it becomes evident as to the Progressive agenda on same-sex marriage and special protections for those who are sexually confused.

In June 2010 US ambassador to the United Nations Susan Rice issued a glowing statement on the importance of "Lesbian, Gay, Bisexual and Transgender (LGBT) Pride Month."

Rice detailed the Obama administration's support for the LGBT political agenda, which included extending federal benefits to same-sex couples, and for Secretary of State Hillary Clinton extending benefits for overseas State Department authorities who claim to be homosexuals, cross-dressers, or transsexuals.

According to Rice, LGBT individuals experience persecution around the globe, but she was pleased that the UN had issued a revolution in 2009 that condemned human rights violations based on a person's sexual orientation.

She also indicated that the Obama administration was supportive of the International Gay and Lesbian Human Rights Commission (IGLHRC) becoming a consultative organization to the UN on human rights issues.[29]

In an era when Christians are the single most persecuted group in the world, with tens of thousands killed each year for their faith and millions more driven from their homes, the United States government focuses on supporting "rights" for homosexuals and cross-dressers at the United Nations. At the same time the Obama administration was pushing for these LGBT rights, it refused to label the Boko Haram in Nigeria a terrorist organization even as it targeted and killed thousands of Christians a month.

As Christians were being discriminated against and murdered in Islamic nations, the Obama administration actually moved forward to support at the United Nations blasphemy laws encouraged by those nations. Human rights attorney Brooke Goldstein in 2013 said that the United States must stop supporting blasphemy laws. "The Obama administration co-sponsored with the Muslim Brotherhood and the Organization of Islamic Cooperation, a resolution at the UN that criminalizes the use of the media to condemn Islam. We are supporting the pretext under which Christians are being murdered."[30]

Religious freedom comes second, if at all, to sexual freedom in the current sales pitch for centrally controlled utopian societies. The logic is clear if flawed: if everyone gets to have lots of orgasms and have no children to bother with, they will not notice that all of their other freedoms are repressed.

UTOPIAN NATIONS

The bottom line is that the United Nations is staffed from top to bottom with utopian dreamers who have found the perfect outlet for their totalitarian impulses. These are unelected, unaccountable career bureaucrats who work day and night to create a web of treaties, agreements, and initiatives that are all designed for one purpose: to destroy the sovereignty of individual nations and to establish an all-powerful one-world government ruled by the UN.

There must be constant vigilance to guard true liberty, which has an ever-increasing sphere, rather than the shrinking sphere of personal liberty brought about by collectivist utopian thought.

10

THE FAILURE OF UTOPIAN SYSTEMS

As we have seen throughout previous chapters, utopian thinkers and political leaders, widely separated in time and place, have much in common. The similarities are amazingly uniform and are based on several false premises, mental attitudes, and behaviors they all share.

First, utopians are typically either atheists or they have created for themselves what I would call false, vengeful gods. An example would be Muhammad, who created a vengeful "god" out of his own mental torment. By rejecting God, utopians also reject biblical morality and civilized behavior. Karl Marx, certainly an atheist, worshipped his own intellect and openly rejected God. Mao clearly worshipped power and Marxist political theories, and he too was an atheist. Another atheist, Joseph Stalin, sought to control the lives of hundreds of millions of people according to his version of a "just society." Adolf Hitler, an occultist with his own version of God, sought the perfect Aryan society, a utopia of his design that would last a thousand years. Robespierre wanted "virtue" in society, so he imposed terrorism and used the guillotine on the French people.

To the end of creating their versions of a perfect society, a utopia on earth, these tyrants collectively caused the murders of tens of millions of people and the suffering of hundreds of millions.

These particular central planners were uniformly filled with pride and possessed a ruthless sense of destiny. Their delusions of grandeur propelled them to relentlessly pursue their objectives—despite any obstacles (most of the time these "obstacles" were other human beings who were in disagreement, and they were slaughtered by the millions).

Like the central planners of today, they were amoral and had no concern for the well-being of individuals, as their goal was an overall perfect society in their image. The society model was all-important, not the individual within it. These utopians were willing to kill millions of their fellow human beings in order to achieve these goals. The gulags, concentration camps, and torture chambers were the earmarks of their utopian agendas.

They were, and many others still are today, energized by a demonic hatred of all those who oppose them. Their hatred was and is so complete that they stand ready to kill even their own wives and children to maintain totalitarian power. Joseph Stalin killed his second wife and let his own son die in a Nazi prison camp instead of exchanging a Nazi general, who had been captured by the Soviet Army, for him. Stalin told the Nazi official who had offered the exchange that he wasn't going to trade a general for a low-ranking Russian officer! Mao made his wife abandon their baby during the infamous "Long March" of 1934–1935. Pol Pot's Khmer Rouge killers buried children up to their necks, and then publicly bashed the children's heads until they died.

To achieve their goals utopians must abandon all conscience and become capable of the most unspeakable crimes against their fellow human beings, all to achieve the perfect society. To the mass-murdering utopians of the twentieth century, killing people was inconsequential, as anything was seen as permissible to achieve their utopian goals.

As utopian central planners are today, those in the past were pathological liars. As Paul Johnson noted in *Intellectuals*, both Marx and Engels faked statistics[1] and outright lied in order to justify their irrational theories about capitalism and the perfect world they were supposedly creating. The real world wouldn't conform to their flawed theories, so they imposed their theories on an unwilling world—and with tragic and ongoing consequences.

Utopian tyrants were also disloyal to their closest associates and paranoid about how these associates might work to undermine their totalitarian empires. Stalin, for example, routinely used purges to kill off anyone he thought might threaten his power. Many of those he killed were totally loyal to him, but they became victims of his hatred. During one purge, he wiped out nearly all of the senior officers in the Russian military!

Utopian tyrants—whether simply philosophers or politicians—create their delusional systems of governing with no relationship to reality. Karl Marx, for example, theorized that once the Communist Party overthrew the capitalists, they would set up a dictatorship of the proletariat—which would eventually fade away, and everyone would live in peace and harmony—without the "evil" profit motive and human greed. But his dictatorship never really involved the proletariat in the Soviet Union, in China, or anywhere else. It consisted of the elitists claiming to represent the "proletariat."

Communism, the fruit of Marx and Engels, didn't bring peace or prosperity to the world. It never liberated the workers. It brought misery, slavery, famine, and death to more than 100 million people around the globe during the twentieth century. During that time more people died at the hands of atheist central planners than died in all the wars in all the history of mankind.

IRRATIONAL IDEALISM AND RUTHLESSNESS

Utopian systems always fail because they are based on faulty premises about human nature and the law of supply and demand in a free-market economy.

Utopians think that "profit" and the "profit motive" result in greed, oppression, and economic imperialism. They wrongly believe that if the free enterprise system—any system of barter or trade between individuals—is abolished, everyone will share with their neighbors and we will all live in Mr. Rogers' Neighborhood. The utopian economic goal is perhaps best stated in Karl Marx's famous quote, discussed earlier: "From each according to his ability, to each according to his need."

The phrase "according to his ability" has nothing to do with the profession the individual may desire, but the one the state deems best exploits his ability and usefulness to the state. Likewise, "to each according to his need" indicates that the state, not the individual, chooses food and shelter. Utopianism and liberty are not compatible.

Daniel Hager, a writer for the journal *Ideas on Liberty*, described the failure of utopianism this way:

> Utopianism has a long-running history that includes turning the 1900s into the bloodiest century in human experience. Typically utopian schemes are founded on the premise that individual self-interest must be subjugated for the purported greater public good. As such, utopianism is fit for only a utopia: the term derives from the Greek words ou ("not") and topos ("place") and means simply "not a place."
>
> Real-world social experiments that seek to achieve a communitarian ideal generally lead either to disintegration or repressive rule. Utopia turns into cacotopia, a "bad place." The utopian Soviet Union, according to ample documentation, was a kakistotopia, a "worst place."[2]

Economist and social commentator Thomas Sowell, speaking of the devastating consequences of socialism upon the lives of people around the globe, wrote, "Socialism is a wonderful idea. It is only as a reality that it has been disastrous." He then noted that, among every people and every nation around the world, socialism has inevitably led to hunger in countries that used to export food. In Communist countries, it led to the killing of more civilians during peacetime than Hitler killed in death camps during World War II.

Even though socialism has continually been a failure, Sowell continued, its advocates have explained away the failures as being the fault of particular leaders who weren't implementing it correctly. If only the correct leaders were in power, they would make socialism work, according to socialist "intellectuals."[3]

Neoconservative author and professor Joshua Muravchik titled his 2002 book after a statement made by a German Communist named Moses Hess, who declared in 1846 that it was the goal of socialists to create a "heaven on earth." What they created, however, was a hell on earth, with more than 100 million dead during the twentieth century.[4]

Of course, a few eggs have to be broken to make an omelet—and that's what utopian tyrants Lenin, Stalin, and Hitler did in the march to create utopian states. In the case of these Communist utopian oppressors the broken eggs were tens of millions of human deaths and the suffering of hundreds of millions more.

In tracing the bloody chaos that emerged from seventeenth-century France, Muravchik described the life and philosophy of the French revolutionary François Noël Babeuf, a figure not well known to most. Yet, it was Babeuf who became the brains behind the French Revolution's "Conspiracy of Equals." Babeuf called himself Gracchus, after a Roman tribune who seized so-called surplus land from the rich and gave it to the poor.

Like the twentieth-century Communists, Babeuf wanted to abolish private property and believed that the French Revolution would bring about peace and joy to the French citizens. He wrote, "The sans-culottes [workers] want to be happy, and I don't think it is impossible that within a year, if we carry out our measures aright and act with all necessary prudence, we shall succeed in ensuring general happiness on earth." This is just one example of the incredible delusional thinking of utopians.

According to Babeuf, the Conspiracy of Equals was going to eradicate "once and for all the desire of a man to become richer, or wiser, or more powerful than others." He envisioned his brilliance single-handedly remaking human nature and the aspiration to better oneself.

Babeuf's goal was an all-powerful central government to oversee the lives of French citizens from cradle to grave. He advocated that "the great principle of equality, or universal fraternity, would become the sole religion of the peoples."

The "good intentions" of the first European utopian revolution went terribly wrong, and France was plunged into decades of war, poverty, and death. The terror of the guillotine became the enforcer of "equality."

Babeuf and his fellow conspirators published a "Manifesto of Equals," which stated, "We demand real equality, or Death; that is what we must have. . . . For its sake, we are ready for anything; we are willing to sweep everything away. Let all the arts vanish, if necessary, as long as genuine equality remains for us."[5]

The Conspiracy of Equals demanded that all private property be abolished; all property was to be communal and distributed by a cadre of "superiors." Of course, Babeuf would be among the "superiors." In addition, they demanded universal compulsory labor. They proclaimed that "the fatherland takes control of an individual from his birth till his death." Citizens who were a bad example to the communal society would be banished to prison islands.

Babeuf and his Conspiracy of Equals wanted a society where everyone would eat in common mess halls and where travel was forbidden without the leaders' permission. Entertainment would be banned as well as religious belief. The similarities between Babeuf's perfect society and that of Sparta and Thomas More's Utopia are striking.

In the end, Babeuf had his head removed by the guillotine—a victim of his own revolution. But the socialist agenda he advocated helped inspire two German revolutionaries, named Karl Marx and Friedrich Hegel. After observing the horror of the attempt to create a utopia amid the French Revolution, Karl Marx devised what he thought would be a plan that worked. It did not.

David Horowitz, the former New Left Communist who recanted and is now a fearless fighter against Marxists, socialists, and Islamists, has noted of utopians:

> All the totalitarian movements of modernity have been inspired by the
> same fantasy of a world made right and finally brought into harmony

with itself. This utopian delusion is not restricted to aspiring commissars or religious fanatics. . . .

The desire to make things better is an impulse essential to our humanity. But taken beyond the limits of what is humanly possible, the same hope is transformed into a destructive passion, until it becomes a desire to annihilate whatever stands in the way of the beautiful idea. Nihilism is thus the practical extreme of the radical project.[6]

When such "idealistic" nihilism blossoms, it is inevitable that millions will die.

UTOPIAN SOCIALISM VERSUS THE FREE MARKET

A basic truth that never seems to penetrate the mind of the utopian tyrant is that collectivist (socialist) concepts don't work in the real world to make people happier, freer, or more prosperous, regardless of how many times they are tried and fail.

Rather than redistribute wealth, as promised by Marx and others, socialism actually distributes poverty. Collectivism kills incentives and thus the pooling of wealth that is needed for invention.

Under socialism, the rich are diminished and the poor continue to be poor without freedom of thought or initiative to climb out of poverty. In the more extreme cases, the socialist system becomes a police state, and terror becomes a way of life.

Milton Friedman, one of the foremost conservative economists, believed that economic arrangements play a dual role in the promotion of a free society. Economic freedom is an end in itself, and it is indispensable in guaranteeing political freedom.[7]

Friedman noted that competitive capitalism promotes political freedom because it separates economic power from political power.[8] He concluded that free enterprise is a necessary condition for political freedom, and that one can't exist without the other. A central government that controls an economy, whether feudal or Marxist, in effect controls the individual and diminishes his individual freedom.

As Friedrich Hayek reminds us in *The Road to Serfdom*, "We have progressively abandoned that freedom in economic affairs without which personal and political freedom has never existed in the past. Although we had been warned by some of the greatest political thinkers of the nineteenth century, by Tocqueville and Lord Acton, that socialism means slavery, we have steadily moved in the direction of socialism."[9]

Friedman pointed out that there are only two ways of coordinating the economic activities of millions of people: (1) through central planning, using coercion to enforce; and (2) through voluntary exchange or free enterprise exchange, which is most often referred to as "competitive capitalism."[10]

Friedman states that an example in the free enterprise exchange model would be each household using the resources it controls to create goods and services it can then use to exchange for others in the marketplace. In a free market, people freely produce goods and services and others freely pay for these goods and services.[11]

The government's role in a competitive free society is to maintain law and order, prevent coercion of one individual by another, and enforce contracts voluntarily entered into by parties. The system works well if the government does not interfere between the producer of value and the purchaser. It's a self-sustaining system that transacts between tens of millions of individuals each day in the relatively free society in the United States.

The free market, says Friedman, gives people what they want instead of what a particular group, or a central planner, believes they need. He noted: "Underlying most arguments against the free market is a lack of belief in freedom itself."[12]

The government is to be an umpire, not a player, in the free marketplace. It determines the rules of the game in a political free society, and the players go by the rules. If those selling the value of their labors or capital don't abide by those rules, they are either punished through government actions or by the consumers of their products. Those that overcharge on a level playing field that is not monopolistic or produce inferior products soon find their customers going elsewhere.

However, in a communistic central planning system, such as that which once existed in the Soviet Union, the government becomes both the business owner and the producer of the goods and services. No private businesses existed in the Soviet Union, and the result was virtually no choice between products, and poor quality. In some socialist nations a modified socialist system may control what a business owner can produce, the quantities to produce, and even the prices. Individuals find their choices limited or nonexistent. The most current example of that model is Venezuela, where individuals stand in line to get whatever toilet paper may be available that day.

Unfortunately, government interference with the marketplace that provides the best value is not limited to outright Communist or socialist nations; there is also totalitarian democracy. This occurs when elected officials create bureaucracies that can never be unseated and rule over the people of a nation like despots. The best American examples of this are the EPA (Environmental Protection Agency), the Food and Drug Administration (FDA), and the Department of Health and Human Services (HHS), which all now maintain SWAT teams to enforce their regulations that were never approved by Congress in the first place. The three monsters not mentioned in this list are the tax-money eaters that are forcing millions of Americans to receive inferior medical care: Medicare, Medicaid, and Obamacare.

THE WORLDWIDE FAILURE OF COMMUNISM, SOCIALISM, AND PROGRESSIVISM

Utopian tyrants never seem to learn from the real-life failures of their so-called solutions for the problems of mankind. Whenever one collectivist system fails, their reaction isn't to reconsider their worldview, but to try the same insanity somewhere else. It's to claim that more money, time, or centralized control is needed to "make it work this time." The Soviet Communists had seventy years to "perfect" Communism, and there it wound up in the dump heap of history.

The nations making up the European Union finally had to face up to the reality of many of their failed socialist policies after World War II. Countless nations, facing financial and social meltdowns because their welfare states were collapsing, were forced to sell off all the state enterprises that they had either purchased or confiscated in the past to raise money for promised services. Margaret Thatcher summed up the problem in Europe thus: "Socialist governments traditionally do make a financial mess. They always run out of other people's money."[13]

European Parliament member Daniel Hannan has watched this ongoing collapse of European socialism, and he's been warning America not to follow in Europe's foolishness. In his *The New Road to Serfdom*, in a chapter titled "Don't Copy Europe," Hannan wrote, "Europeanization is incompatible with the vision of the founders and the spirit of the republic. Americans are embracing all the things their ancestors were so keen to get away from: high taxes, unelected lawmakers, pettifogging rules."[14]

Hannan warns America against Europeanizing its welfare system, its health care system, its immigration system, its culture, and more. To do so will result in the destruction of the Republic and the engine of progress known as the free enterprise system.

Europe is experiencing what can clearly be observed as a social collapse as a result of its long-term experiment with socialism, multiculturalism, and a rejection of state sovereignty under the EU. Patriotism has died in most nations in Europe, and social relationships between citizens are falling as the birthrate declines.

As European nations try desperately to dig out from their failed welfare state experiments, whom do they turn to for bailouts? Why, the "wicked" United States, with its still-functioning free enterprise system (at least, what's left of it). The United States has apparently become the ATM for the world's socialists, who continually fail to achieve economic progress in their welfare states.

In late 2011, for example, the Federal Reserve engaged in a bailout of the European Central Bank (ECB) that went largely unreported in the United States. The gimmick was called a "temporary U.S. dollar liquidity swap arrangement." The Fed swapped billions of

American dollars for euros! In effect, the Federal Reserve—without legal authority—indirectly bailed out the profligate socialist nations of Europe through this "liquidity swap."[15]

This illegal bailout isn't the only covert operation engineered to bail out failed socialist policies in Europe. In late 2011, President Obama promised that the United States "stands ready to do its part" in bailing out Europe. This was done through the International Monetary Fund (IMF) by donating an additional $100 billion of American taxpayer dollars. Currently, the United States pays 17 percent of the IMF's budget, which allows it to dole money out to failing socialist nations around the globe.

As conservative author Phyllis Schlafly noted:

> We the people who end up paying for IMF donations only found out after the fact, because of our federal courts enforcing Freedom of Information Act requests and a congressionally authorized audit of the Fed, that trillions of dollars of emergency loans have already been given to foreign banks. In addition, the Fed simply printed $442.7 billion out of thin air to buy back flaky mortgage-backed securities from overseas institutions that were heavily invested in U.S. housing.
>
> Obama has no business using U.S. taxpayers' dollars, through the IMF, the Fed or any other secretive agency to bail out foreign banks.[16]

The United States has poured billions of dollars into failed experiments of social and economic engineering not only overseas but in the United States as well. The Obama administration's attempts at "green" energy that yet lacked the technical know-how cost taxpayers billions of dollars, with the Solyndra affair being just one example.[17] Several new energy-source enterprises also lost huge amounts of tax dollars, including First Solar, Ener1, and Fisker Automotive.

CONTRAST NORTH KOREA WITH SOUTH KOREA

In late 2012 *Wall Street Journal* reporter Melanie Kirkpatrick published a sobering book on North Korea and the horrific quality of life that

Koreans suffer, under one of the most brutal central planning totalitarian governments on the planet. Kirkpatrick's book, *Escape from North Korea: The Untold Story of Asia's Underground Railroad*, tells the story of North Koreans who have risked their lives to escape from the living hell created by the Communist system that rules that nation. She stated in her introduction:

> This is a book about personal courage and the quest for liberty. These qualities are embodied in the North Koreans who dare to escape from their slave-state of a nation to the neighboring, but unwelcoming, country of China. They are embodied, too, in Christian missionaries and other humanitarian workers who help the North Korean runaways flee China and reach sanctuary in free countries. They travel along a secret route known as the new Underground Railroad.[18]

In Kirkpatrick's account of life in the North Korean socialist paradise (sarcasm intended), foreigners and foreign goods are kept out of North Korea. Its citizens may not travel without permission, and their education and employment are chosen by the government. There is no selection of products, except, of course, for the ruling elite, as was the case in Thomas More's *Utopia* and rings so true in all of these centrally planned utopias.

Since 2009, when one of many famines swept through North Korea because of its socialist agricultural policies, only 128 North Koreans are known to have escaped and gotten as far as America. Tragically, since the end of the Korean War in 1953, only 25,000 North Koreans have managed to escape from their hellish existence; tens of thousands more have died trying.

The North Korean government, says Kirkpatrick, is "so short of electricity that much of the country is switched off in the early evening."

While North Koreans experience a daily existence of misery, starvation, torture, and death, the totalitarian central planners who run this Communist tyranny began in 2012 to force schoolchildren and the elderly to construct huge monuments in honor of their leaders.

The enslaved in Hoeryong city, for example, were compelled to build a "student palace for idolization" of the Communist dictators. In addition, North Koreans have been forced to construct more than two thousand murals and statues to sing the praises of their slave masters.

Kindergarten children in Hoeryong were made to travel to a construction site to build an elaborate mosaic as a show of loyalty to Kim Jong II, the criminal mastermind who ruled over the centrally planned criminal enterprise, in which one of the largest industries is the counterfeiting of American and European currencies.[19]

While all of this building is going on, an estimated 3 million North Koreans are starving and are desperately in need of food aid.[20]

At the same time North Korea's citizens are routinely starved to death, tortured, or forced to build monuments to their slave masters, South Korea enjoys robust economic growth, with surpluses of foods and manufactured goods it sells around the world.

The Heritage Foundation, a conservative think tank in Washington, DC, published an analysis of South Korea's economic and social freedom in 2012. According to their analysis:

> South Korea is one of Asia's liveliest democracies and the world's 15th largest economy. It has experienced decades of impressive economic growth since the early 1960s and has sophisticated electronics, telecommunications, automobile, and shipbuilding industries. Having implemented economic reforms, South Korea was not hurt as severely by the 1997–1998 Asian financial crisis as many of its neighbors. President Lee Myung-bak took office in 2008 with a large electoral majority, vowing further economic liberalization through freer trade, deregulation, and privatization of major industries.[21]

South Korea's per capita income is $29,936 and its gross domestic product stands at $1.5 trillion.

And what of North Korea's economic well-being? According to Heritage:

> North Korea's dictatorial leadership remains unwilling to open or restructure its economy. It has experimented with a few market

reforms but mainly adheres to the system of state command and control that has kept the country and its people in near bankruptcy for decades. The Communist Party controls every aspect of economic activity. The impoverished population is heavily dependent on food rations and government subsidies in housing. Deprivation is widespread. In recent years, the government has phased out or clamped down on existing private markets, reducing the already very limited free-market experimentation.

The North Korean economy has contracted for two consecutive years, with a negative growth rate of 0.5 percent in 2010 estimated after a 0.9 percent decline in 2009. The Hermit Kingdom may be attempting to allow limited foreign direct investment, but the dominant military establishment and ongoing leadership change make any significant near-term change unlikely. Normal foreign trade is minimal, with China and South Korea being the most important trading partners.[22]

In addition, what food aid free governments do provide to North Korea is seized by military and government officials, who demand bribes before distributing food to starving North Koreans.

The CIA *World Factbook* on North Korea states that the per capita income in that centrally planned collectivist nation is just $1,800 (based on 2011 estimates). Contrast that to the South Korea per capita income of $29,936 per year. The differences are staggering.[23]

North Korea is now considered the least free country on the planet that is not Islamic. Its citizens live in fear, starvation, and poverty. Citizens living in South Korea's free enterprise environment are prosperous and have a growing economy and individual liberty. Which system works better for its citizens, collectivism or free enterprise? The answer is obvious.

RONALD REAGAN REMINDS US OF OUR RENDEZVOUS WITH DESTINY
In a speech delivered in March 1984, President Ronald Reagan reminded his listeners of the hope that our political and economic systems offer to America and to the world.

He noted:

> We offer an optimistic society. More than 200 years after the patriots fired that first shot heard 'round the world, one revolutionary idea still burns in the hearts of men and women everywhere: A society where man is not beholden to government; government is beholden to man. The difference between the path toward greater freedom or bigger government is the difference between success and failure; between opportunity and coercion; between faith in a glorious future and fear of mediocrity and despair; between respecting people as adults, each with a spark of greatness, and treating them as helpless children to be forever dependent; between a drab, materialistic world where Big Brother rules by promises to special interest groups, and a world of adventure where everyday people set their sights on impossible dreams, distant stars, and the Kingdom of God. We have the true message of hope for America.[24]

Speaking of the destructive chaos that Jimmy Carter had created during the four years of his dismal occupation of the White House, President Reagan stated:

> The spendthrifts who mangled America with the nightmare of double-digit inflation, record interest rates, unfair tax increases, too much regulation, credit controls, farm embargoes, gas lines, no-growth at home, weakness abroad, and phony excuses about "malaise" are the last people who should be giving sermonettes about fairness and compassion.
>
> Their failures were not caused by erratic weather patterns, unusual rotations of the moon, or by the personality of my predecessor. They were caused by misguided policies and misunderstanding human nature. Believe me, you cannot create a desert, hand a person a cup of water, and call that compassion. You cannot pour billions of dollars into make-work jobs while destroying the economy that supports them and call that opportunity. And you cannot build up years of dependence on government and dare call that hope.[25]

The contrast between Reagan's policies and those of his failed predecessor Jimmy Carter were stark. They are reminders of the difference between free markets/limited government and the utopian concepts of equal outcome promoted by the Carter administration.

President Carter had quickly led the United States into double-digit inflation, gasoline rationing, and foreign policy failures of immense proportions. It was Carter's policies that led to the expulsion of the pro-Western shah of Iran and the rise of the Islamic mullahs in Iran. Thanks to Carter's utopian foreign policies of "we are all one big, happy family," the world today faces some very complex problems with Iran that would not exist had the secular-leaning government not been overthrown in favor of Islamic extremists.

President Reagan believed in America as a shining light on the hill and in the superior nature of its limited constitutional government and its free enterprise system. Holding those beliefs as his standard, he was able to lead America out of Carter's self-proclaimed "malaise" and weakness.

Reagan's vision for America is one that the utopian tyrants reject. One vision leads to freedom and prosperity; the other, to economic disaster, famine, and slavery.

THE FOUNDING FATHERS' REALISTIC VIEW

The Founders of the United States realized that man was imperfect and prone toward sin and the love of power. For this reason they designed a system of government with checks and balances to protect the American people from those who might want to establish despotism.

In his farewell address to Congress, President George Washington observed:

> It is important . . . that the habits of thinking in a free Country should inspire caution in those entrusted with its administration, to confine themselves within their respective Constitutional spheres; avoiding in the exercise of the powers of one department to encroach upon another. The spirit of encroachment tends to consolidate the powers

of all the departments in one, and thus to create whatever the form of government, a real despotism. A just estimate of that love of power, and proneness to abuse it, which predominates in the human heart is sufficient to satisfy us of the truth of this position.

The necessity of reciprocal checks in the exercise of political power; by dividing and distributing it into different depositories, and constituting each the Guardian of the Public Weal against invasions by the others, has been evinced by experiments ancient and modern, some of them in our country and under our own eyes. To preserve them must be as necessary as to institute them.

If in the opinion of the People, the distribution or modification of the Constitutional powers be in any particular wrong, let it be corrected by an amendment in the way which the Constitution designates. But let there be no change by usurpation; for though this, in one instance, may be the instrument of good, it is the customary weapon by which free governments are destroyed. The precedent must always greatly overbalance in permanent evil any partial or transient benefit which the use can at any time yield.[26]

These were clearly statements warning of the centralization of power and of central planning. Washington clearly understood that people can't be trusted with unrestrained political power because of a propensity to abuse it. Likewise, President Washington warned that the nature of our government shouldn't be altered by usurpation, which President Obama routinely does through executive orders as that office leans more and more toward the imperial.

In the next chapter, we'll go into greater detail about the vision our Founding Fathers had for creating the most unique political system to ever exist—and one we must preserve.

11

THE VISION OF THE FOUNDING FATHERS

Our nation's Founders were the antiutopians of their time. They were breaking free from authoritarian control of the British Parliament and the King of England and were embarking on the creation of a unique Republican form of government. They purposed in their hearts and minds to create a new form of government that would restrict the power of the federal government, while providing a framework for ordered freedom for the separate states and for individuals.

From their studies of the works of John Locke and other pro-freedom philosophers who had defended the concept of personal liberty, freedom of conscience, and freedom of religion, their concept of a new nation arose. Personal liberty was an upmost goal.

Overwhelmingly Christian, the Founders held that mankind were collectively sinners and that they had to create a governmental system of checks and balances to keep government leaders from acquiring a single source of central control. They wanted to diffuse federal power to protect liberty for everyone.

Virtually all of the Founders were Christians, and a few who worked directly on the Declaration of Independence and Constitution were pastors who believed that they had a purpose in creating this new system of government. They sensed what they called Divine Providence in shaping the American Republic, and they believed they had to be faithful to that calling.

Founder James Madison put it well: "We have staked the whole future of American civilization, not upon the power of government, far from it. We have staked the future of all of our political institutions upon the capacity of mankind for self-government; upon the capacity of each and all of us to govern ourselves, to control ourselves, to sustain ourselves according to the Ten Commandments of God."[1]

In their wisdom, the Founders developed a system that consisted of three separate branches of government—each with checks and balances. Each branch could hold the other two branches accountable, although Congress, which is the House of the people, held special powers over the other two branches. The people, of course, had close contact with and could regularly vote out of office those in Congress who were deemed power hungry, incompetent, corrupt, or inept.

In the Constitution as originally ratified, a system was created wherein the senators represented the states and were appointed by state legislatures. The House was to represent the interests of the people within the states. Unfortunately, in 1913, under the reign of "progressive" Woodrow Wilson, the Seventeenth Amendment changed the Senate from the original intent of the Founders and made it a body that is directly elected, thus mostly eliminating the senators' drive to represent their respective state governments. Senators would now be less concerned over state issues and more concerned with being reelected. It was a major break with what the Founders envisioned for their Republic, and of course the process of limiting the rights of the various states began immediately.

The Founders knew about the history of European tyrannies, and they wanted to set up a system of government that would make it difficult for a leader, elected or otherwise, to gather all power in the executive branch. What they feared most of all was for America to descend into despotism similar to the monarchies of Europe.

As Thomas Jefferson so eloquently stated in the "Kentucky

Resolutions" of 1798, "In questions of power then, let no more be heard of confidence in man, but bind him down from mischief by the chains of the constitution."[2]

James Madison, who is considered the chief architect of the US Constitution, wrote twenty-nine of the eight-five *Federalist Papers* that argued in favor of ratifying the Constitution. In the fifty-first paper, he noted that "if men were angels, no government would be necessary. If angels were to govern men, neither external nor internal controls on government would be necessary. In framing a government which is to be administered by men over men, the great difficulty lies in this: you must first enable the government to control the governed; and in the next place oblige it to control itself. A dependence on the people is, no doubt, the primary control on the government; but experience has taught mankind the necessity of auxiliary precautions."

This is precisely the reason the Founders put so many checks and balances into the Constitution. This is also the reason Progressives, Marxists, and liberals have worked so diligently to turn the Constitution into a "living document" that can be changed to assign ever more power to a central government. There exist too many restrictions in the Constitution as originally created for a despot to create an all-powerful central regime. If there weren't, the central planners and collectivists would eliminate the Senate and create a single chamber to allow the major cities and their welfare recipients to control the entire Congress. Constant diligence must be exercised to counter this desire.

THE CALL FOR INDEPENDENCE

In April 1776 William Henry Drayton, the chief justice of South Carolina, urged his fellow American patriots to pursue independence from England as a divine calling. He noted:

> I think it my duty to declare, in the awful seat of justice, and before Almighty God, that in my opinion, the Americans can have no safety, but by divine favor, their own virtues, and their being so prudent, as not to leave it in the power of British rulers to injure them. Indeed,

the ruinous and deadly injuries received on our side, and the jealousies entertained, and which in the nature of things must daily increase against us, on the other, demonstrate to a mind the least given to reflection, that true reconcilement can never exist between Great Britain and America the latter being subject to the former. . . .

The Almighty created America to be independent of Great Britain: let us beware of the impiety of being backward to act as instruments in the Almighty hand, now extended to accomplish his purpose, and by the completion of which, alone, America, in the nature of human affairs, can be secure against the crafty and insidious designs of her enemies, who think her favor and prosperity already by far too great. In a word, our piety and political safety are so blended, that to refuse our labor in this divine work, is to refuse to be a great, a free, a pious and a happy people.[3]

Drayton was prophetic in his belief that God was calling upon America to be free of British oppression. He envisioned that the patriots who were gathering to discuss independence from England were going to create an entirely new—and unique—system of government, unlike anything ever seen before in world history: one that would stand by biblical principles.

THE DECLARATION OF INDEPENDENCE

In June 1776 the Second Continental Congress voted to appoint five men to write the Declaration of Independence from England. The five men chosen were: Thomas Jefferson, John Adams, Benjamin Franklin, Roger Sherman, and Robert Livingston.

John Adams dominated the committee and assigned Thomas Jefferson to write up the Declaration. The wording of the Declaration was approved on July 2; the Congress delegates then voted to approve it on July 4, 1776. On July 8 the Declaration was read aloud outside of Independence Hall in Philadelphia. And on August 2, 1776, the fifty-six members of the Continental Congress signed the document.

The Declaration begins with these powerful words:

The unanimous Declaration of the thirteen united States of America,

When in the Course of human events, it becomes necessary for one people to dissolve the political bands which have connected them with another, and to assume among the powers of the earth, the separate and equal station to which the Laws of Nature and of Nature's God entitle them, a decent respect to the opinions of mankind requires that they should declare the causes which impel them to the separation.

We hold these truths to be self-evident, that all men are created equal, that they are endowed by their Creator with certain unalienable Rights, that among these are Life, Liberty and the Pursuit of Happiness.

—That to secure these rights, Governments are instituted among Men, deriving their just powers from the consent of the governed, — That whenever any Form of Government becomes destructive of these ends, it is the Right of the People to alter or to abolish it, and to institute new Government, laying its foundation on such principles, and organizing its powers in such form, as to them shall seem most likely to effect their Safety and Happiness. Prudence, indeed will dictate that Governments long established should not be changed for light and transient causes; and accordingly all experience hath shewn, that mankind are more disposed to suffer, while evils are sufferable, than to right themselves by abolishing the forms to which they are accustomed.

But when a long train of abuses and usurpations, pursuing invariably the same Object evinces a design to reduce them under absolute Despotism, it is their right, it is their duty, to throw off such Government, and to provide new Guards for their future Security.

Notice the key elements of these first few paragraphs of this Declaration of Freedom:

1. Men are entitled by the Laws of Nature and Nature's God to be free.

2. They have the God-given rights of life, liberty, and the pursuit of happiness.

3. Governments are created by men to protect these God-ordained rights from tyrants.

4. Whenever a government becomes despotic and destroys these rights, it is the absolute right of the people to alter or abolish a tyrannical government in order to restore those rights.

5. A government should not be overthrown for "light and transient causes."

After describing the right of Americans to be free from tyranny, the Declaration details the abuses of the King of England against the American colonists. It ends with these words:

We, therefore, the Representatives of the united States of America, in General Congress Assembled, appealing to the Supreme Judge of the world for the rectitude of our intentions, do, in the Name, and by the Authority of the good People of these Colonies, solemnly publish and declare, That these United Colonies are, and of Right ought to be Free and Independent States; that they are Absolved from all Allegiance to the British Crown, and that all political connection between them and the State of Great Britain, is and ought to be totally dissolved; and that as Free and Independent States, they have full Power to levy War, conclude Peace, contract Alliances, establish Commerce, and to do all other Acts and Things which Independent States may of right do.

And for the support of this Declaration, with a firm reliance on the protection of divine Providence, we mutually pledge to each other our Lives, our Fortunes and our sacred Honor.

On July 3, the day before the Declaration was approved, John Adams wrote to his wife Abigail and told her, "I am apt to believe that it will be celebrated by succeeding generations as the great anniversary Festival. It ought to be commemorated, as the day of deliverance, by solemn acts of devotion to God Almighty."[4]

On August 2, 1776, the day the parchment copy of the Declaration of Independence was signed, Samuel Adams declared, "We have this day restored the Sovereign to Whom All men ought to be obedient. He reigns in heaven and from the rising to the setting of the sun, let His kingdom come."

On the celebration of the 150th anniversary of the signing of the Declaration of Independence on July 5, 1926, President Calvin Coolidge delivered an amazing speech entitled "The Inspiration of the Declaration." In it, Coolidge described America's religious heritage that eventually led to the creation of the Declaration, complete with its acknowledgment that our rights come from God, not from government. He observed:

> It was not because it was proposed to establish a new nation, but because it was proposed to establish a nation on new principles, that July 4, 1776, has come to be regarded as one of the greatest days in history. Great ideas do not burst upon the world unannounced. They are reached by a gradual development over a length of time usually proportionate to their importance. This is especially true of the principles laid down in the Declaration of Independence.
>
> Three very definite propositions were set out in its preamble regarding the nature of mankind and therefore of government. These were the doctrine that all men are created equal, that they are endowed with certain inalienable rights, and that therefore the source of the just powers of government must be derived from the consent of the governed. . . .
>
> No one can examine this record and escape the conclusion that in the great outline of its principles the Declaration was the result of the religious teachings of the preceding period. The profound philosophy which Jonathan Edwards applied to theology, the popular preaching of George Whitefield, had aroused the thought and stirred the people of the Colonies in preparation for this great event. No doubt the speculations which had been going on in England, and

especially on the Continent, lent their influence to the general sentiment of the times. . . .

About the Declaration there is a finality that is exceedingly restful. It is often asserted that the world has made a great deal of progress since 1776, that we have had new thoughts and new experiences which have given us a great advance over the people of that day, and that we may therefore very well discard their conclusions for something more modern. But that reasoning cannot be applied to this great charter. If all men are created equal, that is final. If they are endowed with inalienable rights, that is final. If governments derive their just powers from the consent of the governed, that is final. No advance, no progress can be made beyond these propositions.[5]

In this statement, Coolidge was responding to those in America who were claiming that the Declaration and the Constitution were outdated for a modern society and needed to be updated or changed. These were the so-called Progressives of the 1920s, almost all followers of Karl Marx who were pushing for a greatly expanded federal government at the expense of states' rights and individual liberty. Their plans were at least partially achieved by the elections of Woodrow Wilson and Franklin Roosevelt. By this time the anarchists, who also declared themselves as Progressives, were discredited by the assassination of President McKinley in 1901.

Coolidge clearly explained that the Declaration's principles were solid and inviolable. Government is not God; human rights come from heaven; and governments are to protect those God-given rights. Progressives, of course, believed then and still believe today that God doesn't exist or is not relevant and that central government is the entity that creates, gives, or takes away "rights." In short, Progressives do not believe that personal liberty is granted by the Divine, and therefore the degree of liberty can be directly controlled by those who are deemed "progressive" enough to understand human need.

Coolidge believed that America had a God-ordained destiny to fulfill. While serving as vice president under President Warren G.

Harding, he delivered a Memorial Day speech on May 31, 1931, in which he noted:

> If there be a destiny, it is of no avail to us unless we work with it. The ways of Providence will be of no advantage to us unless we proceed in the same direction. If we perceive a destiny in America, if we believe that Providence has been the guide, our own success, our own salvation require that we should act and serve in harmony and obedience . . .
>
> They [the Founding Fathers] were intent upon establishing a Christian commonwealth in accordance with the principle of self-government. They were an inspired body of men. It has been said that God sifted the nations that He might send choice grain into the wilderness. . . . Who can fail to see in it the hand of destiny? Who can doubt that it has been guided by a Divine Providence?[6]

PLEDGING THEIR LIVES, FORTUNES, AND SACRED HONOR

The courageous men who signed the Declaration of Independence knew that they were possibly signing their own death warrants. The King of England and his officials in the colonies considered this an act of treason punishable by death.

What happened to these brave men—who were willing to risk everything to give us the freedoms we have today?

In 1848, B. J. Lossing published *Biographical Sketches of the Signers of the Declaration of American Independence*. In it he revealed that, although most of the Declaration's signatories survived the war and went on to live productive lives, a great number of them lost everything—including their wives and children.

Richard Stockton of New Jersey, for example, was a wealthy landowner who was elected to the Continental Congress in 1776. Stockton had to flee from his estate with his wife and children to avoid being captured by the British, but he was betrayed by a British loyalist. According to Lossing:

He remained a prisoner for some time, and, on account of his position as one of the signers of the Declaration of Independence, he was treated with great severity. The hardships he endured shattered his constitution, and when he found himself almost a beggar, through the vandalism of the British in destroying his estate, and by the depreciation of the continental paper currency, he was seized with a despondency from which he never recovered. A cancer in his neck also hurried him toward the grave, and he died on the twenty-eighth of February, 1781, in the fifty-first year of his age.[7]

John Hart of New Jersey also suffered great loss during the War for Independence.

The signers of the Declaration everywhere were marked for vengeance, and when the enemy made their conquering descent upon New Jersey, Mr. Hart's estate was among the first to feel the effects of the desolating inroad. The blight fell, not only upon his fortune, but upon his person, and he did not live to see the sunlight of Peace and Independence gladden the face of his country. He died in the year 1780 (the gloomiest period of the War of Independence), full of years and deserved honors.[8]

After adding his signature to the Declaration, Joseph Hewes of North Carolina had to return home swiftly to protect his life's work from being destroyed by the British. His health failed rapidly and he died eleven days after resigning his seat in the Continental Congress. He was only fifty. "He was the first and only one of all the signers of the Declaration, who died at the seat of Government, while attending to public duty," Lossing wrote. "His remains were followed to the grave by Congress in a body, and a large concourse of the citizens of Philadelphia."[9]

Arthur Middleton of South Carolina lost his property and his family was scattered. He was eventually taken prisoner by the British and was sent to a prison in Florida. In time, he was exchanged for a British prisoner and was later elected to Congress.

According to Lossing: "By exposure he contracted an intermittent fever, which he neglected until it was too late to check its ravages upon his constitution. He died on the first day of January, 1788. He left his wife a widow with eight children." Fortunately, his wife lived until 1814, and "had the satisfaction of seeing her offspring among the honored of the land."[10]

These men were willing to lose everything to help create a new nation based on the belief that God is the author of human freedom. Our inalienable rights don't come from an all-powerful central government. They are God-given, and our system of government was created to protect those rights from tyrants—including one of our recent presidents.

THE CONSTITUTIONAL CONVENTION

After gaining independence from Britain in a hard-fought war and the failure of the original pact, the Articles of Confederation, the Founders gathered in Philadelphia in May 1787 and labored through September to craft a new Constitution for the United States of America.

The first order of business was choosing George Washington to preside over the Constitutional Convention. Another order of business was to institute three basic rules for the Convention: voting was to be by state, each with one vote; proper decorum was to be maintained; and the proceedings were to be secret.

Free and open discussion was encouraged by shifting back and forth during the Convention between a "Committee of the Whole" and the Convention itself. Delegates could freely debate the issues in the committee and then vote on the proposals during the Convention portion of the meeting.

James Madison took copious notes of the convention, which were not published until 1840. Madison had also worked on a proposal for the national government, which was to consist of separate branches of government: executive, legislative, and judicial.[11]

After months of debate and drafts of the Constitution, it was sent to the states for ratification. In submitting the Constitution to the states, George Washington sent along a letter with it. It read:

September 17, 1787

Sir: We have now the honor to submit to the consideration of the United States in Congress assembled, that Constitution which has appeared to us the most advisable. The friends of our country have long seen and desired, that the power of making war, peace and treaties, that of levying money and regulating commerce, and the correspondent executive and judicial authorities should be fully and effectually vested in the general government of the Union: but the impropriety of delegating such extensive trust to one body of men is evident— Hence results the necessity of a different organization.

It is obviously impracticable in the federal government of these States, to secure all rights of independent sovereignty to each, and yet provide for the interest and safety of all— Individuals entering into society, must give up a share of liberty to preserve the rest. The magnitude of the sacrifice must depend as well on situation and circumstance, as on the object to be obtained. It is at all times difficult to draw with precision the line between those rights which must be surrendered, and those which may be reserved; and on the present occasion this difficulty was increased by a difference among the several States as to their situation, extent, habits, and particular interests.

In all our deliberations on this subject we kept steadily in our view, that which appears to us the greatest interest of every true American, the consolidation of our Union, in which is involved our prosperity, felicity, safety, perhaps our national existence. This important consideration, seriously and deeply impressed on our minds, led each State in the Convention to be less rigid on points of inferior magnitude, than might have been otherwise expected; and thus the Constitution, which we now present, is the result of a spirit of amity, and of that mutual deference and concession which the peculiarity of our political situation rendered indispensable.

That it will meet the full and entire approbation of every State is not perhaps to be expected; but each will doubtless consider, that had her interests been alone consulted, the consequences might have been particularly disagreeable or injurious to others; that it is liable to as few exceptions as could reasonably have been expected, we hope and believe; that it may promote the lasting welfare of that country so dear to us all, and secure her freedom and happiness, is our most ardent wish.

With great respect, We have the honor to be, Sir, Your Excellency's most Obedient and humble Servants,

George Washington, President By unanimous Order of the Convention.[12]

During the time when the states were considering ratifying the Constitution, Alexander Hamilton, James Madison, and John Jay wrote a series of essays under the pen name "Publius" to explain the purposes of the Constitution and its design to protect state sovereignty and human freedom. The series became known as the Federalist Papers.

In 1788 New Hampshire became the last state to ratify the Constitution, and the new Congress set a date for choosing presidential electors and the opening session of the Congress.[13]

In 1791 a Bill of Rights was also added to the Constitution. These amendments clearly spell out restrictions on the federal government's powers and on the rights of states and individuals. The First Amendment, for example, protects a free press, free speech, and religious liberty.

James Madison pointed out in Federalist No. 45, that "the powers delegated by the proposed Constitution to the federal government are few and defined. Those which are to remain in the state governments are numerous and indefinite."

Justice Joseph Story, who spent nearly twenty-five years on the US Supreme Court, wrote a detailed analysis of the Constitutional Convention in 1840. His *Familiar Exposition of the Constitution* is a thorough examination of the Constitution and its design to restrict federal power while maximizing human freedom.

In Story's section on the importance of the separation of powers, he wrote:

The first thing, that strikes us, upon the slightest survey of the national Constitution, is, that its structure contains a fundamental separation of the three great departments of government, the legislative, the executive, and the judicial. The existence of all these departments has always been found indispensable to due energy and stability in a government. Their separation has always been found equally indispensable, for the preservation of public liberty and private rights. Whenever they are all vested in one person or body of men, the government is in fact a despotism, by whatever name it may be called, whether a monarchy, or an aristocracy, or a democracy.[14]

INTERPRETING THE CONSTITUTION

Joseph Story explained in clear language how judges are to interpret the Constitution:

> It is to be interpreted, as all other solemn instruments are, by endeavoring to ascertain the true sense and meaning of all the terms; and we are neither to narrow them, nor to enlarge them, by straining them from their just and natural import, for the purpose of adding to, or diminishing its powers, or bending them to any favorite theory or dogma of party. It is the language of the people, to be judged of according to common sense, and not by mere theoretical reasoning. It is not an instrument for the mere private interpretation of any particular men. The people have established it and spoken their will; and their will, thus promulgated, is to be obeyed as the supreme law. Every department of the Government must, of course, in the first instance, in the exercise of its own powers and duties, necessarily construe the instrument. But, if the case admits of judicial cognizance, every citizen has a right to contest the validity of that construction before the proper judicial tribunal; and to bring it to the test of the Constitution. And, if the case is not capable of judicial redress, still the people may, through the acknowledged means of new elections, or proposed amendments, check any usurpation of authority, whether wanton, or unintentional, and thus relieve themselves from any grievances of a political nature.[15]

Of course, the current crop of Progressives, including President Barack Obama and Supreme Court justices such as Elena Kagan or Sonia Sotomayor, believe this too restrictive. They claim there is an "evolving," "emerging," or "living" Constitution, which is subject to their own current interpretations as a way of promoting their social justice or redistributive justice political agendas. In their thinking, the Constitution is an Etch A Sketch toy that can be used to mean whatever they need it to mean for their current purposes. This process of course would provide a would-be despot with a way to redefine the meaning of liberty and to enslave people under the guise of operating under a constitutional government. What Obama, Kagan, Sotomayor, and the like would create would be a lawless government subject only to their political whims.

Mark Levin, author of *Liberty and Tyranny,* wrote:

> The Constitution is the bedrock on which a living, evolving nation was built. It is—and must be—a timeless yet durable foundation that individuals can count on in a changing world. It is not perfect but the Framers made it more perfectible through the amendment process.
>
> The Conservative seeks to divine the Constitution's meaning from its words and their historical context, including a variety of original sources—records of public debates, diaries, correspondence, notes, etc. While reasonable people may, in good faith, draw different conclusions from the application of this interpretative standard, it is the only standard that gives fidelity to the Constitution.
>
> And where the Constitution is silent, states and individuals need not be. The Constitution and, more particularly, the framework of the government it establishes are not intended to address every issue or answer every perceived grievance. This is not a defect but a strength, because the government was intended to be a limited one.[16]

Heritage Foundation scholar David Forte devoted an entire chapter to the concept of "originalism" in *The Heritage Foundation Guide to the Constitution*. Originalism means that anyone trying to determine what the Constitution means must look to the Founders' *original* wording and meaning, at the time the Constitution was written—not to current political views or personal agendas. Therefore, originalists look for the evident meaning of the words used; the meaning according to the lexicon of the times; the meaning in context with other sections of the Constitution; the meaning according to the words by the Framer who suggested the language; and more.

Forte wrote, "Originalism comports with the understanding of what our Constitution was to be by the people who formed and ratified that document. It affirms that the Constitution is a coherent and interrelated document, with subtle balances incorporated throughout. . . . In short, it is a remarkable historical achievement, and unbalancing part of it could dismantle the sophisticated devices it erected to protect the people's liberty."[17]

Mark Levin correctly labels "Statists" as those who reject the concept of limited federal power as outlined in the Constitution. He notes that the Statist

> is not interested in what the Framers said or intended. "He is interested only in what he says and he intends. Consider the judiciary, which has seized for itself the most dominant role in interpreting the Constitution. When asked by a law clerk to explain his judicial philosophy, the late Associate Supreme Court justice Thurgood Marshall responded, "You do what you think is right and let the law catch up." The late Associate justice Arthur Goldberg's answer was no better. A law clerk recounts Goldberg telling him that his approach was to determine "what is the *just* result." Still others are persuaded by the Statist's semantic distortions, arguing that the judge's job is to spread democracy or liberty.[18]

It is not the judge's job to redefine the Constitution to pursue his notions of what's right or just. His job is to correctly discern what the Founders intended in the Constitution when rendering a decision.

LIMITED FEDERAL GOVERNMENT UNDER THE TENTH AMENDMENT

Joseph Story explained the importance of the Tenth Amendment and how it protects our freedoms under the Constitution at all levels of government by designated power to the states and people:

> The next and last amendment, which has not been already considered, is, "The powers not delegated to the United States by the Constitution, nor prohibited by it to the States, are reserved to the States respectively, or to the People."
>
> This amendment follows out the object of the preceding; and is merely an affirmation of a rule of construction of the Constitution, which, upon any just reasoning, must have existed without it. Still, it is important as a security against two opposite tendencies of opinion, each of which is equally subversive of the true import of the Constitution. The one is to imply all powers, which may be useful to the National Government, which are not expressly prohibited; and the other is, to deny all powers to the National Government, which are not expressly granted. We have already seen, that there are many implied powers necessarily resulting from the nature of the express powers; and it is as clear, that no power can properly arise by implication from a mere prohibition.
>
> The Government of the United States is one of limited powers; and no authority exists beyond the prescribed limits, marked out in the instrument itself.
>
> Whatever powers are not granted, necessarily belong to the respective States, or to the people of the respective States, if they have not been confided by them to the State Governments.[19]

In his concluding remarks in his amazing book on the Constitution, Story offered this warning to the American people:

> The structure [of the Constitution] has been erected by architects of consummate skill and fidelity; its foundations are solid; its compartments are beautiful, as well as useful; its arrangements are full of wisdom and order; and its defenses are impregnable from without.

It has been reared for immortality, if the work of man may justly aspire to such a title.

It may, nevertheless, perish in an hour, by the folly, or corruption, or negligence of its only keepers, THE PEOPLE. Republics are created by the virtue, public spirit, and intelligence of the citizens. They fall, when the wise are banished from the public councils, because they dare to be honest, and the profligate are rewarded, because they flatter the people, in order to betray them.[20]

A WARNING FROM GEORGE WASHINGTON

In President George Washington's 1796 Farewell Address to the American people, he warned against those in the federal government encroaching upon other areas of government in violation of the US Constitution. Such encroachments, noted Washington, will result in "a real despotism." His warning is as timely today as it was then—and probably even more urgently needed now than when he was in office. Washington warned:

> It is important, likewise, that the habits of thinking in a free country should inspire caution, in those entrusted with its administration, to confine themselves within their respective constitutional spheres, avoiding in the exercise of the powers of one department to encroach upon another.
>
> The spirit of encroachment tends to consolidate the powers of all the departments in one, and thus to create, whatever the form of government, a real despotism. A just estimate of that love of power, and proneness to abuse it, which predominates in the human heart, is sufficient to satisfy us of the truth of this position. The necessity of reciprocal checks in the exercise of political power, by dividing and distributing it into different depositories, and constituting each the Guardian of the Public Weal against invasions by the others, has been evinced by experiments ancient and modern; some of them in our country and under our own eyes. To preserve them must be as necessary as to institute them. If, in the opinion of the people, the distribution or modification of the

constitutional powers be in any particular wrong, let it be corrected by an amendment in the way, which the constitution designates.

But let there be no change by usurpation; for, though this, in one instance, may be the instrument of good, it is the customary weapon by which free governments are destroyed. The precedent must always greatly overbalance in permanent evil any partial or transient benefit, which the use can at any time yield.

Of all the dispositions and habits, which lead to political prosperity, Religion and Morality are indispensable supports. In vain would that man claim the tribute of Patriotism, who should labor to subvert these great pillars of human happiness, these firmest props of the duties of Men and Citizens. The mere Politician, equally with the pious man, ought to respect and to cherish them.

A volume could not trace all their connections with private and public felicity. Let it simply be asked, Where is the security for property, for reputation, for life, if the sense of religious obligation desert the oaths, which are the instruments of investigation in Courts of Justice? And let us with caution indulge the supposition, that morality can be maintained without religion.

Whatever may be conceded to the influence of refined education on minds of peculiar structure, reason and experience both forbid us to expect, that national morality can prevail in exclusion of religious principle.[21]

George Washington clearly understood the importance of checks and balances in the Constitution to prevent the federal government from morphing into a utopian tyranny. He knew that if the executive branch of the government began infringing on the duties of the other two, power would eventually be concentrated in one all-powerful despot.

The self-proclaimed Progressives who find themselves in powerful positions in Washington, DC, seem propelled by their totalitarian impulses to always seek to centralize power in one branch of the government, normally the executive. Leftist presidents have viewed Congress as an impediment to their goals, unless both the House and Senate are in their part's hands as well. They also view the Supreme Court as an impediment unless they have stacked the deck with totalitarian justices who view the Constitution itself as an impediment to social justice and income redistribution.

Liberals reject checks and balances and any other restrictions in the Constitution designed to protect Americans from a despotic government, particularly those provided to the states and to the people. In Progressive elitist thinking, most Americans are too stupid to self-govern and need an army of bureaucrats and social engineers to herd them like sheep to do whatever the statists think is good for them.

The battle to preserve and defend our God-given freedoms will never end. There will always be social totalitarians, not always labeled by a single political party, working to create a utopian tyranny where social engineers will control our lives from the moment we're born until we're told to die as was done in the failed Soviet experiment of collectivism. Rather than seeking liberty of the individual we often find the Democratic and Republican parties in the United States arguing over which set of rules they want the American people to abide by.

The defense of the principles outlined in the Declaration of Independence and our US Constitution, which define liberty as from God rather than government, must be constantly defended. Eternal vigilance is called for in the defense of liberty at all levels of government, from town hall meetings to sessions of the Senate.

12

COMBATING FUTURE UTOPIAN PLANNERS

A truly free society cannot exist collectively if its individual citizens do not have personal liberty. Freedom of the individual in areas of religion, speech, assembly, and work must come first or the society as a whole cannot be free.

Throughout this book, we have looked at utopian activists, utopian political philosophies, and utopian governmental systems that have uniformly destroyed human freedom, killed millions, and subjected the populations of numerous countries to untold suffering and poverty. Whenever a utopian political or cultural leader is able to place his belief of perfecting mankind and human relations into action, the result has been the enslavement or death of human beings. Utopian terrorism has continued for thousands of years. The utopian tyrant functions more like the exterminator of humanity than a savior of humanity. The outcome of his actions is always carnage.

From Sparta to the destructive collectivist policies of progressive American presidents such as Wilson, Roosevelt, Johnson, and Obama, the consequence is always the same—economic and moral destruction. People are treated as members of an unthinking beehive instead of as individuals with God-given talents and the unalienable right to freedom of action, thought, and religion.

Of course, not all utopianism is relegated to the West. There were numerous revolts—most inspired by Taoism—in China to create utopian societies, some recorded as early as AD 100 to 200. Such revolts continued in China on and off for nearly two thousand years until a successful culmination by Mao Tse-tung's Communist Party of China in 1949. As an example, the great Sichuan peasant insurrection of 993 maintained the slogan "level the rich and poor."[1] In whatever territory central planning utopians have controlled, the people have been herded like cattle into programs and economic systems that kill creativity, stifle innovation, and punish the productive while rewarding the indolent.

The utopians, with their fanatical and unworkable ideas, impose their plans on unwilling populaces, and the victims of utopian tyranny are given little choice in the matter. They either submit or they're tortured, starved, or killed. Even when the people do submit, they usually end up starving because central planning redistributes poverty and misery. There never has been a successful, productive central-planned collectivist system, and never will be. This is because socialism violates fixed laws of human nature. People have an intrinsic need to be rewarded for hard work. But why work hard if the system is only going to rob you of the fruits of your labors? In fact, why work at all when you can simply stand in line and obtain your necessities for free? Collectivism kills the basic human desire to be rewarded for one's work.

THE PILGRIMS' FAILED EXPERIMENT WITH COLLECTIVISM (COMMUNISM?)
Upon arriving in the New World, the Pilgrims attempted collectivist/communal living based on what they believed, in error, was a biblical principle. The model could easily be called Communist, as no private property was permitted. All worked for the common good with the belief that no one would take more than was needed from their production.

Oddly, this ideology is still alive today and is actually referred to as Christian Communism. The basis in the New Testament is Jesus's account of the Last Judgment in Matthew: "Then shall [the King] answer [the wicked], saying, Verily I say unto you, Inasmuch as ye did it not to one of the least of these, ye did it not to me. And these shall go away into everlasting punishment; but the righteous into life eternal" (25:45–46).

Christian Communists believe this scripture applies not only to individuals but to societies and governments as well. From this point of view, it is easy to see why collectivists, religious or atheistic, believe in collective punishment as well.

The Pilgrims, as do the Christian Communists of today, used Acts 2:44–46 and 4:32–36 as evidence of the communal societies of the early church. In the Old Testament they cite Leviticus 25:35–38 as proof of God's approval of collectivism. When collectivists attempt to apply these scriptures to societies as rules for central planners, the result is always failure. The Bible is intended by God as a spiritual guide, not a reference work for central planners.

In the Pilgrims' case, the communal experiment began in 1622 and involved approximately two dozen families. The system prohibited private property, and all were to share equally regardless of the amount any one individual produced. Starvation and death resulted. Some took what they wanted while producing little or nothing, and the productive soon became disheartened.

Governor William Bradford described the Pilgrims' failed communal experiment and how productive the society became once this attempt was abandoned in favor of free enterprise with private ownership.

> At length after much debate, the Governor, with the advice of the chief among them, allowed each man to plant corn for his own household, and to trust to themselves for that; in all other things to go on in the general way as before. So every family was assigned a parcel of land, according to the proportion of their number with that in view—for present purposes only, and making no division for inheritance—all boys and children being included under some family. This was very successful. It made all hands very industrious, so that much more corn was planted than otherwise would have been by any means the Governor or any other could devise, and saved him a great deal of trouble, and

gave far better satisfaction. The women now went willingly into the field, and took their little ones with them to plant corn, while before they would allege weakness and inability; and to have compelled them would have been thought great tyranny and oppression.

The failure of the experiment of communal service, which was tried for several years, and by good and honest men proves the emptiness of the theory of Plato and other ancients, applauded by some of later times, —that the taking away of private property, and the possession of it in community, by a commonwealth, would make a state happy and flourishing; as if they were wiser than God.

For in this instance, community of property (so far as it went) was found to breed much confusion and discontent, and retard much employment which would have been to the general benefit and comfort. For the young men who were most able and fit for service objected to being forced to spend their time and strength in working for other men's wives and children, without any recompense. The strong man or the resourceful man had no more share of food, clothes, etc., than the weak man who was not able to do a quarter the other could. This was thought injustice. The aged and graver men, who were ranked and equalized in labour, food, clothes, etc., with the humbler and younger ones, thought it some indignity and disrespect to them. As for men's wives who were obliged to do service for other men, such as cooking, washing their clothes, etc., they considered it a kind of slavery, and many husbands would not brook it.

This feature of it would have been worse still, if they had been men of an inferior class. If (it was thought) all were to share alike, and all were to do alike, then all were on an equality throughout, and one was as good as another; and so, if it did not actually abolish those very relations which God himself has set among men, it did at least greatly diminish the mutual respect that is so important should be preserved amongst them. Let none argue that this is due to human failing, rather than to this communistic plan of life in itself. I answer, seeing that all men have this failing in them, that God in His wisdom saw that another plan of life was fitter for them.

These matters premised, I will now proceed with my account of affairs here. But before I come to other things I must say a word about their planting this year. They felt the benefit of their last year's harvest; for by planting corn on their own account they managed, with a great deal of patience, to overcome famine. This reminds me of a saying of Seneca's (Epis. 123): that an important part of liberty is a well-governed belly, and patience in want.

The settlers now began to consider corn more precious than silver; and those that had some to spare began to trade with the others for small things, by the quart, pottle, and peck, etc.; for they had not money, and if they had, corn was preferred to it. In order that they might raise their crops to better advantage, they made suit to the Governor to have some land apportioned for permanent holdings, and not by yearly lot, whereby the plots which the more industrious had brought under good culture one year, would change hands the next, and others would reap the advantage; with the result that manuring and culture of the land were neglected. It was well considered, and their request was granted.

Every person was given one acre of land, for them and theirs, and they were to have no more till the seven years had expired; it was all as near the town as possible, so that they might be kept close together, for greater safety and better attention to the general employments.[2]

Note Bradford's comment about the failure of Plato's theories on communal living. He learned firsthand what it was like to experiment with Plato's utopian concepts and how the experiment with it nearly doomed the Pilgrims' settlement in the New World. Communal sharing didn't bring about harmony and productivity; it brought about disillusionment, starvation, and discord. Private property appears to be an imperative in all cultures that seek to be prosperous. The collectivist, central planning model has been shown repeatedly to be a failure. Had Bradford had access to the later writings of Karl Marx, he surely would have seen them in the same light as Plato's.

Today the very obvious comparison of collectivism versus free enterprise can be seen on a small Asian peninsula. The differences between the economies, food production, and per capita income of North and South Korea are staggering. The collectivist North is in a state of perpetual famine, while South Korea is one of the most prosperous nations in the world today. North Korea keeps its citizens permanently enslaved by centrally planning their lives, while South Koreans are free to pursue their careers and dreams. The totalitarian central planning system of North Korea redistributes nothing more than poverty. The free enterprise system of South Korea enables each individual to prosper based on his or her abilities and allows the creation of wealth pooling to allow investment and growth. Those of the North are banned from travel for fear they will not return to the slavery they endure, while those of the South use their wealth earned in a free society to travel the world.

One noted aspect of Bradford's description of the early years of the Pilgrims is how men and women reacted to having to produce value others had access to without any personal reward. It bred resentment and rewarded laziness. Once the communal experiment was banished and private property reinstated, the settlement began to thrive and families went willingly to work to provide for their own needs.

Fortunately, the Pilgrims were not enslaved in a totalitarian Communist system from which there was no escape—unlike the hapless North Koreans. The Pilgrims were a small, self-governing unit at the time and were able to change their system quickly. If they'd been under a utopian dictatorship, however, they would undoubtedly have continued to starve, and this early settlement of America would have failed to be one of the cornerstones of the vibrant nation that still exists today.

One can only wonder what the world would be like today had the Pilgrims not turned from this Communist type of experiment and the rest of the nation had followed it. It is entirely conceivable that North America and perhaps the whole world would be under the domination of wicked utopian tyrants such as Robespierre, Lenin, Hitler, or Mao, with slavery and mass starvation. It would be, as O'Brien told Winston Smith in *1984*, a future with the image of a boot stamping on a human face forever.

DANGERS TODAY, FROM THE NSA TO GOOGLE

In the world of technology today, utopians have access to vast powers that can be used to suppress all forms of freedom throughout the world. Just a few decades ago, these technological powers did not exist but are now available to be used as forms of suppression and coercion. With the tracking power of microchips, GPS devices, and armed drones, the likelihood of utopian tyrannies lasting for centuries should they come to power once again is a current reality. Those who love liberty must be at the forefront of defending against the use of technology as a means of limiting those rights endowed upon us by our Creator.

KILL SWITCHES FOR PEOPLE

Many believe that microchips are used just to track lost pets. The time may come when a utopian tyrant will use implanted microchips to track and control the life of every person in the United States. We could be living in a time when no one can vote, buy, or sell unless he has a microchip implanted inside—much like the mark of the beast referred to in the book of Revelation. (See Revelation 13:15–16.)

This is no paranoid delusion of a conspiracy theorist. A school district in Texas came under scrutiny in late 2012 for forcing its students to wear microchip-embedded identification cards at all times. Students at John Jay High School and Anson Jones Middle School have been required to wear these radio-frequency identification (RFID) chips so that school officials can track their individual locations. Students who refused to wear the microchip were denied access to common areas, such as cafeterias and libraries. One student, Andrea Hernandez, was told she couldn't vote in school elections because she refused to wear the tracking device. According to Hernandez, having to wear the microchip was like being branded with the mark of the beast.[3] After legal threats the school agreed to remove only her chip but still required that she wear the badge. Feeling that this was intimidating for her the family continued the lawsuit but lost. Although she refused on religious grounds, a judge sided with the school's ruling: "Plaintiff's objection to wearing the Smart ID badge without a chip is clearly a secular choice, rather than a religious concern."[4] As a result, schools nationwide have begun this tracking process.

Imagine this technology in the hands of a regime of utopian central planners bent on absolute uniformity of the citizens such as existed under Stalin or Mao. A microchip could be surgically implanted by force in every subject of their rule and be easily tracked. And that's not all.

Researchers have developed a workable microchip that automatically releases medicines into the body of its host. The programmable microchip was first developed by MicroCHIPS of Massachusetts and was tested in early 2012 on eight women from Denmark. Each of the implanted microchips contained twenty doses of the bone-building drug Forteo. The inventors of this medical microchip hope to develop a version that has enough medicine for a year of automatic treatments.[5]

This may be a wonderful device for patients in need of long-term care for certain illnesses, such as cancers or chronic pain; however, there could be a darker side to this technological breakthrough. A utopian tyrant could force the implantation of this type of microchip filled with poison that could be remotely released to kill should the individual disobey the state. The effect would be like a kill switch the police use in a "bait car," which are placed in high-theft neighborhoods with the key in the ignition to attract potential criminals. Suspected enemies of the state could easily be controlled by the constant threat of instant death. The use of such a kill switch would probably be used first in prisons or on pedophiles to gain public acceptance, and then introduced into the general population for "security" reasons.

KILL SWITCHES FOR CELL PHONES

In early 2012 President Obama's secretary of transportation, Ray LaHood, suggested that the government develop technology that could turn off cell phones when a person is driving. This totalitarian proposal was suggested as a "safety" measure to keep drivers from texting or talking on their cell phones while driving.

This proposal has *1984*'s Big Brother written all over it. Millions of Americans use their cell phones for safety purposes when they're driving.

If a car breaks down, they can immediately call for help. If they're lost, they can use the GPS software in their smart phones to find their destination. Losing cell phone access while driving could result in a serious loss of lives—rather than supposedly saving lives. LaHood got so much flak for his absurd proposal that he dropped it.[6]

Sadly, concepts such as this one from delusional utopian thinkers who want to "protect" us all from ourselves never die. This proposal will undoubtedly be brought up again—once utopians think public opinion has shifted enough to accept it.

POLICE STATE USE OF YOUR CELL

In 2014 it was revealed that the NSA (National Security Agency) had hacked the cell phone of German chancellor Angela Merkel, as well as other of our allies. The NSA headquarters is located in Fort Meade, Maryland, a northern suburb of Washington, DC. In 2013 the NSA employed about thirty-three hundred people, and its known budget was $10 billion. Its sole purpose is intercepting and analyzing the communications of people around the world.

In June 2013 Ed Snowden, a contract employee of the NSA who became a whistle-blower and now lives in Moscow, Russia, released documents that revealed the extent of the domestic surveillance activities of the agency. The NSA has been collecting the phone records of millions of Americans, as well as private user data from online services.

In March 2013 the then head of the NSA under the Obama administration, Dr. James Clapper, lied to Congress about the data collection. At a hearing on surveillance, Sen. Ron Wyden asked Clapper whether the NSA collected "any type of data at all on millions or hundreds of millions of Americans." Clapper responded, "No, sir. . . Not wittingly."[7]

In reality he was well aware at the time of the extent of the collection of data. If this outrage can occur under a constitutional framework, imagine the damage, intimidation, and coercion that could be done under a utopian central planning regime.

CAR KILL SWITCH AND BLACK BOX

Utopians using new technology can learn an individual's location and actions even if he turns off a cell phone and removes the battery. In some European nations, car manufacturers are being required to fit their automobiles with "black boxes" that record the habits and locations of drivers and transmit that information to insurance companies and to the police. In the United States legislation was proposed in mid-2012 that would force automobile manufacturers to install black boxes in all cars. As usual, in the beginning the use can seem reasonable to many. The black boxes, now used by almost all automakers to find faults, would also record "vehicle miles traveled" or VMT. Fees would then be levied on drivers depending on how far they traveled rather than on (or in addition to) a tax on gasoline. The concept came from the fact that, with increased fuel efficiency, states are getting less revenue from motorists for more miles driven.

According to the Heritage Foundation, "A VMT would be expensive to implement because every car would need to be fitted with a device that both records miles driven and transmits the information to a government database. This complicated system would cost millions and raise concerns of big brother watching our every movement. Americans don't like paying the gas tax, but they are sure to be even more unhappy having to deal with the administrative nightmare the VMT promises."[8] Other legislation made black boxes mandatory in all new cars sold in the United States beginning in 2015.

These new mandatory black boxes could eventually include kill switches that law enforcement agencies could use to automatically shut down specific cars or, for that matter, all cars in an area over which the government wanted to impose more control.

OnStar, a system available on General Motors cars, already has such a kill switch because it has its own cellular phone system rather than using the driver's. The OnStar service can work with law enforcement officials to stop cars being driven by car thieves or carjackers. Of course, such a system could also be used by utopian tyrants to deal with political dissidents who may try to flee persecution. Imagine the government having the power to remotely stop or even control your car.

DRONES AS KILL SWITCHES

The normalization of the use of drones for domestic police surveillance is upon us. Federal agencies and more and more state, county, and city law enforcement agencies have added drones. Currently used for surveillance in the United States, drones were used by both the George W. Bush and the Barack Obama administrations to target foreign enemies such as Taliban terrorists in Pakistan.

However, Barack Obama was the first president ever to sign a death warrant against an American citizen without trial. Anwar al-Awlaki was killed by a CIA drone attack in Yemen on September 30, 2011.[9] Two weeks later, al-Awlaki's seventeen-year-old son, Abdulrahman al-Awlaki, a US citizen born in Denver, was also killed in a drone strike.[10] Both were in Yemen, apparently promoting terror, although neither had been directly involved in a terrorist act himself. There was an apparent element of embarrassment to President Obama and the Pentagon with al-Awlaki, as he was the spiritual guide to Islamic terrorist killer Nidal Malik Hasan, a US Army major and psychiatrist who killed thirteen service members and an unborn child at Fort Hood in 2009 while shouting, "Allah Akbar."[11] It was then learned that al-Awlaki was invited to the Pentagon to speak about the "religion of peace" shortly after the jihad attack against the United States on 9/11.[12] He may have been targeted simply to shut him up about his contacts in the US military, which is a sign that drone use is already out of control with the Congress still in place. Once American citizens can be targeted by drones for death without trial, the obvious question arises about drone use in the United States with the continued militarization of the police and massive increase in use of SWAT teams. Imagine this drone technology in the hands of an out-of-control utopian-minded dictator who believes he alone can solve the problems of humankind.

INTERNET KILL SWITCHES

As mentioned earlier, the National Security Agency (NSA) has a massive budget of $10 billion per year to tap into communications. This "tapping" is not just for collection of cell phone data. The NSA maintains—and uses—the ability to track virtually all computer transactions in the world. The NSA claims that in the United States it collects only "metadata" to watch for terrorist interactions from abroad; however, as already noted, NSA director Clapper was caught lying to Congress about the collection of data in 2013.

During the first term of the Obama administration, his operatives sought legislation that would give the Department of Homeland Security the power to shut down parts of the Internet—for "national security" purposes. The plan became known as the "Internet kill switch" and alarmed many in Congress. No such legislation was ever passed; however, local police authorities have ordered cell phone providers to shut off services during "stand-offs," indicating that police powers are beginning to trump individual rights in the United States.

SMART GRID KILL SWITCHES

The central planners may think your home is kept too warm or too cool, and they want to be able to "fix" that for you against your will. The Obama administration used $3.4 billion in "stimulus" dollars to subsidize the creation of "smart grid" projects across America. The ultimate goal is to have a network of smart grids in place that can remotely control home appliances and heating systems in the name of stopping global warming. Big Brother can then control the overall use of electricity in your home, thus controlling "greenhouse gases." While supposedly done in the name of energy efficiency, it really gives government power over the choices of the individual. It is a form of government coercion that could truly be abused in the wrong hands. A central planning tyrant could simply turn off the heat in a home during the winter if someone there disagreed with the despot's policies.

THE EVER-PRESENT CAMERAS

The United Kingdom has become the model surveillance society in the last decade or so. There are now an estimated 5 million CCTV (closed circuit TV) cameras in service in the UK, or one for every fourteen citizens. These cameras monitor every aspect of daily life in Britain, Scotland, and Wales, both indoors and out.[13] London alone has ninety-one thousand CCTV cameras.

There are also six thousand CCTV cameras being operated in Manhattan alone by the New York Police Department, and more are to be added.[14] In the summer of 2012, the NYPD announced a new surveillance program called the Domestic Awareness System. This new system links the city's extensive surveillance system with law enforcement databases to track suspected terrorists. Of course, the same technology can also be used by utopian tyrants to track political enemies of the regime or coerce most into submission.[15]

***

All of these technologies are useful when in the hands of political leaders who love the Constitution and believe in America's place in the world as a beacon of freedom. But these same technologies can be used by utopians to create an electronic surveillance prison for all, a sort of high-tech version of North Korea.

A few years ago, Will Smith, Gene Hackman, and Jon Voight appeared in the film *Enemy of the State*, which portrayed a rogue element inside the federal intelligence community using tracking devices and satellite surveillance to kill off those it considered enemies to national security. The bad guys were conservatives, of course, which is typical Hollywood liberalism in action. In reality, the utopian tyrants who have already used oppressive measures to kill enemies of the state are utopian "liberals," not conservatives. While the Nazi Party is often pointed to as being a part of the "Right," keep in mind that it was in fact a national socialist party of central planners trying to create a utopia. As discussed in previous chapters, these utopian central planners have killed millions upon millions—and will do so again if given the power.

The technology is now in place to make our lives a hell on earth if in the hands of utopians.

THE LEFT'S STRANGLEHOLD ON AMERICA

Regardless of how they may refer to themselves, central planners have no place in government, the founding purpose of which was personal liberty. They may call themselves liberals, progressives, socialists, or even Communists, but if their stated goal is "social justice" or "economic justice" or any form of collective punishment based on religion, race, or economic standing, they are a danger to freedom. Those who would restrict jobs based on race in the name of some misguided view of justice are no less racist and intolerant than the Ku Klux Klan, but far more dangerous because often they have obtained positions of power. They have a worldview that is opposed to the American Constitution and the Founding Fathers' vision for a society free of government coercion of the individual.

A recent example of this is the misguided passage of a Houston, Texas, ordinance that would allow men to enter the women's restroom at any time if they "considered" themselves women or transgender. Of course, age was not taken into consideration in the ordinance, and as a result, an adult male claiming to feel like a female that day would be permitted to walk into a restroom full of young girls. This in itself would seem bad enough of an idea, but when pastors in the city of Houston attempted to obtain an initiative on the ballot to strike down the ordinance promoted by the lesbian mayor and her "wife," religious freedom came under direct assault. The lesbian mayor demanded in court copies of sermons, with the intent of taking away tax exemption of churches that disagreed with her homosexual, transgender agenda. Suddenly the concepts of religious freedom and freedom of speech were to be tossed aside in the name of "social justice" for the LGBT movement.[16]

It is not just within the federal government that a cadre of anti-freedom zealots works day and night to undermine the liberties outlined in the Constitution. Even at the city and county levels, those who wish to transform our nation into a tightly controlled society, conformed to their vision of justice and perfection, work toward central planning that would rule from the moment of birth (if, in fact, a birth is allowed) until the day that one of their death panel decides it has become too expensive for the government to keep an individual alive.

On the federal level there are individuals who want almost unlimited power for a Progressive president who will ignore the Constitution. In Congress they are the same individuals who would do anything to stop the agenda of a president promoting free enterprise and true racial equality that is blind to color at all levels of government. They desire Philip Dru, Administrator (mentioned in chapter 7) to rule with unelected bureaucratic czars.

At the federal level these utopians can easily be identified. In Congress they can be found proudly exhibiting themselves in the Congressional Progressive Caucus. Most are elected from "safe" liberal districts that most often have more people receiving benefits from government than paying taxes. They operate collectively, like a permanent Soviet-style Politburo working with leftist "think tanks" to craft policies to rob Americans of their liberties in the name of "social justice" or "economic justice."

The Congressional Progressive Caucus (CPC) could be considered the socialist wing of the Democratic Party and consisted of sixty-nine members as of 2014. The CPC works hand in glove with the Institute for Policy Studies (IPS), a radical organization promoting communistic-type collectivism, and with the Democratic Socialists of America. It is also considered an ally by the Communist Party USA. Many far-left radical groups in the United States have links from their Internet sites to the CPC.

The CPC was founded in 1991 by then representative Bernie Sanders of Vermont. Sanders is now a senator, an openly admitted socialist, and a candidate for president in 2016. Sanders caucuses with but is not officially a member of the Democratic Party, which he considers too conservative. Some of Sanders's cofounders of the CPC are former representative Ron Dellums, an ally of Fidel Castro and other

Latin American dictators, and Maxine Waters, the rabid California leftist who claims the CIA spread cocaine into black communities in order to kill off minorities.[17] As time went on, the opinions and charges out of the CPC became even more bizarre. During the 2014 election cycle, a CPC member stated that the Republican Party still believed in slavery. Anything to create fear and give government more central power to create "social justice."

Some of the things done by members of the CPC in the name of equality and justice go as far as to protect and promote Islamic terrorists. In 2013 the Congressional Progressive Caucus was cochaired by Muslim leftist Keith Ellison, a congressman from Minnesota, and Rep. Raúl Grijalva of Arizona. Ellison has close ties to the Council on American Islamic Relations (CAIR), a Muslim Brotherhood front. Grijalva is a former member of MEChA, a radical Chicano group that seeks the reconquest of the American Southwest by Mexico. As a cochair of the Congressional Muslim Staff Association, he has invited numerous radical Muslims to speak, several with terror ties, including the late Anwar al-Awlaki. One of the fundamentals of Islam is the creation of a utopian state under a caliphate, so it should be of no surprise that Ellison is, of course, a member of the Congressional Progressive Caucus.

Both Raúl Grijalva and Keith Ellison have expressed hatred for some of America's basic institutions, as they believe they are fundamentally "unjust." Former speaker of the House Nancy Pelosi was a member of the CPC as late as 2012 but appears to have dropped out to be more of a stealth radical.

Many of those in the CPC are also members of the Congressional Black Caucus (CBC), which claims to be a caucus for African American congressmen, though no black Republican congressmen or senators have even been members of the CBC. There is a reason for that. Mostly from inner cities, the congressmen in the CBC are for the most part assorted Marxists, socialists, and self-proclaimed Progressives who seek the destruction of the free enterprise system, to replace it with one that creates "social and economic justice." Although the vast majority of

African Americans are against abortion on demand and homosexual marriage, as a group the CBC promotes a cultural revolution that includes legalization of homosexual marriage and protecting abortion on demand. The CBC also works to expand the welfare state and promotes racial division with racial quotas.

The CBC was founded by radical leftists John Conyers, Ron Dellums, Shirley Chisholm, and others in 1969. To understand how far left this caucus really is, consider the fact that in April 2009, a CBC delegation visited Havana to meet with Communist dictator and mass murderer Fidel Castro. After the meeting, CBC members praised Castro for his hospitality and called for a normalization of relations with this brutal tyrant who has cost the lives of so many trying to impose his vision of a utopia.

CBC member Barbara Lee described Castro as being warm and receptive. Another CBC member, Rep. Bobby Rush of Illinois, said, "In my household, I told Castro he is known as the ultimate survivor." Rep. Laura Richardson said of Castro, "He looked right into my eyes and he said, 'How can we help? How can we help President Obama?'" Isn't that special? Fidel Castro became a survivor by killing or imprisoning his opponents and turning his island nation into what amounted to a giant prison camp that many still risk their lives to escape on small boats and rafts—and he wants to help America?

After meeting with the CBC members, the brutal killer Castro announced that some in the delegation from America had expressed to him that a segment of American society "continues to be racist." Emanuel Cleaver, a key CBC member, denies that anyone made such a statement to Castro. But, who knows? CBC members routinely cry "racism" whenever anyone tries to promote free-market ideas or biblical morality in Congress. Of course, to criticize their leftist politics is to be automatically accused of racism.[18]

Regrettably, many of the radical anti-American politicians in the CPC and the CBC are safely entrenched in congressional districts where they are guaranteed a lifetime in Congress to work for the destruction of our system of government. The CBC is not an African American caucus; it is just an extension of the Congressional Progressive Caucus, which allows radical leftists to have larger staffs and federal monies to spend promoting their utopian concepts.

Men and women such as these prove that those desiring a central planning model can't be trusted with any power over American lives. They must be defeated and removed from public office if possible, and if not, then isolated by maintaining a majority in Congress that desires to maintain individual liberty with the least amount of government coercion possible.

MEDIA THAT KNOW BETTER THAN THE PEOPLE: ENEMY OF THE REPUBLIC

The so-called mainstream media have proved beyond doubt that they are not independent or honest in how they report political news. Many of the largest outlets have become propaganda arms of the Progressive movement and function more as censors than news gatherers and dispensers of fact.

In 2010 the *Daily Caller* exposed an underground network of newspaper reporters, TV personalities, and online journalists who claimed to be neutral, known as the JournoList. The *Daily Caller* showed that this was a group of several hundred mainstream "journalists" who strategized frequently about how they could attack John McCain and Sarah Palin in order to ensure an Obama victory. The JournoList zealots worked together to make sure no bad news surfaced about Obama and that McCain and Palin were regularly smeared for every misstep they might make. Aside from the obvious, such as Paul Krugman of the *New York Times*, the group included writers from the *Washington Post, Newsweek, Time*, the *Boston Globe,* the *Chicago Tribune*, CNN, and dozens of more outlets.

At the earliest establishment of newspapers, the media were viewed as "the Fourth Estate" and the defenders of liberty, always questioning government and standing for freedom of speech, press, and assembly. Sadly, most major news outlets today stand only for their own freedom of speech and press and are willing to stand by as government silences any voices they do not agree with on the right.

One good example occurred when current major media outlets actually allowed a man to be jailed rather than tell the known truth in his defense because it interfered with their ideology. Just before the presidential election in 2012 and on the anniversary of the 9/11 jihad attack on the United States, armed terrorists stormed an American diplomatic compound in Benghazi, Libya, killing the ambassador, his aide, and two former Navy SEALS. Because it was before the election, and President Obama was running a campaign claiming he had defeated al-Qaeda and terror in general, he simply could not admit that Islamic terror was alive, growing, and killing Americans.

A story was invented in the West Wing of the White House blaming the attack on a small-time Egyptian Copt's short YouTube film. To mask the truth, the US government ran paid apologies for the video on Arab TV networks, and the filmmaker, Nakoula Basseley Nakoula, was literally jailed without trial on the basis of an alleged parole violation. Secretary of State Hillary Clinton had publicly vowed to jail him and blamed the attack and deaths on him.[19]

The mainstream media were aware of the cover-up from day one, simply because of the nature of the attack and the lack of any demonstrations anywhere about the fourteen-minute film that literally no one had seen until the White House called attention to it. Why? The truth could have had a negative effect on the presidential election, and the "JournoList" organization supported Barack Obama's programs of "social justice."

This may seem like an extreme case, but unfortunately there are many more as the media have become a bastion for those making a lot of money promoting "social justice" at the cost of others. The media refusals to debate global warming or report on the costs of alternate energy are other examples. The Obama administration's green energy corruption, resulting in the waste of billions of dollars on wind and solar power projects that eventually went belly up, was not widely reported. On Election Day 2012, the Heritage Foundation listed nineteen "green graveyard" boondoggles that Obama had funded to the tune of $2.6 billion. All nineteen of these green energy projects have since gone bankrupt.[20]

The issue for Barack Obama and his followers was never global warming or green energy, but rather, government control over individuals' lives and the ability to limit their freedom using any means to achieve some strange concept of equal outcome rather than equality under the law.

Tragically, in 2012 Barack Obama, a central planner and utopianist, won four more years in the White House and continued to wield his pen to expand government power over the lives of individuals. As the welfare state expands in the name of social equality, a tipping point will be reached. Productive, gainfully employed voters will be outnumbered at the polls by the welfare class, who will vote for ever more so-called Progressives to give them ever more and greater handouts. Those who call themselves Progressives, who are actually leading us back to the Dark Ages, will have created a permanent majority of those receiving government aid who will keep them in office. That situation will, of course, be unsustainable, resulting in the same draconian force as was seen in Stalinist times.

James Madison, the Father of our Constitution, warned against a federal government that had the power to do whatever it wished with the taxes it took from American citizens. "If Congress can do whatever in their discretion can be done by money, and will promote the general welfare" he said, "the government is no longer a limited one possessing enumerated powers, but an indefinite one subject to particular exceptions."[21]

In a letter to James Robertson, Madison wrote, "With respect to the two words 'general welfare,' I have always regarded them as qualified by the detail of powers connected with them. To take them in a literal and unlimited sense would be a metamorphosis of the Constitution into a character which there is a host of proofs was not contemplated by its creators."[22]

Yet, that's exactly what Progressives such as President Barack Obama have done. They have taken the words "general welfare" to mean that the federal government may transform human society and individual will to create a "just" society in which there is equal outcome. However, to achieve equal outcome, the more intelligent and productive must have the value of their work taken from them and given to others whom President Obama refers to as the "less fortunate." This is the definition of a tyranny—a government unrestrained by the rule of law to create an outcome against the will of the people. A president who believes the Constitution is a "living document" that can be changed by executive order is indeed a tyrant.

THE INTENT OF THE FOUNDERS

On September 17, 1796, President George Washington delivered his famous Farewell Address to Congress. In it, Washington distilled a great deal of wisdom and warnings about defending our Republic from internal and external enemies. He also made it very clear that he considered the Christian religion to be a key component in holding together the new republic.

Washington warned his audience that the time would come when "unprincipled men" would try to subvert the power of the people: "One method of assault may be to effect, in the forms of the [C]onstitution, alterations, which will impair the energy of the system, and thus to undermine what cannot be directly overthrown."[23]

One of the ways the Constitution was altered for the worse was in 1913 during Wilson's administration when it was amended to have direct election of senators. The Founders wanted senators to represent the interests of each state in order to protect them from being overrun by states with larger populations. The senators were appointed by the state legislatures under the original Constitution. The Founders were deeply concerned about states' rights and deliberately created a federal government with limited powers.

CONSTITUTIONAL SUBVERSION

Today, the Constitution has been subverted and too much power has gone to the federal level, just as the Founders, including President Washington, warned. The misuse and misinterpretation of the "Interstate Commerce Clause" of the Constitution has transferred far too much power to the central government, which has used that power to limit liberty of the individual. This clause was intended to regulate trade between the states, but it was reinterpreted by Roosevelt's stacked liberal Supreme Court in 1942 to greatly expand the power of the federal government to regulate nearly every aspect of our economy.

The case setting the precedent was *Wickard v. Filburn*. It involved a small dairy farmer who was charged for growing more wheat than the federal government permitted. The wheat he grew wasn't sold across state lines. The farming family was using it to make flour for their own household and to feed cattle. The Supreme Court, stacked by Roosevelt, ruled that "even though [his] activity be local and though it may not be regarded as commerce, it may still . . . be reached by Congress if it exerts a substantial economic effect on interstate commerce." In effect, this ruling gave Congress and the executive branch power to regulate virtually all human activity in the United States, and that is pretty much the case today.[24]

Attorney and author Mark Levin noted that "Wickard swept away 150 years of constitutional jurisprudence, decentralized governmental authority, and private property rights protection. And with it the judiciary seized a role for itself—the manipulation of law to promote a Statist agenda—that continues to this day. Indeed, through a succession of laws and rulings, all three branches—the judicial, the legislative, and the executive—now routinely exercise power well beyond their specific, enumerated authority under the Constitution."[25]

George Washington also warned about the dangers of political parties to good government. He observed:

> The alternate domination of one faction over another, sharpened by the spirit of revenge, natural to party dissension, which in different ages and countries has perpetrated the most horrid enormities, is itself a frightful despotism. But this leads at length to a more formal

and permanent despotism. The disorders and miseries, which result, gradually incline the minds of men to seek security and repose in the absolute power of an individual; and sooner or later the chief of some prevailing faction, more able or more fortunate than his competitors, turns this disposition to the purposes of his own elevation, on the ruins of Public Liberty.[26]

Washington also cautioned that, once in power, those parties could create dangers by allowing a particular branch of the federal government to overstep its bounds:

It is important, likewise, that the habits of thinking in a free country should inspire caution, in those entrusted with its administration, to confine themselves within their respective constitutional spheres, avoiding in the exercise of the powers of one department to encroach upon another. The spirit of encroachment tends to consolidate the powers of all the departments in one, and thus to create, whatever the form of government, a real despotism. A just estimate of that love of power, and proneness to abuse it, which predominates in the human heart, is sufficient to satisfy us of the truth of this position.[27]

Washington's most famous statement about religion and political prosperity is worth reprinting:

Of all the dispositions and habits, which lead to political prosperity, Religion and Morality are indispensable supports. In vain would that man claim the tribute of Patriotism, who should labor to subvert these great pillars of human happiness, these firmest props of the duties of Men and Citizens. The mere Politician, equally with the pious man, ought to respect and to cherish them. A volume could not trace all their connections with private and public felicity. Let it simply be asked, where is the security for property, for reputation, for life, if the sense of religious obligation desert the oaths, which are the instruments of investigation in Courts of Justice? And let us with caution indulge the supposition, that morality can be maintained without

religion. Whatever may be conceded to the influence of refined education on minds of peculiar structure, reason and experience both
forbid us to expect, that national morality can prevail in exclusion of
religious principle. It is substantially true, that virtue or morality is
a necessary spring of popular government. The rule, indeed, extends
with more or less force to every species of free government. Who, that
is a sincere friend to it, can look with indifference upon attempts to
shake the foundation of the fabric?[28]

THE FOUNDERS' DEFENSE OF LIBERTY TODAY

The warnings of President George Washington and the other Founders
of the Republic are today ignored not only by the vast citizenry but by
our elected officials as well. The future of our nation is currently in
jeopardy from utopian tyrants who wish to enslave Americans through
a system of draconian central planning. Not understanding the value
of pooled wealth for investment, these utopians desire to make us all
equally poor—that is, except for high-paid bureaucrats who will administer our poverty.

Often referred to as "social justice," what is really meant is the
replacement of the individual's liberty to use the value or earnings he
creates as he sees fit. Instead, the utopians want to transfer the value
produced or earnings of the individual to others, as the state deems
necessary, to satisfy a perceived social need. The same term is used to
eliminate another form of liberty through coercion in the form of collective punishment, such as white males being required to have significantly
higher grades and SAT scores to be admitted to colleges, because of
the sins of less than a one-hundredth of a percent of whites 150 years
ago. Even Asian males fall victim to colleges and universities making
amends for the crimes of this tiny minority. According to a December 4,
2011, article in *USA Today*, "A study by Princeton sociologist Thomas
Espenshade examined applicants to top colleges from 1997, when the
maximum SAT score was 1600 (today it's 2400). Espenshade found that
Asian-Americans needed a 1550 SAT to have an equal chance of getting

into an elite college as white students with a 1410 or black students with an 1100."[29] More often than not, the families of those collectively punished did not even arrive in the United States until after the Civil War, but that means nothing to those who preach collective social justice.

Collectivists cannot see the error in collective punishment because they do not understand the need for individual liberty and responsibility. Rather than the citizen being responsible for his well-being and his actions, collectivists like Marx believe it is the central responsibility of government to cause the "well-being" of those they deem less capable.

But within the Anglo-American political tradition, freedom has been characterized quite differently. F. A. Hayek defines it as "always the possibility of a person's acting according to his own decisions and plans, in contrast to the position of one who was irrevocably subject to the will of another, who by arbitrary decision could coerce him to act or not to act in specific ways. The time-honored phrase by which this freedom has often been described is therefore 'independence of the arbitrary will of another.'"[30]

Freedom from the "arbitrary will of another" is key to understanding true liberty as the Founding Fathers envisioned it. The Constitution called for the least coercion of the individual possible to maintain the rules—such as government weight and measurement standards for trade—for society to function. Of course, that was before revisionism by federal courts.

The Founders created a document that was not arbitrary, but rather uniform in governance. Other than those victimized by the sin of slavery in the South, the same rules governed everyone, and citizens could freely operate their own lives in a sphere of freedom. Compare that to today, where government maintains many different, arbitrary rules for various groups of people or entities, such as corporations. Some farmers may grow one crop but not another. A farmer may have his property taken for growing too much of a crop, or a businessman may find his competitor more favored by government and paying less or no tax at all, or even receiving money from the Treasury to help compete against him.

These types of arbitrary rules coerce individuals and destroy free society.

Because central planners desire a certain cultural outcome, different members of society must be coerced to varying degrees to obtain that desired "equal" outcome.

While there is still a degree of liberty in the United States, we must resist the taking of our individual liberty, regardless of the promised reward of financial security—a security that will never come, as evidenced by the dwindling Social Security and Medicare programs today. The danger is in voting in the despot that promises all and then takes all.

The Founders created a republic in the Constitution rather than a democracy, knowing full well that the latter would quickly turn to mob rule, and those with minority opinions would eventually be deprived of their rights. Believing God, not government, is the giver of human rights, the Founders conceived a government in which individuals had a large sphere of liberty that included freedom of religion, speech, press, and assembly. These rights could not be removed by a simple majority vote because people were "endowed by their Creator with certain unalienable Rights."

Every American needs to read the *original* writings of those who produced the documents of America's founding, not the interpretations of so-called Progressive "historians," who deliberately skew the facts to promote a statist agenda. We must learn for ourselves why the defense of religious freedom was the foundation of our Republic.

DEFENDING LIBERTY'S FUTURE

Milton Friedman's proposition, that there is a unity between political and economic liberty and that one cannot exist without the other, is accepted today to the point of being taken for granted or even ignored. Friedman's *Capitalism and Freedom* followed F. A. Hayek's *The Constitution of Liberty*, which was released in 1960. In the two works both men argued that political freedom could not exist without economic freedom, and that argument should never be ignored. The chief examples of the twentieth century, of course, are the Soviet Union, Communist China prior to reforms, and nations such as Cuba and North Korea today.

Both Hayek and Friedman saw government at most as an economic referee that kept the playing field level rather than an interventionist with the duty of picking winners and losers and thus stifling innovation. Laws regarding competition and industry should be more like traffic laws, which allow people to drive to their destinations without harming the ability of others to do the same. When this concept is not applied to economic endeavors and burdensome restrictions become the norm, spillover into political freedom is inevitable. An example was the Obama administration's use of the Internal Revenue Service to suppress opposition from Tea Party and other conservative groups in the 2012 election.

The original purpose of the IRS was totally economic. It was created to collect, according to Woodrow Wilson, a small tax from only the highest of earners. In 1913 an individual had to earn more than $8,945.00 before paying tax. In 2013 dollars that equates to $207,725.00. However, Americans earning 10 percent of that amount are taxed today. The IRS also controls the actions of businesses and now even monitors health care under Obamacare. Virtually all aspects of Americans' lives now fall under the jurisdiction of the IRS, and it is just one of many agencies originally brought into existence to deal with economic measures that now, directly or indirectly, adversely affect the liberty of the individual in other areas.

To protect our liberty and avoid the inevitable utopian attempt to create yet another state modeled on central planning and collectivism, citizens must be on eternal guard. Every proposed law, regardless of whom it is designed to affect, must be regarded as a probable attempt to further restrict personal liberty. It should be closely examined, not only at the federal level, but at the state, county, and city levels as well. One need not look far to see examples, such as the new totalitarian control over students at public schools, which demand that virtually no emotions be shown lest there be punishment. What children are taught to accept in the schools today—no freedom of speech or religion—is what they will be willing to accept from government as adults.

It is the duty of every parent who believes in personal liberty to teach their children the Founders' intent in authoring the Constitution and their logic behind establishing a republic. Without this knowledge instilled in future generations, this nation is doomed to follow the models of central planning and collectivism that have brought mass starvation, slavery, and death to untold millions.

Ronald Reagan, in his first inaugural speech as governor of California, echoed a warning from President George Washington and other Founders: "Freedom is a fragile thing," he said, "and is never more than one generation away from extinction. It is not ours by inheritance; it must be fought for and defended constantly by each generation, for it comes only once to a people. Those who have known freedom and then lost it have never known it again."

The pledge of the signers of the Declaration of Independence gave that promise as well:

"And for the support of this Declaration, with a firm reliance on the Protection of Divine Providence, we mutually pledge to each other our Lives, our Fortunes and our sacred Honor."[31]

We can do no less for future generations.

DEFENDING THE LIBERTY IN CHRIST

The battle for the future is the same one that Christians have been fighting against utopian socialists, Communists, Progressives, and those who call themselves liberals today, since the Ascension of Jesus. It is a battle between personal and spiritual liberty, and slavery.

It is, in reality, a battle between Satan, who wants to rule every aspect of life in his own "utopia" on earth, and the forces of God, who bring the promise of eternal freedom in this fallen world. The Bible says that "the thief"—that's Satan—comes to steal, kill, and destroy (John 10:10). It is always his goal to enslave humans—to bring them into bondage and misery. He, like his human servants, enjoys creating cultural and political institutions that bring about suffering and bondage. A centralized government does just that. It is easy to envision the Antichrist's government, as described in the book of Revelation, being a centrally planned collectivist regime that would torment every soul to force strict obedience. One could imagine this as living in a worldwide high-tech version of North Korea, facing eternity with no possibility of escape.

Whether they realize it or not, collectivists are satanically motivated, which explains why every major centrally planned collectivist government to date has been atheistic and has caused the misery and death of tens of millions. Rather than understanding human beings as created in the image of God, they view man as just another mammal, a living cog in their collective's machine. Instead of each man and woman having a spirit with a free will, collectivists see each person as a part of the Borg as depicted in the TV series *Star Trek*, a mere cell of the collective. Those of us from a Judeo-Christian heritage know better. We see each person as having God-given, intrinsic value, with the ability to reach as high spiritually and economically as he is willing and able to.

The names may change in this ongoing battle to enslave mankind, but the collectivist philosophy that drives them is always the same. Whether it was Lycurgus, or even the more extreme examples of Muhammad, Mao, Lenin, Stalin, Hitler, Mussolini, or Robespierre, the philosophy that motivates them is totalitarian. They, as a group, reject the individual right to free choice and view the "state" as god rather than almighty God.

Let's be realistic. Right here in America, the battle will never end between utopian tyrants and those who value our Constitution and the republican government that the Founders crafted. The reason the battle continues is easily defined. Collectivists want to create a utopia on earth that rivals God's in heaven.

What can be done to protect our personal freedoms?

Freedom and democracy are not synonymous and there is no such thing as a democratic form of government. Democracy is a process by which leaders are elected and has nothing to do with the form of governance. Corporations elect boards of directors through a democratic process. This process makes them neither free nor democratic.

It was Friedrich Hayek who coined the phrase "totalitarian democracy" to describe governments having a democratic process but little or no freedom. Examples of this can easily be seen in Canada, Germany, France, Iran, and the United Kingdom, where if individuals are publicly critical of Islam they may be arrested, fined, or even imprisoned. Canadian television is so censored by the government that Christian programming made in the United States often cannot be shown there. Yet Canada, as well as France, the United Kingdom, and Iran, elects officials at the provincial, city, and national levels. By pure definition of process, Iran is indeed a democratic nation with little or no real freedom. In the democratic nation of Germany, Christian homeschooling families have had to choose between sending their children to the government schools and permanently losing custody of them.

Some other examples of this contrast between democracy and freedom: A small businessman in Shanghai, China, has more economic freedom than a small businessman in Milan, Italy. A Christian who is critical of homosexuality in Russia has more personal freedom to express opinions in that area than a Christian in Canada, where graduates of Christian colleges have been forbidden to take a bar examination to become lawyers because they are presupposed to be bigoted against gays.

Laws in many Western nations are arbitrary in nature, suiting the environment at the moment with no respect to the sphere of freedom of the individual. When laws are arbitrary, there exists no rule of law, which is the basis of freedom in a civil society.

The general public often does not realize how arbitrary laws are. In the United States a farmer can go to prison for killing an eagle on his property to plow new land, but if he builds a large "green" commercial windmill that same famer will receive a permit to kill dozens of eagles a year without penalty. In a bar fight, if a serious injury occurs, an assault charge could get a five-year sentence, but the sentence could be double or triple that if a racially derogatory term is used during the fight.

In the United States today a man can use the women's dressing room at a department store or a public restroom if he "feels" like a woman that day, but a teenage boy can get arrested for looking up a girl's skirt. It is not racist for a black rap artist to say "nigger" over and over again in a song, but a white student can be barred from public schools for uttering the term once in a heated argument.

These arbitrary laws can become personal more quickly than most realize. If your cousin says his company is about to do something big, don't buy the stock or you could wind up in jail for insider trading. Don't carry cash on your way to buy a new car, because during a traffic stop the cops may seize the money and your current car, claiming that the only reason people carry large amounts of cash is to commit a crime.

Not only may a citizen in his own car not be safe from unwarranted search and seizure in violation of the Fourth Amendment protections, but now the Fourth Amendment doesn't seem to protect a person's home from being entered without a search warrant anymore. Because of the new "no knock" laws predominately passed by Republican legislators and approved by a "conservative" Supreme Court, some innocent families have experienced having their front doors bashed down in the middle of the night by a SWAT team whose guns and flash grenades have severely injured and even killed children in the home.

Want to run your business without paying state income tax? Move it from Maryland to New York. For a ten-year period, your new business will owe no state income tax while the unlucky guy who already owned a business there pays a higher tax to cover what you don't pay. Sadly, this is true of far more states than New York. In many instances sweetheart tax deals are cut with a specific business, to encourage it either to move in or to stay put.

Want a green card? Buy a "going business" such as the Subway restaurant owned by your cousin for $500,000, or just put $1 million into an investment trust. Why sneak over the border when you can just buy a green card? Are you a great athlete? You can get instant citizenship by signing up for the US Olympic team. (Yes, that has happened.)

Want to build a golf course for rich liberals in California? Water is no problem. Want to get water for your family farm in California's Great Valley? Forget about it.

Where there is arbitrary law there is no consistent, equal freedom for all. Living in a "democracy" does not guarantee freedom. The United States, with its militarized police forces, is becoming a totalitarian democracy rivaling those of Canada, France, and Iran.

What can you do to protect your personal sphere of freedom?

Just voting is not the answer. Both major political parties in the United States promote laws restricting freedom. The Democrats want to restrict your economic freedom in the name of social justice and your freedom of speech in the name of political correctness. The Republicans want to subject you to a militarized police force with Gestapo-like powers and jail you for life for the slightest infractions of obscure laws you were probably never aware of. It was a Republican Congress that passed the laws allowing police to seize and sell private property without due process and no proof of any crime having been committed. Taking property without just process is about as anti–personal freedom as it can get.

Just showing up to vote is not enough; the demand for true freedom must be a constant concern for the citizen regardless of the nation he resides in. In the United States that means showing up at county-, city-, and state-level government meetings to voice his opposition against new laws that restrict economic and personal freedoms. Those who want to take away freedom of the individual and replace it with central planning are always present at town hall gatherings to have their opinions heard, because they believe that, in the end, this route will bring them a free lunch along with a free education and guaranteed income for life.

If citizens who understand the true nature of freedom through the rule of law are not willing to face arrest in demanding that their ever-shrinking sphere of freedom be protected and expanded, then that sphere will vanish. Surely freedom-loving peoples in the West, particularly Christians, should be willing to take some risks at a time when Christians in Indonesia, Pakistan, Syria, and North Korea are dying for refusing to renounce their faith. If Americans are unwilling to take personal risk to stop central planners in their attempt to create an earthly utopia the individual personal sphere of liberty will shrink until all are slaves of the state. Now is not the time for fear or apathy or silence. Now is the time to stand up to the utopians at all levels of government and spheres of influence and say, enough is enough. Those who love their personal liberty must be ready to fight for it.

NOTES

CHAPTER 1: Satanic Influence in Utopian Tyrannies

1. Richard Wurmbrand, *Tortured for Christ* (Bartlesville, OK: Living Sacrifice, 1967), 37.
2. Ibid, 38.
3. Richard Wurmbrand, *Marx and Satan*, 6th ed. (Westchester, IL: Crossway, 1986; repr., 1990), 24.
4. Ibid., 12–13.
5. Ibid., 13.
6. Ibid., 15.
7. Ibid., 18.
8. Ibid.
9. Eugene Methvin, *The Rise of Radicalism: The Social Psychology of Messianic Extremism* (New Rochelle, NY: Arlington House, 1973), 172.
10. Ibid., 173.
11. Cleon Skousen, *The Naked Communist* (Salt Lake City: Ensign, 1962), 305.
12. Ibid., 307.
13. Wurmbrand, *Marx and Satan*, 59.
14. Ibid., 52.
15. Ibid., 53.
16. Ibid., 65–66.
17. Ibid., 74–75.
18. Walter C. Langer, *The Mind of Adolf Hitler: The Secret Wartime Report* (New York: Basic Books, 1972), 36–37.
19. Ibid., 37.
20. Ibid., 36.
21. Hermann Rauchning, *The Voice of Destruction* (Gretna, LA: Pelican, 1940), 49–50.
22. Ibid., 256–57.
23. Ibid., 258.
24. William L. Shirer, "The Strange Life and Works of H. S. Chamberlain," in *The Rise and Fall of the Third Reich*, electronic ed. (New York: RosettaBooks, 2011), chap 4.
25. Paul Roland, *The Nazis and the Occult: The Dark Forces Unleashed by the Third Reich,* Google eBook ed. (London: Arcturus, 2011).
26. Bill Yenne, *Hitler's Master of the Dark Arts: Himmler's Black Knights and the Occult Origins of the SS*, Kindle edition, 90–93). Motorbooks International n.p.: MBI. Kindle Edition, 3.

CHAPTER 2: Sir Thomas More's *Utopia*

1. F. A. Hayek, *The Road to Serfdom*, 50th anniv. ed. (University of Chicago Press, 1994), 63.
2. *Encyclopedia of Science, Technology, and Ethics*, s.v. "Utopia and Dystopia," January 1, 2005.
3. Thomas More, *Utopia* (London et al.: Cassell, 1909; public domain), 6.
4. *Encyclopedia of Philosophy*, s.v. "More, Thomas," by Edward Surtz, January 1, 2006.
5. The History Learning Site, "Sir Thomas More," http://www.historylearningsite.co.uk/thomas_more.htm.
6. John Guy, "The Search for the Historical Thomas More," *History Review*, March 2000.
7. Karl Kautsky, *Thomas More and His Utopia* (New York: Russell & Russell, 1959), 159.
8. Guy, "The Search for the Historical Thomas More."
9. More, *Utopia*, 69.
10. Ibid., 89.
11. Ibid., 80.
12. Kautsky, *Thomas More and His Utopia*, 198.
13. John W. Elliott, *Monarch Notes for Thomas More's Utopia* (New York: Simon & Schuster, 1966).
14. More, *Utopia*, 98.
15. Ibid., 151.
16. Ibid., 163, 111.
17. James Mackinnon, *A History of Modern Liberty*, vol. 2 (London; New York and Bombay, Longmans, Green, 1906), 40.
18. More, *Utopia*, 166.
19. James R. Stoner Jr., "God's Bestseller," *First Things*, April 2004, http://www.firstthings.com/article/2004/04/gods-bestseller.
20. George Orwell, "Review of Yevgeny Zamyatin's *We*," *Tribune*, January 4, 1946.

CHAPTER 3: Sparta and Plato's *Republic* **Inspire Utopian Tyrants**

1. *Plutarch's Lives*, vol. 2, trans. Aubrey Stewart and George Long (London: George Bell, 1894), "Life of Lykurgus," sec. 5. Public domain.
2. Ibid., sec. 8.
3. Ibid., sec. 9.
4. Ibid., sec. 14.
5. Ibid., sec. 17.
6. Ibid., sec. 27.
7. Ben Kiernan, *Blood and Soil: A World History of Genocide and Extermination from Sparta to Darfur* (Chicago: R. R. Donnelley, 2007), 46.
8. Friedrich Schiller, *Poet of Freedom*, vol. 2 (New Benjamin Franklin House, 1988), 285–86.
9. Ibid., 283.
10. Ibid., 284–85.
11. Stephen Hodkinson and Ian Macgregor Morris, eds., *Sparta in Modern Thought* (Classical Press of Wales, 2012).
12. Anton Powell and Stephen Hodkinson, *Sparta: The Body Politic* (Classical Press of Wales, 2009).
13. Jung Chang and Jon Halliday, *Mao: The Unknown Story* (New York: Random House, 2005; 2006; Anchor, 2011), Kindle edition, 1118–19.
14. *New World Encyclopedia*, s.v. "Prussia," accessed December 6, 2014, http://www.newworldencyclopedia.org/entry/Prussia.

15. Paul Johnson, *Intellectuals*, rev. ed. (New York: Harper Collins, 2009), Kindle edition, 547.

16. Toivo Koivukoski and David Edward Tabachnick, *Confronting Tyranny: Ancient Lessons for Global Politics* (New York: Rowman & Littlefield, 2005), 239–40.

17. Johnson, *Intellectuals*, 82–83.

18. Ibid., 106–11.

19. Jennifer Tolbert Roberts, *Athens on Trial: The Antidemocratic Tradition in Western Thought* (Princeton, NJ: Princeton Univ. Press, 1994), 194.

20. Simon Schama, *Citizens: A Chronicle of the French Revolution* (New York: Vintage, 1989), 809, 840.

21. Daniel Hager, "Utopia versus Eutopia," Foundation for Economic Education (FEE) website, accessed December 7, 2014, http://fee.org/the_freeman/detail/utopia-versus-eutopia/.

22. Philipp Blom. *A Wicked Company: The Forgotten Radicalism of the European Enlightenment* (Philadelphia: Basic, 2010), xvii.

23. James Billington, *Fire in the Minds of Men: Origins of the Revolutionary Faith* (Philadelphia: Basic, 1980), 94.

24. Plato, "History" website, accessed December 8, 2014, http://www.history.com/topics/ancient-history/plato.

25. Mark R. Levin, *Ameritopia*, repr. ed. (New York: Threshold Editions), 28.

26. Harry W. Laidler, *Socio-Economic Movements: An Historical and Comparative Survey of Socialism, Communism, Co-operation, Utopianism; and Other Systems of Reform and Reconstruction* (New York: Thomas Y. Crowell, 1944), 13.

27. "The Nazi Party: The 'Lebensborn' Program," Jewish Virtual Library, accessed December 8, 2014, http://www.jewishvirtuallibrary.org/jsource/Holocaust/Lebensborn.html.

28. Laidler, *Social-Economic Movements*, 15.

29. Laidler, Ibid, 15.

30. Levin, *Ameritopia*, 33.

CHAPTER 4: Utopian Totalitarian Rulers

1. *New Catholic Encyclopedia*, 2nd ed., s.v. "Supreme Being, Cult of the."

2. Paul Halsall, "Maximilien Robespierre: Justification of the Use of Terror," *Modern History Sourcebook*, accessed December 8, 2014, http://origin-rh.web.fordham.edu/Halsall/mod/robespierre-terror.asp.

3. Marisa Linton, "Robespierre and the Terror," *History Today* 56, no. 8 (August 2006).

4. Edmund Burke, "Reflections on the Revolution in France," 1790, available online at the website of the Constitution Society, accessed December 8, 2014, http://www.constitution.org/eb/rev_fran.htm.

5. Paul Johnson, *Intellectuals* (New York: Harper Collins, 2009), Kindle edition, 1174–75.

6. Ibid., 1304–8.

7. W. Cleon Skousen, *The Naked Communist*, Ensign Publishing Co., 1962, 37.

8. Karl Marx and Friedrich Engels, *The Communist Manifesto* (London: Communist League, 1848), Kindle edition (2005), 312–17.

9. J. Edgar Hoover, *Masters of Deceit* (n.p.: Henry Holt, 1958), Kindle edition, 470–78.

10. Ibid., 520–27.

11. Victor Kravchenko, *I Chose Freedom: The Personal and Political Life of a Soviet Official* (New York: Charles Scribner's Sons, 1946), 118.

12. Ibid., 129.

13. Stéphane Courtois, et al., *The Black Book of Communism: Crimes, Terror, Repression* (Harvard Univ. Press, 1999), 4.

14. Jung Chang and Jon Halliday, *Mao: The Unknown Story* (New York: Random House, 2005; 2006; Anchor, 2011), Kindle edition.

15. Andrew Roberts, "Whitewashing Mao: A mealy-mouthed new biography goes immorally easy on the 'Great Helmsman,'" Wall Street Journal, October 6, 2012, C9, http://www.wsj.com/articles/SB10000872396390444813104578016243142147194.

16. Ibid.

17. Richard M. Ebeling, "Mao: The Unknown Story," *Freeman*, September 1, 2005.

18. Peter Ford, "Falling Blackbirds in Arkansas: In Mao Zedong's China It Was Falling Sparrows," *Christian Science Monitor*, January 3, 2011.

19. Michael Fathers, "A Most Secret Tragedy: The Great Leap Forward aimed to make China industrial giant—instead it killed 45 million," *Wall Street Journal*, October 26, 2012.

20. Benito Mussolini, World War II Reference Library, Ed. Barbara C. Bigelow, George Feldman, Christine Slovey, and Kelly King Howes. Vol. 3: Biographies. Detroit: UXL, 1999,167-174. COPYRIGHT 1999-2000 U*X*L, COPYRIGHT 2006 Gale, Cengage Learning, accessed 1/24/15, http://go.galegroup.com/ps/i.do?id=GALE%7CCX3411800065&v=2.1&u=skok85085&it=r&p=GVRL&sw=w&asid=b7628253f16279196288eabd3354975c.

21. *International Encyclopedia of the Social Sciences*, 2008, s.v. "Nietzsche, Friedrich," accessed December 9, 2014 from Encyclopedia.com, http://www.encyclopedia.com/doc/1G2-3045301750.html.

22. *Encyclopedia of Philosophy* online, s.v. "Sorel, Georges," accessed January 1, 2006.

23. *Encyclopedia of Philosophy*, s.v. "Max Stirner," January 1, 2006.

24. Benito Mussolini, *The Doctrine of Fascism* (1932); Kindle edition (2012), 60–62.

25. Ibid., 72–74.

26. Ibid., 82–84.

27. Ibid., 126–29.

28. Ibid., 273–77.

29. "Adolf Hitler," *World War II Reference Library*, January 1, 1999, http://www.highbeam.com/doc/1G2-3411800058.html.

30. Clive Pearson, "Hitler and the Law," *History Review*, March 1, 2008.

31. "World War II Casualty Statistics," SecondWorldWarHistory.com, http://www.secondworldwarhistory.com/world-war-2-statistics.asp.

CHAPTER 5: The Cultural Utopians

1. William Booth, Salvation Army Torrance Corps website, accessed December 9, 2014, http://www1.usw.salvationarmy.org/usw/www_usw_torrance2.nsf/vw-sublinks/FCD98CD6A8BFB1B68825771D00178DE1.

2. Killer Angel: A Biography of Planned Parenthood's Margaret Sanger (Franklin, TN: Standfast Books, 2014), 37.

3. Rebecca Messall, "The Long Road of Eugenics: From Rockefeller to Roe v. Wade," *Human Life Review*, October 1, 2004.

4. Dave Andrusko, "Dr. Angela Franks Will Conduct Two Workshops on PPFA at National Right to Life 2011," National Right to Life News Today, May 17, 2011, http://www.nationalrighttolifenews.org/news/2011/05/dr-angela-franks-will-conduct-two-workshops-on-ppfa-at-national-right-to-life-2011/#more-1813.

5. John Elvin, "Did Mother of Free Love Urge Selective Breeding?" *Insight on the News*, December 16, 1996.

6.   Carl Mitcham (Editor) *Encyclopedia of Science, Technology, and Ethics*, Macmillan Reference USA, "Margaret Sanger," January 1, 2005.

7.   Alan Sears and Craig Osten, *The ACLU vs. America* (Nashville: Broadman & Holman, 2005), 13.

8.   Roger N. Baldwin, *Liberty under the Soviets* (New York: Vanguard, 1928), 216.

9.   Ibid., 194.

10. Ibid., 180.

11. Ibid.

12. "C250 Celebrates Columbians ahead of Their Time: John Dewey," Columbia University's C250 site, accessed December 9, 2014, http://c250.columbia.edu/c250_celebrates/remarkable_columbians/john_dewey.html.

13. John Dewey, *Impressions of Soviet Russia and the Revolutionary World* (1928), chap. 3, available online at http://ariwatch.com/VS/JD/ImpressionsOfSovietRussia.htm#chapter3.

14. Ibid.

15. Bill O'Reilly, "What a Friend Terrorists Have in the ACLU," *Herald News*, March 5, 2005.

16. Bill O'Reilly, *Talking Points Memo*, March 1, 2005.

17. Sears and Osten, *The ACLU vs. America*, (Nashville, TN: B&H Publishing Group, 2006), 174.

18. Tait Russell, "Honoring a Killer," *FrontPage Magazine*, February 16, 2011, http://www.frontpagemag.com/2011/tait-trussell/honoring-a-killer/.

19. Gordon Edwards, "The Lies of Rachel Carson," *21ˢᵗ Century* magazine, summer 1992, http://www.21stcenturysciencetech.com/articles/summ02/Carson.html.

20. Henry I. Miller, "Rachel Carson's Deadly Fantasies," *Forbes*, September 5, 2012.

21. Ibid.

22. Saul Alinsky, *Rules for Radicals*, unabr. ed. (New York: Knopf Doubleday, 2010), xi.

23. John Perazzo, "Saul Alinsky, Obama's Political Guru," *FrontPage Magazine*, October 22, 2009, http://www.frontpagemag.com/2009/john-perazzo/saul-alinsky-obamas-political-guru/.

24. Saul Alinsky profile at DiscoverTheNetworks.org, accessed December 11, 2014, http://www.discoverthenetworks.org/individualProfile.asp?indid=2314.

25. John Gallagher, "Harry Hay's Legacy," *Advocate*, November 26, 2002.

26. Anne-Marie Cusac, "Harry Hay: Gay Activist Interview," *Progressive*, September 1, 1998.

27. Charles Socarides, *Homosexuality: A Freedom Too Far* (Phoenix: Adam Margrave, 1995), 46.

28. Encyclopedia of Lesbian, Gay, Bisexual, and Transgendered History in America, s.v. "Homophile Movement."

29. Gallagher, "Harry Hay's Legacy."

30. "Obama's Buggery Czar: Jennings' Group Made Sex between Children and Adults Look Normal," *Washington Times*, December 8, 2009, http://www.washingtontimes.com/news/2009/dec/08/obamas-buggery-czar/.

31. *St. James Encyclopedia of Popular Culture*, s.v. "Timothy Leary."

32. Ibid.

33. Aleister Crowley, *Book of the Law*, reissue ed. (York Beach, ME; Boston: Weiser, 2012), 9.

34. Barbara Krantz, "The Changing Face of Older-Adult Addiction," *Addiction Professional*, March/April 2008.

35. George Soros, Underwriting Democracy: Encouraging Free Enterprise and Democratic Reform among the Soviets and in Eastern Europe (New York: Public Affairs, 2004), 3.

36. George Soros profile at DiscoverTheNetworks.org; accessed December 11, 2014, http://www.discoverthenetworks.org/individualProfile.asp?indid=977.

37. "The Shared Agendas of George Soros and Barack Obama," DiscoverTheNetworks, February 2011, http://www.discoverthenetworks.org/viewSubCategory.asp?id=1276.
38. Ibid.

CHAPTER 6: The Collectivist Road to Poverty and Slavery
1. F. A. Hayek, *The Road to Serfdom*, Routledge Classic repr., rev. (Abington, UK: Psychology Press, 2001), 13.
2. Ibid., 13–14.
3. Ibid., 25.
4. Rebecca Kaplan, CBS News, January 14, 2014, www.cbsnews.com/news/obama-i-will-use-my-pen-and-phone-to-take-on-congress.
5. Barack Obama, speech, Lorain County Community College, Elyria, OH, April 18, 2012.
6. Hayek, *The Road to Serfdom*, 26–27.
7. Ibid., 75–76.
8. Ibid., 78.
9. Ibid., 82.
10. F. A. Hayek, "The Intellectuals and Socialism," *University of Chicago Law Review* (Spring 1949), 417–20.
11. Hayek, *The Road to Serfdom*, 86.
12. Alexis de Tocqueville, *Democracy in America*, vol. 2, 808–9.
13. Ibid., 809.
14. Ibid., 810.
15. Ibid., 810–11.
16. Hayek, *The Road to Serfdom*, 158.
17. Frédéric Bastiat, *The Law* (n.p.: CreateSpace, 2013), 9.
18. Ibid., 10.
19. Ibid., 14.
20. Ibid., 18.
21. Ibid., 21.
22. Ibid., 23.
23. Augustine, *The City of God*, bk. 4, chap. 4.
24. Bruce Bawer U.K., "Thought Police Send Man to Prison," *FrontPage Magazine*, March 14, 2012, http://www.frontpagemag.com/2012/bruce-bawer/u-k-thought-police-send-man-to-prison/.
25. George Orwell, *1984* (New York: Houghton Mifflin Harcourt, 1983), Kindle edition, 4144–46; emphasis added.
26. Ibid.
27. "Works Of Aldous Huxley: Brave New World," Monarch Notes, January 1, 1963.
28. Aldous Huxley, *Brave New World Revisited*, Perennial Classics repr. ed. (New York: HarperPerennial, 2006) 2.
29. Daniel Hannan, *The New Road to Serfdom: A Letter of Warning to America*, Broadside Books ed. (New York: HarperCollins, 2011), 115–16.
30. Ibid., 186–87.

CHAPTER 7: Twentieth-Century Utopian Fiction
1. Robert Higgs, "Who Was Edward M. House?" *Independent Review* 13, no. 3 (Winter 2009), available online at http://www.independent.org/newsroom/article.asp?id=2294.

2. Ibid.

3. Ibid.

4. *Columbia Encyclopedia*, 6th ed., s.v. "House, Edward Mandell," *Encyclopedia.com*; accessed December 12, 2014, http://www.encyclopedia.com/doc/1E1-House-Ed.html.

5. Isabelle de Pommereau, "Germany Finishes Paying WWI Reparations, Ending Century of 'Guilt,' *Christian Science Monitor*, October 4, 2010, http://www.csmonitor.com/World/Europe/2010/1004/ Germany-finishes-paying-WWI-reparations-ending-century-of-guilt.

6. Edward M. House, Liberty, September 14, 1935, as quoted in J.B. Matthews, *American Mercury*, November 1954, 140-141.

7. David M. Esposito, "Imagined Power: The Secret Life of Colonel House," *Historian*, Summer 1998.

8. Ibid.

9. Ibid.

10. Edward Mandell House, *Philip Dru: Administrator*, New York, B.W. Huebsch, 1912, 42.

11. Ibid., 57.

12. Ibid., 155-156.

13. Ibid., 182.

14. Ibid., 182.

15. Ibid., 222.

16. Ibid., 276.

17. William Norman Grigg, "A Practical Guide to Reading *Philip Dru: Administrator*," in House, *Philip Dru: Administrator* (n.p.: Robert Welch University Press, 1998), vi.

18. Ibid.

19. Charles Seymour, *The Intimate Papers of Colonel House*, vol. 1 (Boston and New York: Houghton Mifflin, 1926;1928), 152–53.

20. Edward Bellamy, Looking Backward: 2000-1887, The Riverside Library, Houghton Mifflin Co., Boston/New York, 1917, reprinted online by Gutenberg.org, ii-iii.

21. Ibid., 56-57.

22. Ibid., 62.

23. Karl Marx, Critique of the Gotha Programme, part 1 (1875), available online at http://www.marxists.org/archive/marx/works/1875/gotha/ch01.htm.

24. Bellamy, *Looking Backward*, 763–64.

25. Ibid., 1001–4.

26. Ibid., 1087–91.

27. Ibid., 2555–58.

28. Ibid., 1143–47.

29. Ibid., 2171–75.

30. Ibid., 2203–6.

31. Martin Gardner, "Looking Backward at Edward Bellamy's Utopia," *New Criterion*, September 1, 2000.

32. Arthur E. Morgan, *Edward Bellamy* (Columbia Univ. Press, 1944), 369.

33. Ibid., 371.

34. Ibid., 368.

35. Deborah Klezmer, Women in World History: A Biographical Encyclopedia, "Flynn, Elizabeth Gurley," Gale Research Inc., 1st Edition, 1999.

36. Bellamy, *Looking Backward*, 74–75.

37. Heywood Broun, biography by John Simkin, Spartacus Educational, http://spartacus-educational. com/USAbrounH.htm.
38. Gardner, "Looking Backward at Edward Bellamy's Utopia."
39. Robert Higgs, "A Tale of Two Brain Trusts," Foundation for Economic Education (FEE) website, October 1, 2002, http://fee.org/freeman/detail/a-tale-of-two-brain-trusts/.
40. Ibid.
41. John T. Flynn, *The Roosevelt Myth* (Auburn, AL: Ludwig von Mises Institute, 2011), Kindle edition, 2381–83.
42. Ibid. 252–55.
43. Scott Shockford, "The United States of Regulation: Compliance Costs Consume Huge Chunks of Our Economy," *Reason.com* (blog), April 30, 2014, http://reason.com/blog/2014/04/30/the-united-states-of-regulation-complian.

CHAPTER 8: American Utopians in Government
1. Hamowy, Ronald, ed., *The Collected Works of F. A. Hayek,* The University of Chicago Press, 2011(Kindle edition), 2238.
2. Hillsdale College Politics Department, eds., *The U.S. Constitution: A Reader* (Hillsdale College Press, 2012), 617.
3. Ibid., 641.
4. Mark R. Levin, *Ameritopia* (New York: Simon & Schuster, 2012), 189.
5. Woodrow Wilson, "The President of the United States," in *Constitutional Government of the United States* (New York: Columbia Univ. Press, 1908).
6. Susan Jones, "Obama Says He Won't Wait for Legislation: 'I've Got a Pen and I've Got a Phone,'" cnsnews.com, January 15, 2014, http://www.cnsnews.com/news/article/susan-jones/obama-says-he-wont-wait-legislation-ive-got-pen-and-ive-got-phone.
7. Levin, *Ameritopia,* 191.
8. "Progressive Support for Italian and German Fascism," DiscoverTheNetworks.org, accessed December 12, 2014, http://www.discoverthenetworks.org/viewSubCategory.asp?id=1223.
9. "The Progressive Era's Legacy: FDR's New Deal," DiscoverTheNetworks.org, accessed December 12, 2014, http://www.discoverthenetworks.org/viewSubCategory.asp?id=1228.
10. Ibid.
11. Jim Powell, "FDR, The Great Court-Packer," Future of Freedom Foundation, March 10, 2009, http://fff.org/explore-freedom/article/fdr-great-courtpacker/.
12. Mark R. Levin, *Liberty and Tyranny* (New York: Simon & Schuster, 2009), 41.
13. Doris Kearns Goodwin, *Lyndon Johnson and the American Dream* (New York: New American Library, 1991), 155.
14. Martin Tolchin, "How Johnson Won Election He'd Lost," *New York Times*, February 11, 1990, http://www.nytimes.com/1990/02/11/us/how-johnson-won-election-he-d-lost.html.
15. Jonah Goldberg, *Liberal Fascism: The Secret History of the American Left, from Mussolini to the Politics of Meaning* (New York: Random House, 2008), Kindle edition, 4327–31.
16. Ibid., 4336–37.
17. Ronald Kessler, *Inside the White House* (New York: Simon and Schuster, 1996), 33.
18. "LBJ's 'War on Poverty' Hurt Black Americans," National Center for Public Policy Research, press release, January 8, 2014, http://www.nationalcenter.org/P21PR-WarOnPoverty_010814.html.
19. Ibid.

20. Ronald Reagan, *50 of President Ronald Reagan's Most Important Speeches from 1957 to 1994 (formatted for the Kindle)* (Amazon Digital Services, 2010), 175–80, 204–7.

21. Cass Sunstein, *The Second Bill of Rights: FDR's Unfinished Revolution—And Why We Need It More Than Ever* (New York: Basic Books, 2006), 3.

22. Paul R. Ehrlich, Anne H. Ehrlich, and John P. Holdren, *Human Ecology: Problems and Solutions* (San Francisco: W. H. Freeman, 1973), 279.

23. John Holdren and Paul Ehrlich, *Global Ecology: Readings Towards a Rational Strategy for Man* (San Diego: Harcourt Brace Jovanovich, 1971), 3.

24. Jeff Jacoby, "Dangerous to Our Health," *Boston Globe*, June 16, 2010, http://www.boston.com/bostonglobe/editorial_opinion/oped/articles/2010/06/16/dangerous_to_our_health/.

25. Hal Scherz, "Why Donald Berwick Is Dangerous to Your Health," RealClearPolitics, May 26, 2010, http://www.realclearpolitics.com/articles/2010/05/26/why_donald_berwick_is_dangerous_to_your_health_105730.html.

26. Penny Starr, "Obama Once Needed 'to Take a Subway or Bus Just to Find a Fresh Piece of Fruit,'" CNSNews.com, April 18, 2012, http://cnsnews.com/news/article/obama-once-needed-take-subway-or-bus-just-find-fresh-piece-fruit.

27. Liz Klimas, "'Food Swamp': Studies Reveal 'Food Deserts' Not So Parched for Health Food Access," *The Blaze*, April 20, 2012, http://www.theblaze.com/stories/2012/04/20/food-swamp-studies-reveal-urban-food-deserts-not-so-parched-for-health-food-access/.

28. Patrick Richardson, "Wasted Food, Hungry Kids: Michelle Obama's Bill in Action," *PJ Media* (blog), September 24, 2012, http://pjmedia.com/blog/wasted-food-hungry-kids-michelle-obamas-bill-in-action/.

29. Howard Portnoy, "NYC Food—Police Chief Michael Bloomberg's Latest Ban: Jumbo Soft Drinks," *Hot Air* (blog), May 31, 2012, http://hotair.com/greenroom/archives/2012/05/31/nyc-food-police-chief-michael-bloombergs-latest-ban-jumbo-soft-drinks/.

30. "Mommy Bloomberg: Nanny-State Policies in New York City," *Washington Times*, August 7, 2012.

31. Eliza Strickland, "The New Face of Environmentalism," *East Bay Express*, November 2, 2005, http://www.eastbayexpress.com/gyrobase/the_new_face_of_environmentalism/Content?oid=290098&showFullText=true.

32. EPA Abuse, "Van Jones Is the Ultimate Watermelon (Green Outside, Red Inside)," EPAAbuse.com, September 22, 2011, http://epaabuse.com/537/watermelon-patch/van-jones-is-the-ultimate-watermelon-green-outside-red-inside/.

33. Green for All's official website, accessed December 15, 2014, http://greenforall.org/.

34. EPA Abuse, "Van Jones Is the Ultimate Watermelon."

35. "NASA Scientist Accused of Using Celeb Status among Environmental Groups to Enrich Himself," FoxNews.com, June 22, 2011, http://www.foxnews.com/politics/2011/06/22/nasa-scientist-accused-using-celeb-status-among-environmental-groups-to-enrich/.

36. "2010 Blue Planet Prize: Announcement of Prize Winners, Tokyo, Japan," EWire, June 17, 2010, http://www.ewire.com/news-releases/2010-blue-planet-prizeannouncement-of-prize-winners/.

37. "The Sophie Prize 2010," official website of the Sophie Prize, accessed December 15, 2014, http://www.sofieprisen.no/Prize_Winners/2010/index.html.

38. "Mission Statement," the Sophie Prize website, accessed December 15, 2014, resourceshttp://www.sofieprisen.no/The_Sophie_Prize/Mission_Statement/index.html.

CHAPTER 9: The Utopian Nations (UN)—a Threat to America's Sovereignty
1. G. Edward Griffin, *The Fearful Master: A Second Look at the United Nations* (Belmont, MA: Western Islands, 1964), 68.

2. Ibid., 70.

3. Ibid., 71.

4. Ibid., 87–89.

5. Ibid., 127.

6. James Delingpole, *Watermelons: The Green Movement's True Colors* (New York: Publius, 2011), Kindle edition, 3181–83.

7. Ibid., 3140–42.

8. Ibid., 3188–91.

9. Ron Taylor, *Agenda 21: An Expose of the United Nations' Sustainable Development Initiative and the Forfeiture of American Sovereignty and Liberties* (Amazon Digital Editions, 201), Kindle edition, 47–50.

10. Ibid., 262–67.

11. United Nations, *Agenda 21: Earth Summit: The United Nations' Programme of Action from Rio*, (United Nations, 1992); available online at http://www.keepourrights.org/agenda_21_pdf.pdf.

12. Ryan Balis, "World Heritage Areas: A Critical Analysis," National Center for Public Policy Research, January 2005.

13. Mary Ann Cunningham, Environmental Encyclopedia, Third Edition (Farmington Hills, MI: Gale Publishing, 2003).

14. Naomi Mapstone, "Ransom: Rainforest Held Hostage by Oil Interests Unless the World Pays to Preserve Biosphere," Amazon Watch, November 28, 2011, http://amazonwatch.org/news/2011/1128-ransom-rainforest-held-hostage-by-oil-interests-unless-the-world-pays-to-preserve-biosphere.

15. Inés Benítez, "Drilling Threatens Spain's Renewable Energy Paradise," Inter Press Service, April 5, 2012, http://www.ipsnews.net/2012/04/oil-drilling-threatens-spains-renewable-energy-paradise/.

16. John R. Bolton, *How Barack Obama Is Endangering Our National Sovereignty* (New York: Encounter, 2010), 9.

17. William F. Jasper, "LOST: Law of the Sea Treaty: Although LOST Would Threaten American Sovereignty by Giving the UN Control of the Oceans, Ratification of the Treaty Is Still a Top Priority of the Obama Administration," *New American*, March 2, 2009.

18. Ibid.

19. James M. Inhofe and Jim DeMint, "INHOFE AND DEMINT: U.N. treaties mean LOST U.S. sovereignty," *Washington Times*, July 25, 2012, http://www.washingtontimes.com/news/2012/jul/25/un-treaties-would-separate-americans-from-the-cons/?page=all.

20. Patrick J. Buchanan, "Should the U.N. Be Lord of the Oceans?" American Cause, February 28, 2005, http://www.theamericancause.org/a-pjb-050228-lordoftheoceans.htm.

21. Jonathan Turley, "Shut Up and Play Nice: How the Western World Is Limiting Free Speech," *Washington Post*, October 12, 2012.

22. Ibid.

23. Patrick Goodenough, "Religious Tolerance Resolution Backed by Obama Administration Aligns with Islamic Bloc's Interests," CNSNews.com, December 16, 2011, http://cnsnews.com/news/article/religious-tolerance-resolution-backed-obama-administration-aligns-islamic-bloc-s.

24. David Horowitz and Robert Spencer, *Islamophobia: Thought Crime of the Totalitarian Future* (Sherman Oaks, CA: David Horowitz Freedom Center, 2011), Kindle edition, 55–57.

25. Ibid., 699–702.

26. Ibid., 294–95.

27. Michael Farris, "New World Playpen: The United Nations' Parental Power Grab," *American Conservative*, October 1, 2009, http://www.theamericanconservative.com/articles/new-world-playpen/.

28. Donna Laframboise, *The Delinquent Teenager Who Was Mistaken for the World's Top Climate Expert* (Toronto: Ivy Avenue Press, 2011), Kindle edition, 2425–28.

29. United States Mission to the United Nations, "Statement by Ambassador Susan E. Rice, U.S. Permanent Representative to the United Nations, on Lesbian, Gay, Bisexual and Transgender (LGBT) Pride Month," Briefing Room, June 30, 2010, http://usun.state.gov/briefing/statements/2010/143808.htm.

30. "Human Rights Attorney: 'Obama Admin Supporting Blasphemy Laws Used to Murder Christians,'" Fox News *Insider*, October 22, 2013, http://insider.foxnews.com/2013/10/22/human-rights-attorney-obama-admin-supporting-blasphemy-laws-used-murder-christians.

CHAPTER 10: The Failure of Utopian Systems

1. Paul Johnson, *Intellectuals* (Harper & Row: New York, 1988), 62-70.

2. Daniel Hager, "Utopia Versus Eutopia," FEE, March 1, 2003, http://fee.org/freeman/detail/utopia-versus-eutopia/.

3. Thomas Sowell, "How Good Intentions Pave the Road to Ruin: Socialism Redistributes Only Poverty," *Charleston Daily Mail*, December 5, 2002.

4. Ronald Radosh, "The Dream and Death of an Idea: Socialism across Two Centuries," *Washington Times*, April 21, 2002.

5. Algis Valiunas, "The Good Intentions Paving Co," *American Spectator*, September 1, 2002.

6. David Horowitz, *Radicals: Portraits of a Destructive Passion* (Washington, DC: Regnery, 2010), 1.

7. Milton Friedman, *Capitalism and Freedom*, 40th ann. ed. (University of Chicago Press, 2009), Kindle edition, 308–12.

8. Ibid., 333–36.

9. F. A. Hayek, *The Road to Serfdom*, Routledge Classic repr., rev. (Abington, UK: Psychology Press, 2001), 13.

10. Friedman, *Capitalism and Freedom*, 397–402.

11. Ibid., 403–7.

12. Ibid., 431–32.

13. Margaret Thatcher, TV Interview for Thames TV *This Week*, February 5, 1976.

14. Daniel Hannan, *The New Road to Serfdom: A Letter of Warning to America*, Broadside Books ed. (New York: HarperCollins, 2011), 118.

15. Gerald P. O'Driscoll, "The Federal Reserve's Covert Bailout of Europe," *Wall Street Journal*, December 28, 2011.

16. Phyllis Schlafly, "Bailing Out the European Union," *Human Events*, January 12, 2012.

17. Solyndra was a solar company in Fremont, California, that went bankrupt in 2011 after receiving $535 million in federal loan guarantees from the Obama administration. Unfortunately, the cost to taxpayers was much higher.

18. Melanie Kirkpatrick, *Escape from North Korea: The Untold Story of Asia's Underground Railroad* (New York: Encounter, 2014), Kindle edition, 41–44.

19. D. Wolman, "How the U.S. Could Pressure North Korea Tomorrow: Quit the $100 Bill," *Time*, February 24, 2012, http://business.time.com/2012/02/24/how-the-u-s-could-pressure-north-korea-tomorrow-quit-the-100-bill/.

20. "North Koreans of All Ages Are Being Enlisted to Construct Pricey Memorials to the Country's Leaders," State News Service, October 12, 2012.
21. Terry Miller, Kim R. Holmes, and Edwin J. Feulner, "2012 Index of Economic Freedom," Heritage Foundation and *Wall Street Journal*, 2012.
22. Ibid.
23. CIA *World Factbook*, North Korea, Central Intelligence Agency website, accessed December 15, 2014, https://www.cia.gov/library/publications/the-world-factbook/geos/kn.html.
24. Ronald Reagan, *50 of President Ronald Reagan's Most Important Speeches from 1957 to 1994 (formatted for the Kindle)* (Amazon Digital Services, 2010), 4031–38.
25. Ibid., 4048–53.
26. Hillsdale College Politics Department, eds., *The U.S. Constitution: A Reader* (Hillsdale College Press, 2012), 146–47.

CHAPTER 11: The Vision of the Founding Fathers
1. William J. Federer, *America's God and Country Encyclopedia of Quotations* (St. Louis: Amerisearch, 2000), 411.
2. Barbara E. Oberg, ed., *The Papers of Thomas Jefferson*, vol. 30, *January 1798 to January 1799*, (Princeton Univ. Press, 2003).
3. Benson John Lossing, *Lives of the Signers of the Declaration of Independence* (n.p.: Tales End Press, 2012), Kindle edition, 3498–507.
4. Federer, *America's God and Country*, 200.
5. Hillsdale College Politics Department, eds., *The U.S. Constitution: A Reader* (Hillsdale College Press, 2012), 708, 711–12.
6. Federer, *America's God and Country*, 180–81.
7. Lossing, *Lives of the Signers*, 1122–27.
8. Ibid., 1251–56.
9. Ibid., 2967–69.
10. Ibid., 3198–200.
11. Edwin Meese, ed., *The Heritage Guide to the Constitution* (Washington, DC: Heritage Foundation, 2005), 9.
12. Hillsdale College Politics Department, *The U.S. Constitution*, 209–10.
13. Meese, *Heritage Guide*, 10.
14. Joseph A. Story, *Familiar Exposition of the Constitution of the United States* (New York: Harper & Brothers, 1847), 47.
15. Ibid., 36–37.
16. Mark R. Levin, *Liberty and Tyranny* (New York: Threshold Editions, 2010), 52–53.
17. Meese, *Heritage Guide*, 15.
18. Levin, *Liberty and Tyranny*, 53.
19. Joseph A. Story, *Familiar Exposition of the Constitution* (n.p.: Packard Technologies, 2005), Kindle edition, 3950–59.
20. Ibid., 4004-9.
21. George Washington, "Farewell Address," September 1796, archived online on the Early America website, at http://www.earlyamerica.com/milestone-events/wahsingtons-farewell-address/.

CHAPTER 12: Combating Future Utopian Planners

1. Ngo Van Xuyet, "Ancient utopia and peasant revolts in China," July 20, 2004, posted online at libcom.org/library/ancient-utopia-peasant-revolts-china-ngo-van-xuyet.

2. Harold Paget, *Bradford's History of the Plymouth Settlement; 1608–1650,* American Heritage ed. (San Antonio: Mantle Ministries, 1988).

3. Catholic Online, "Students Who Refused Microchip Surveillance at Texas School Punished," October 10, 2012, http://www.catholiconline.com/news/hf/faith/story.php?id=47959.

4. Michael Santo, "Judge: Student's objection to location tracking ID badge secular, not religious," *Examiner.com,* January 9, 2013, http://www.examiner.com/article/judge-student-s-objection-to-location-tracking-id-badge-secular-not-religious.

5. Salynn Boyles, "Drug-Delivery Microchip Could Replace Daily Injections," WebMD Health News, February 16, 2012, http://www.webmd.com/osteoporosis/news/20120216/drug-delivery-microchip.

6. "LaHood Seeks Automatic 'Kill Switch' for Cell Phones," *Heartlander Magazine,* January 17, 2012.

7. "James Clapper's 'least untruthful' statement to the Senate," *Washington Post,* posted by Glenn Kessler, June 12, 2013, http://www.washingtonpost.com/blogs/fact-checker/post/james-clappers-least-untruthful-statement-to-the-senate/2013/06/11/e50677a8-d2d8-11e2-a73e-826d299ff459_blog.html.

8. "Cravaack Passes Amendment to Prohibit Federal Driving Tax," State News Service, June 29, 2012.

9. "Anwar al-Awlaki Targeted by U.S. Drones after Osama Bin Laden Raid," ABC News, May 6, 2011, http://abcnews.go.com/Blotter/anwar-al-awlaki-targeted-us-drones-osama-bin/story?id=13549218.

10. Laura Kasinov, "Fatal Strikes Hit Yemen as Violence Escalates," *New York Times,* October 15, 2011.

11. Robert D. McFadden, "Army Doctor Held in Ft. Hood Rampage," *New York Times* front page, November 10, 2009.

12. Catherine Herridge, "Exclusive: Al Qaeda Leader Dined at the Pentagon Just Months after 9/11," Fox News, October 20, 2010, http://www.foxnews.com/us/2010/10/20/al-qaeda-terror-leader-dined-pentagon-months/.

13. David Barrett, "One surveillance camera for every 11 people in Britain, says CCTV survey," *Telegraph* (UK), October 7, 2013, http://www.telegraph.co.uk/technology/10172298/One-surveillance-camera-for-every-11-people-in-Britain-says-CCTV-survey.html.

14. Jane Timm, "Drop a bag in NYC? Cue the bomb squad," MSNBC, April 22, 2013, http://www.msnbc.com/morning-joe/drop-bag-nyc-cue-the-bomb-squad.

15. Mario Tama, "Total Surveillance: NYPD Launches New All-Seeing 'Domestic Awareness System,'" RT News online, July 30, 2012, http://rt.com/usa/nypd-surveillance-awareness-cameras-433/.

16. Jesse Lee Peterson, "Houston's Lesbian Mayor Turns Tyrant," WND, October 19, 2014, http://www.wnd.com/2014/10/houstons-lesbian-mayor-turns-tyrant/.

17. Maxine Waters, letter to Attorney General Janet Reno, August 30, 1996, available online at narconews.com/darkalliance/drugs/library/32.htm.

18. Alex Isenstadt, "CBC Members Praise Castro," *Politico,* April 7, 2009, http://www.politico.com/news/stories/0409/21008.html.

19. Joshua Rhett Miller, "Jailed filmmaker vows to finish film wrongly blamed for Benghazi attack," Fox News, June 16, 2013, http://www.foxnews.com/us/2013/06/16/exclusive-jailed-filmmaker-vows-to-finish-film-wrongly-blamed-for-benghazi/.

20. Rachael Slobodien, "Green Graveyard: An In-Depth Look at Government's Bad Bets on 19 Now-Bankrupt Companies," *Daily Signal,* November 6, 2012, http://dailysignal.com/2012/11/06/green-graveyard-an-in-depth-look-at-governments-bad-bets-on-19-now-bankrupt-companies/.

21. James Madison, "Letter to Edmund Pendleton," January 21, 1792, in *The Papers of James Madison*, vol. 14, Robert A. Rutland et. al., eds. (Charlottesville: University Press of Virginia, 1984).

22. James Madison, *The Writings of James Madison*, vol. 9 (1819–1836), ed. Gaillard Hunt (New York: G. P. Putnam's Sons, 1900).

23. Franklin Roosevelt et al., *15 Documents and Speeches That Built America, "Four Freedoms" speech, given in January, 1941 to the 77th Congress*, (Amazon Digital Services, 2011), Kindle edition, 1135–36.

24. James Holland, "Peeling Back Congressional Overreach," Heritage Action for America, December 23, 2010, http://heritageaction.com/2010/12/peeling-back-congressional-overreach/.

25. Mark R. Levin, *Liberty and Tyranny* (New York: Simon & Schuster, 2009), 54.

26. Roosevelt et al, *15 Documents and Speeches That Built America*, 1147–52.

27. Ibid., 1162–67.

28. Ibid., 1173–81.

29. "Some Asians' college strategy: Don't check 'Asian'," *USA Today*, December 4, 2011, http://usatoday30.usatoday.com/news/education/story/2011-12-03/asian-students-college-applications/51620236/1.

30. F. A. Hayek, *The Constitution of Liberty* (Chicago: Univ. of Chicago Press, 1960).

31. Roosevelt et al., *15 Documents and Speeches That Built America*, 497–498.

INDEX